MANCHURIA

HEILONGJIANG

JILIN

LIANING

Sea of
Japan

NORTH
KOREA

SOUTH
KOREA

Tokyo

Chengde

EI MONGGOL

Beijing ★
Datong

HEBEI

Jinan

SHANDONG

Yellow
Sea

JAPAN

XIA

SHANXI

River

Yellow

Xian

SHAANXI

HENAN

JIANGSU

ANHUI

Hefei

Nanjing

Shanghai
Huangpu River

East
China
Sea

Jialing River

HUBEI

Wuhan

ng

Yangtse River

ZHEJIANG

JIANGXI

FUJIAN

Taipei

GUANGXI

GUANGDONG

Guangzhou
(Canton)

Shenzhen

TAIWAN

Nanning

Hong Kong

AM

Hainan
Island

South
China
Sea

PHILIPPINES

China
in Search of
Its Future

CHINA

in Search of

Its Future

Years of Great Reform, 1982–87

JOHN WOODRUFF

Foreword by Michel Oksenberg

UNIVERSITY OF WASHINGTON PRESS

Seattle and London

Library of Congress Cataloging-in-Publication Data

Woodruff, John.
    China in search of its future: years of great reform, 1982–87
John Woodruff: foreword by Michel Oksenberg.
        p.   cm.
    Bibliography: p.
    Includes index.
    ISBN 0-295-96803-6
    1. China—History—1976– I. Title.
DS779.2.W66 1989
951.05'8—dc19   88-29027
                                                            CIP

In memory of

Frank Reed

without whose teaching I might have found some
much less interesting way to make a living

Contents

Foreword

John Woodruff covered China for *The Baltimore Sun* from the fall of 1982 to the summer of 1987. Based in Beijing, he traveled widely, and his reporting was comprehensive. During his five years on the mainland, his stories peppered all the sections of *The Sun:* features, food, entertainment, health, and frequently the front page. From July 1970 to July 1973, long prior to his Beijing assignment, Woodruff had been posted to Hong Kong, where he covered the Cultural Revolution and honed his skills as a China watcher. During his mainland and Hong Kong assignments, he spent long stints in Taiwan, where, among other activities, he studied Mandarin. He also spent the academic year 1973–74 in the University of Michigan Journalism Fellows program, where he studied East Asian culture and history. At the time of his departure from Beijing, Woodruff was widely regarded as among the most insightful of the foreign correspondents covering one of the major stories of our time: the reforms of the Deng Xiaoping era.

Woodruff's China assignment coincided with the reform-oriented era, from the landmark 1982 Twelfth National Congress of the Chinese Communist party (CCP) to the 1987 Thirteenth Congress. The author's experience therefore coincides roughly with the apex of Deng Xiaoping's power, for the Twelfth Central Committee elected in 1982 and its leading bodies were largely Deng's creation, balanced by more cautious forces somewhat skeptical of the reform. When Woodruff arrived in Beijing, Deng and his associates were dismantling the rural communes and were taking their first experimental steps to expand the role of the market place in the urban sector. The opening to the outside world, proclaimed four years earlier, was beginning to be felt through an increased Western presence in the major cities. A legal infrastructure that would attract foreign businessmen to China was beginning to be erected. Western and Chinese negotiators were hammering out the details of the first joint ventures. The Sino-American relationship had just weathered a period of tension that was resolved through the August 1982 joint agreement between the United States and the People's Republic governing American arms sales to Taiwan. The subsequent five years saw the rapid expansion of Sino-American relations, highlighted by the 1984 visit to Beijing by that previously outspoken critic of normalization, Ronald Reagan. Trade, scholarly and cultural exchanges, and tourism between China and the United States grew rapidly from 1982 to 1987. These were good years for Americans to be in China.

They were good years for the Chinese as well, particularly when one recalls the turmoil of China's modern history: the Boxer Rebellion of 1900, the revolution of 1911, the May Fourth Movement of 1919, the Northern Expedition of 1927, the war against Japan (1937–45), the civil war (1945–49), the collectivization of agriculture and nationalization of industry (1955–56), the Great Leap Forward and its aftermath (1958–61), and the Cultural Revolution and its aftermath (1966–76). The decade from 1978 to 1988, particularly the five years Woodruff experienced, was probably the most sustained period of domestic tranquility that China has experienced in a century. In many respects, the pace and extent of change has no parallel in China's entire long history. From 1978 to 1988 China's gross national production doubled, television became commonplace in most urban cities and began its rapid spread to the countryside, clothing fashions underwent enormous change, and a building boom swept the nation. At the same time, blatant corruption joined the use of personal connections as a major way to grease the wheels of bureaucracy. In addition, environmental degradation, such as air and water pollution, began seriously to detract from the quality of urban life.

In a very real sense, Woodruff was in China when the nation's political agenda shifted profoundly from how to *launch* the nation onto the path of modernization—the issue that had confronted the leaders for a century—to how to *sustain* a modernization effort and handle the cascading, unanticipated consequences of that effort. Future historians may look back upon the 1980s and judge the decade to have been a decisive one in China's quest for modernity. It is a period in Chinese history that deserves to be recorded by an observant Westerner whose business it is to make sense of daily events.

This book joins a time-honored genre. For decades, foreign correspondents in China as elsewhere have written books interpreting the national mood during the time of their assignments. It is worth recalling the difficulties foreign correspondents face in attempting to cover a country as diverse, secretive, restrictive, and authoritarian as China. They have little access to the top leaders. To a certain extent, they must rely on other foreigners, especially in the diplomatic and business communities. They are under surveillance by undercover agents, their telephones are quite likely tapped or bugged, and many of their native informants speak to them at personal risk. Ethical correspondents go to great lengths to ensure that no harm comes to their sources, as Woodruff has done in this book. They must eschew the easy stories in the capital and must somehow overcome the barriers to discovering the country at large, where their travel is subject to severe constraints. They depend on local research assistants and, to greater or lesser extents, on guides and translators to introduce them to the nation, and they must compensate for the consequent biases and distortions that creep into their work. They must escape the pack mentality of many of their peers, avoiding victimization by the gossip network that infests the community—while knowing how to use it. They usually do not have the luxury of studying a single subject in depth, as social scientists do, nor do they have much access to policy documents, as subsequent historians do. They rely on their ability to question, to see, to listen, and to record. It is a challenging craft.

The public is the beneficiary when newsmen overcome these constraints and write books about the setting in which they have worked for several years. Daily newspaper dispatches simply do not give foreign correspondents the opportunity to capture the complexity and subtlety of the country in which they have been immersed. Of necessity, the daily dispatch must simplify events. The medium itself constrains reporters from providing extensive interpretations that place events in historical or cultural perspective. Occasionally the editor back home will print an illuminating series of articles by the foreign correspondent or will turn over a whole page to his in-depth account. Such writing is frequently excellent, but the reportage tends to be forgotten in the newspaper morgue. Instead, one goes to classics of the foreign correspondents to capture the mood of the times. One does not go back to read William Shirer's dispatches from Nazi Germany or Hugh Byas's from Japan of the 1930s or Harrison Salisbury's from Moscow. Rather, one reaches for their books.

The same is true for China, where for decades foreign correspondents have provided important interpretations of this kaleidoscopic country. The tradition can be traced at least to G. H. C. Morrison, the eminent *Times* of London correspondent at the turn of the century, and to Edmund Backhouse, whose roguish qualities have been so delightfully unearthed in *The Hermit of Peking* by Hugh Trevor-Roper.

China reportage matured in the 1930s with Edgar Snow's classic account of the Chinese Communists in *Red Star Over China.* The war years then saw a series of influential books from the correspondents: Theodore White and Annalee Jacoby's *Thunder Out of China,* Jack Belden's *China Shakes the World,* and Harrison Froman's *Report from Red China,* to name a few. These books still are required reading by those seeking to understand the mood of the times and the sources of Chinese Communist party strength and Kuomintang vulnerabilities as the two sides prepared for their civil war. A. Doak Barnett, a young correspondent who wrote newsletters for the Institute for Current World Affairs and worked for *The Chicago Daily News,* covered the civil war and the early years of Communist rule. The two collections of his writings, *China on the Eve of Communist Takeover* and *Communist China: The Early Years,* are landmark studies of the 1945–55 era.

Then came the drought for American correspondents who, from 1950 to 1979, had to do their China watching from Hong Kong, with sporadic forays into the mainland permissible after 1972. But although Sino-American hostility precluded American journalists from basing themselves inside China, American reporters in Hong Kong did record their impressions. Stanley Karnow's *Mao's China*, for example, provides an excellent account of the Cultural Revolution. Journalists from other countries resided in Beijing in the 1950s and 1960s, and several subsequently wrote informative accounts. For instance, Charles Taylor of *The Toronto Globe and Mail* captured some of the mood of the 1960s in his *Reporter in China*.

For American journalists, the tradition of book-length reportage really could not resume until they had spent several years on assignment inside China. This opportunity did not occur until 1979–80 when, following the resumption of full diplomatic relations during the Carter administration, the major U.S. media opened bureaus in Beijing. Four of that first group published widely read books: from *Time,* Richard Bernstein's *From the Center of the Earth;* from *The New York Times,* Fox Butterfield's *China, Alive in the Bitter Sea;* and from *The Washington Post* and *Los Angeles Times,* Jay and Linda Matthews's *The One Billion.* This foursome produced excellent period pieces on China of the late 1970s and early 1980s: a nation still traumatized by the Cultural Revolution, still fearing political persecution, and still preoccupied by elite-level politics, its bureaucracy unaccustomed to the aggressiveness of American journalists and reluctant to accommodate them. This first wave of journalists also heard the rhetoric of reform and openness to the outside world but did not experience the results. The leaders had promised much more than they had delivered immediately to the populace. Largely confined to Beijing and still very much feeling the ghost of Mao, these earlier journalists—with important differences among them—tended to portray a subdued, often bitter, somewhat stagnant nation. None anticipated, nor did most foreigners or most Chinese, the rapidity and extent of change during the next five years.

That next era, from 1982 to 1987, is the one Woodruff analyzes in this book. Woodruff's China is more alive, less predictable, more open, and less tense than the China described by the first wave of American reporters. In some ways, it is a nation that is less exotic and more familiar to Americans. Woodruff records the fading of Mao's China, the resurrecting of its links to its past, and the emergence of features of a large, developing country reminiscent of India, Brazil, or Indonesia. In short, Woodruff captures a nation in the midst of enormous change, though with substantial elements of continuity. But, as

Woodruff recognizes in his balanced conclusion, where all this will go is uncertain.

Woodruff has written an important book: a thoughtful interpretation of China—not just Beijing—during the apogee of Deng Xiaoping's influence. It joins its honored predecessors as a work students and scholars will turn to frequently to acquire a contemporary "feel" for a decisive moment in the nation's history.

MICHEL OKSENBERG

Acknowledgments,
Disclaimers,
Identities

The reader is entitled to know, first, what this book is not. It is not, to begin with, an attempt to define China. Mercifully for latecomers like myself, that burden fell to earlier reporters, those who took up residence in Beijing in 1979 and 1980 as the first generation of American correspondents in China since the Communist party won power in 1949. They have done that job, and it will not need doing again for some years. Neither is this a work of social science or scholarship. These are times of rapid change in China, and some years must pass before the less hurried, more systematic and studied method of the scholar will provide a satisfying overview. What this is, is a book of journalism about a sea change while it is still in progress. It is one reporter's attempt to describe and to comment upon what he saw of a unique moment in time, the years when Deng Xiaoping's great reform began to yield up discernible changes in the lives of an ancient people. Many years must pass before it will be clear whether this book is also about a truly seminal time in history, but part of the point of writing now is the realization that this possibility exists.

The reader is also entitled to know that the identities of many Chinese people mentioned in this book have been extensively changed. That has been necessary because, despite the substantial relaxation and opening of the society and polity under Deng Xiaoping, China remains a country where it is not yet altogether safe to speak freely, especially to foreigners and very especially to foreign correspondents. The voices heard in this book represent the kinds of people they seem to represent, but elements that might help the authorities discover actual individuals have been systematically changed. To scholars who might wish to know or guess more about speakers in the book, this will be a loss. That loss must be balanced against the personal safety of individuals who have given generously of their knowledge and their time.

This means that many of the people who have been most instrumental in the reporting that went into these pages can be acknowledged only in the broadest generalizations. A first book, as this is, can be a lesson in both the breadth and the depth of one's professional debts. High among mine in this case are those I owe to Professor Michel Oksenberg, a friend from my Hong Kong years, whose idea it was to attempt a book, who was instrumental in arranging the financial and academic support that made it possible, who has read and commented upon every chapter, and who has written the Foreword. Also high among my debts are those I owe to my past and present editors at *The Baltimore Sun,* who have trusted me with three assignments in Asia including the one that led to this book, and who have generously helped to make this writing project possible. During this academic year, I have had financial support from *The Baltimore Sun* and from three sources at The University of Michigan: the Department of Communication, the Center for Chinese Studies, and the Center for Japanese Studies. Faculty and staff members in all three places at Michigan, too numerous to mention individually, have participated generously in this effort. It has been a privilege and a pleasure, as well as a source of personal and professional pride, to have been welcomed as their colleague for an academic year.

I owe lifetime debts to Lynne Duke, who gave me my start in Chinese language at the School for Advanced International Studies (SAIS) of The Johns Hopkins University, and who is the best first-year language teacher I've ever heard of; to faculty members at SAIS and Michigan, who taught the courses that helped to make China and East Asia intelligible to a reporter who came to the subject as a greenhorn; and to teachers at the Mandarin Training Center of National Taiwan

Normal University, who struggled successfully to bring a middle-aged foreigner to a conversational level in a language vastly different from his own. Faculty members of the Center for Chinese Studies at Michigan generously read ample portions of the early drafts and offered suggestions and criticisms that have made this a far better piece of work than I could have made it on my own. If it has virtues, many are due to their contributions. Its failings are my wholly owned property.

JOHN WOODRUFF
Ann Arbor, Michigan
May 1988

China
in Search of
Its Future

1
Cars and Cadres

At a brand-new $250,000 downtown disco, a willowy young man with a pretty face, a punk haircut and billowing Hong Kong pantaloons showed off fluid moves that dominated the strobe-lighted dance floor. A pop singer at the bandstand wore a tuxedo and a maroon sweater-vest and rocked his pelvis as if to imitate Elvis. It was March 1985, and I was in Guangzhou, the capital of Guangdong, the South China province that adjoins Hong Kong. The disco's manager sat with me and my translator at our table, and I asked him whether the dancer or singer might be "Hong Kong compatriots," the official Chinese Communist term for Chinese residents of the British colony. "All the guests and entertainers here are local Cantonese Chinese people," the manager said. The singer's act ended, and in the intermission a tape boomed out American rock songs with lyrics that spoke very explicitly, though in English slang that none of the patrons seemed to understand, about drugs and selected sex acts.

I had lived in Beijing for two and a half years by that time, but I was getting a look at a China I had not previously seen. In South China, where more people can know more about the outside world than anywhere else in the country, I was looking at what some Chinese regarded as a vision of future urban life. In its atmosphere of relative personal freedom, in its accelerated pace of life, and in its economic growth, Guangzhou in 1985 was unlike anything I had ever before associated with China. As if to underscore the depth and breadth of rebellion against the drabness of the Maoist years, which were not yet a decade in the past, the city was awash in suggestions that the fastest-growing line of work might well turn out to be, not work at all, but play. After an introduction by some Chinese friends, a manager of the Oriental Hotel escorted me to the country's only room full of slot machines, known locally as "old tiger machines." The payoffs, though not in cash, ranged from toy plastic dump trucks to real color television sets. Before going back to Beijing, I would see golf courses under construction on land that had once been used to raise rice, roller coasters being put into place in two new amusement parks, multimillion-dollar night clubs going up to serve Japanese and Hong Kong tourists.

I had first seen Guangzhou, the city many people outside China know as Canton, more than twelve years earlier, in October 1972, when I was given a visa to visit the Canton Trade Fair for five days. Those were the years of "ping-pong diplomacy" after President Nixon's visits with Mao Zedong and Zhou Enlai. In those waning years of the late Chairman Mao's Great Proletarian Cultural Revolution, the only dancing I saw in public was in "revolutionary" ballets and operas championed by Jiang Qing, the chairman's wife and cultural tsarina of the radical years. On that 1972 visit, I entered by what was then the standard way of coming from Hong Kong—I took a train to the border, got off, and walked across the bridge at Lowu with my bags. At the midpoint of the bridge, a border guard frowned as he spotted Taiwan visa stamps in my passport. He gave me a memorized speech in English: "This is evidence of U.S. imperialism's plot to create two Chinas, or one China and one Taiwan. I must inform you that there is only one China, the People's Republic of China, and that Taiwan Province is a sacred part of China." Then he smiled professionally, extended his hand and said, "Welcome to visit the People's Republic of China." I carried my bags on into the station on the Chinese side and got on a train to Guangzhou.

During that first visit, an evening's entertainment typically began with a tedious banquet in a big room at the Oriental Hotel. These events ground on through rounds of toasts and speeches honoring "the great friendship of the world's peoples." The billboards outside the hotel carried nothing but paeans to Mao, to the already-fading Cultural Revolution, and to the pet communes and industries of his radical allies. "Down with the American imperialists and their running dogs," a billboard across from the hotel demanded. Virtually every Chinese I saw wore very short, very straight hair, a baggy gray or blue outfit, and a red-and-gold badge bearing an image of the "Great Helmsman" or the "Brilliant Red Sun in Our Hearts," as Chairman Mao was described in just two of more than two dozen glorifying epithets officially bestowed upon him. The fair, essentially a huge collection of halls where China shows off what it wants to export and lets foreigners show off what they want China to import, was a new and exotic experience for the handful of businessmen in the first American contingents ever to attend it. But French, British and Japanese traders who had been coming for years had learned to dread the fair because of after-midnight visits they had sometimes received from Red Guards and other radicals. These late-night seances did not take place in 1972, but old trade-fair hands were still talking about the days when teen-agers had knocked on their hotel-room doors and demanded that they get out of bed in the wee hours to join in "political study" and "self-criticism," activities that were taken seriously in the Cultural Revolution years.

The changes I saw in Guangzhou were one reflection of a sea change in Communist party policy. After the death of Mao Zedong in 1976, a new coalition of modernizers had come to power led by Deng Xiaoping. They threw out the revolutionary rhetoric of the Maoist decades and replaced it with the rhetoric of modernization. They gingerly expanded selected personal freedoms, dismantled Mao's huge farming communes and set out to use incentives to breathe life into a stagnant agriculture. For more than four years, from October 1982 to July 1987, it was my job to report on that sea change for my newspaper, *The Baltimore Sun*. This book is my attempt, before going on to my next reporting assignment, to describe and to comment upon some of what I saw in those years of change.

Guangzhou was far out front among Chinese cities in taking advantage of the new ways. Compared with what I had seen in October 1972, Guangzhou in March 1985 might have been on a different planet. High-speed hydrofoil boats routinely carried Japanese, European, American and Cantonese business commuters on a dozen scheduled runs to and from Hong Kong every day. Scheduled airline flights and direct express trains were equally routine. At the Oriental Hotel, the same cavernous banquet hall where I had winced at the Orwellian Newspeak of memorized toasts to "friendship" had been turned into an oversized bistro. Now, pop singers in sequined gowns stood under multihued spotlights to sing love songs from Taiwan, Hong Kong, and Japan. Billboards all over town advertised, not some officially vetted Maoist aphorism, but Hong Kong computers, American chemicals and the Japanese motorcycles that were already prominent in the city's traffic. The groaning Shanghai sedans and rusting Korean War–era Jeeps that had formed the heart of a hopelessly inadequate motor fleet were replaced by Toyota Crown, Citröen, and Volvo sedans. The miles of shutters that had turned much of the city's old commercial district into a somnolent backwater now came down every day to open the way to shoppers. Thousands of store fronts, turned into impromptu housing in the 1960s after Mao ordered the shops in them closed as "tails of capitalism," were reopening with new commercial tenants.

The Cantonese commercial instinct that dominates many Southeast Asian downtowns was aggressively reasserting itself in this capital city of the Cantonese people. New shops were opening so rapidly that, on mornings the fortunetellers considered auspicious, firecrackers celebrating new business places could be heard from several directions at once. Hong Kong money was finding its way into Guangdong, sometimes on a grand scale, as Cantonese from the neighboring British colony invested in steel-and-masonry towers like the White Swan, the China and the Garden, three international-standard hotels that were among the first in the country to compare with those of Hong Kong or Tokyo. I left Guangdong Province in 1985 to go to Hong Kong by way of Shenzhen, the same town through which almost every visitor had entered and left in 1972, but I went by high-speed jetfoil boat, not by walking across the bridge at Lowu. On my way out, I took a detour to the train station to see a propaganda billboard that had acquired a degree of fame. It was painted in the usual white characters on the usual red background and bore one of the few political slogans I saw on that 1985 visit to Guangdong Province. But it was politics with a difference. "Time," the slogan said, "is money."

That 1985 trip took me to Guangzhou some nine years after Mao Zedong's death had brought the Cultural Revolution irrevocably to its close, and some seven years after Deng Xiaoping had begun to consolidate his position and to dismantle much of what Mao had done in his twenty-seven years in power. For millions, Mao's Cultural Revolution remains today the formative political trauma of a lifetime. Having led the Chinese Communist party through decades of struggle to win power in 1949, Mao had gradually lost out in struggles with other titans of the revolution during the decade and a half after the Communists won the civil war. By the early 1960s, his vision of a radically collectivized society, reorganized into an armylike hierarchy, was rejected by most of the top Communists who had fought alongside him to win power. They sought to replace Mao's vision with a structure more nearly resembling the Soviet system. In 1966, largely in response to this rejection of social goals he had pursued for a decade, Mao and a handful of allies called out the nation's teen-agers, bestowed on selected ranks of them the title "Red Guard," and dispatched them to root out his enemies, real and imagined.

Mao had retained immense personal authority with most ordinary Chinese, despite his problems within the Communist party. In the summer and fall of 1966, Mao and his allies drew upon this personal authority to mobilize ranks upon ranks of his teen-aged Red Guards. The Maoist faction within the party sent these teen-agers as shock troops into the homes and work places of teachers, Communist party officials, monks, bureaucrats, writers and scores of other presumed "enemies" and "capitalist roaders." Red Guards were given free passes to travel on local buses and by bus or train from city to city. The Red Guard movement rapidly ran out of control, as local factions used the teenagers to settle grudges and pursue vendettas while rival units fought pitched battles in the streets of some cities. Red Guards ordered whole families out of their houses and then beat and spit on the alleged "enemy," along with any relative or friend who tried to protect the victim. Many were forced to put on dunce caps and signboards, watch their family books and heirlooms go up in flames and then parade through the streets while the teen-agers kicked and shoved them. Mao was elevated from superhero to cult figure, with literally hundreds of millions of new plastic, porcelain or metal badges issued in his image for occasions that might range from the opening of a new bridge to the explosion of China's first hydrogen bomb. Few city folk dared go out in public without a plastic Mao pinned to the shirt or jacket.

By 1968 the factional fighting was so disruptive that even the Maoists agreed to send in the army to restore order to cities, factories, and campuses. But for four or five more years, schoolchildren were led before some image of the Great Teacher twice every day, to ask for his instructions in the morning and to report back each night. "Lots of kids loved the Cultural Revolution," Ming Yueliang, a Beijing friend, told me twenty years later. "Every time Mao farted, they let us out of school so we could run through the streets waving the Little Red Book of his sayings. Not much work; lots of singing revolutionary songs. But it was weird. I've seen my mother's and father's love letters from those years. They all start with a Mao quote and end with a wish for a long, long life for the Brilliant Red Sun in Our Hearts."

Anyone with a college education, or with a parent or grandparent who had ever owned land or kept a shop, could become a candidate for banishment to farm labor, at minimum, or for imprisonment, beating, and possibly death. Thousands of families were forcibly ripped apart, sometimes with one parent in jail, the other parent and the older children in the countryside and the younger children left to fend for themselves alone in the city for anywhere from a few months to two or three years. University buildings went up in flames in several cities. The entire university system and many institutes and secondary schools closed down, most of the professors and administrators having been sent to farms to "learn from the peasants." The havoc wrought on China's ability to produce the educated Chinese it desperately needs was still not completely undone when I left, twenty-one years after the schools were first closed. By the early 1970s, what remained of the bureaucracy and the Communist party were so intimidated that only the People's Liberation Army seemed able to function fully as a national institution capable of keeping the country unified. Military units, which had been sent to many campuses to restore order in 1968, stayed on in many places for years after 1971 and 1972, when colleges and institutes began to reopen with skeleton student bodies. When I arrived to begin my tour as Beijing bureau chief of *The Baltimore Sun* in October 1982—more than sixteen years after the start of the Cultural Revolution and more than six years after Mao's death—on many university campuses, and in some factories and central government ministries, army units still occupied some of the dormitories, classrooms and offices.

A siege mentality went along with this domestic radicalism, part-and-parcel of a Maoist exploitation of timeless Chinese xenophobia. "Soviet Revisionists" and "American Imperialists" both were presumed ready to attack at any moment. Mao's government saw a world so full of enemies that Beijing eventually recalled its ambassadors from every post but Egypt and Albania. On the northern borders, Chinese and Soviet patrols actually did fight bloody skirmishes in the late 1960s. American troops were a real presence near China's borders in both South Vietnam and South Korea, and American policy still officially recognized the Nationalist party in Taiwan as the legitimate government of all China. "Dig tunnels deep and do everything for the people," Mao ordered, and many cities have spent the last ten years installing movie houses, inns, restaurants, and dance halls in attempts to get some practical use out of the nuclear bomb shelters dug in the Cultural Revolution years. Huge mounds of clay dug out of the earth for these tunnels mar many cities today, including a monumental pile every tourist passes on the way out of the park after visiting Beijing's famous Temple of Heaven. Some members of the first groups of American visitors in the early 1970s would later recall a sense that some Chinese seemed to be heaving a sigh of relief at the prospect of easing relations with a major power in such a hostile world.

Destructive as it was to China's governance and its educational system, and searing as it was for millions of people, the Cultural

Revolution is only one dimension of the trauma the Chinese have experienced since the middle of the nineteenth century. Ever since Western gunboats and armies began, first, to force the country open, and then, to tear off chunks of territory and put them under foreign sovereignty, there have been officials trying to find ways to cope with the outsiders. By the early years of the twentieth century, the Qing, the last of the imperial dynasties that ruled the country for thousands of years, was approaching collapse. But the republic that replaced the dynasty after it fell in 1911 proved too weak to govern. By the 1920s, the country had split into regions controlled by warlords, whose armies often plundered the population when they were not busy fighting one another. The first serious attempt to restore unity came when the Nationalist party moved its armies northward in the middle twenties, defeating each of the major warlords in succession.

But unification was not to last. An eighty-year-old Chinese who has spent a lifetime in, say, Shanghai or Nanjing, has lived since the teen years through times that have included: an all-out slaughter of Communists by Chiang Kai-shek's Nationalists in 1927; recurring natural catastrophes and famines; repeated Nationalist offensives against the Communists in the 1930s; the spreading Japanese bombing and military occupation of China's few relatively modern cities through the late 1930s and early 1940s; the staggering corruption and inflation that debilitated the Nationalists after World War II; the civil war by which the Communists routed the Nationalists to Taiwan and simultaneously, for the first time in a century, freed the country of foreign occupiers; the years of the Communists' early reprisals against their enemies after 1949; Soviet domination of the new industrial economy in the Stalin and Khrushchev years; the repeated mass mobilizations of the Maoist years; the widespread starvation of Mao's Great Leap Forward in the late 1950s—and, only after all of these traumas, Mao's Cultural Revolution of the late 1960s and early 1970s.

No other big country has passed so tumultuously through the past 100 years. Each new tumult has left its own marks, on each generation and on the nation as a whole. Most of the society remains deeply sensitive to this day over past depredations by foreigners, especially the Japanese but also including Westerners. Since 1949, in fields as diverse as literary criticism and political polemics, it is frequently thought a sufficient condemnation simply to brand an idea or a style "foreign" and say little more about it. But of all these national traumas, the deepest marks on the largest numbers living today are those left, not by foreigners, but by the Cultural Revolution, an event conceived and carried out solely by Chinese, using distinctively Chinese methods.

———

I went to Guangdong in March 1985, because that was the year the Communist party chose to extend into the cities some version of the ambitious social, economic, and political changes by which Deng Xiaoping and his reform-minded coalition in Beijing were already dramatically transforming the countryside. Guangdong is South China's window on the outside world, a populous and fertile neighbor of Hong Kong. Much that I had heard and read about this province suggested that it was getting a long head start in using private commerce, foreign business methods and a generally freer atmosphere to bring life to the musty urban economy built during Mao's twenty-seven years in power. It was not altogether surprising that, as Deng Xiaoping discarded Mao's Draconian collectives and set out to write new definitions of socialism, the Cantonese might be among the first to find advantage in the new ways. Cantonese have for centuries gone abroad to live, in Southeast Asia and later in California and New York, in vastly greater numbers than their countrymen. When foreign gunboats began to force the country open in the nineteenth century, it was the Cantonese—living far from any imperial capital, speaking a remote-sounding tongue, and enduring the scorn of northerners because they are shorter and swarthier and include dogs and snakes in their diets—who were chosen to make the first sacrifices. Hong Kong, itself handed over to the British from Guangdong Province's territory after the Opium Wars, would in later years give many Cantonese a window that kept alive an awareness of the outside world even amid the most xenophobic rampages of the Cultural Revolution in 1966 and 1967.

In the 1980s, as Deng Xiaoping reopened foreign contacts and set out to breathe life into the economy, Guangdong's contacts with the modern world gave it advantages that some Cantonese were quick to put to use. Thousands of the province's people already were well ahead of the rest of the country in glimmers of what the outside world was about, if only by dint of watching Hong Kong television for years. The booming economy of the British colony gave Guangdong a ready hard-currency market—unlike any available to other parts of the country—for pork, flowers and even the simpler textile and clothing items Hong Kong's own factories were giving up as they switched upscale to squeeze more cash out of a restricted American market. The Cantonese are as close to Hong Kong ethnically as they are geographically, for the colony's population of some 5.5 million is overwhelmingly dominated by refugees from Guangdong and their children and grandchildren, participants in or descendants of the recurring mass exoduses from Mao's Mainland. As the economy began to open, some of these Hong Kong Cantonese began to bring home some of their riches or family savings, to invest on their own or to help local relatives open shops, restaurants or small factories. A few overseas Cantonese from Southeast Asia, Europe and North America also joined in. Among these Hong Kong and overseas Cantonese investments, the three international-standard hotel towers stand as the most visible examples. But what I saw in Guangzhou in 1985 suggested that Hong Kong and overseas Cantonese investments in small food-processing, entertainment and textile operations, though less visible, probably were changing more lives more rapidly.

The life that was palpably coming to the streets of Guangzhou was one city's day-to-day experience of epochal changes that had taken place at the center of Chinese politics. It is by now more than adequately recorded by several authors that Deng Xiaoping rose to power in the late 1970s after Mao's death partly because he was a shrewd, hard and decisive Communist politician and partly because he had joined the Chinese party branch in France so young, at eighteen, that he simply outlived anyone else who had accumulated comparable credentials and connections over the half-century before Mao died. What sometimes gets less attention is the extent to which Deng's rise to power was powered by something that had also been a major weapon for the Great Helmsman before him—a vision capable of providing at least the general outlines of what his country would be like if he were allowed to recast it. But unlike Mao, whose rivals in the Communist party's early decades in power had their own well-formed and clear view of how to rebuild society, Deng has been further aided by the fact that his chief competitors of the post-Mao years have had nothing comparably appealing to offer.

By the time Mao died in 1976, China gave the impression of a country that knew with painful certainty what it did not want but seemed deeply confused about what it did want. What the country emphatically did not want, what thousands demonstrated or rioted against in several cities as Mao was dying, was a regimented, slogan-chanting, culturally arid society of daily hunger and perpetual shortages—the society it still was after repeatedly pursuing Mao's dream of transforming mankind itself through nationwide surges of political exhortation. Even Hua Guofeng, the man who claimed Mao had personally designated him to be the successor, joined in erasing that vision by arresting Jiang Qing (Mao's widow), the three Shanghai radicals who with Jiang Qing were branded the "Gang of Four," and some of their key supporters. But Hua Guofeng's notion of what to do next consisted mainly of rebuilding the Maoist system, without the class struggle that had energized it. Near the end of the seventies, Deng Xiaoping began to accumulate enough power to effect his own ends. In those years of jockeying for the succession, Deng Xiaoping had one critical asset Hua Guofeng and other rivals lacked—a vision of where to go that had real appeal among both educated and ordinary people.

In the shorthand my colleagues and I often use to summarize events that our papers and newscasts do not have space or time to spell out, Deng's approach to politics and economics is most commonly labeled "pragmatic." The word is not inaccurate, but it falls short of capturing how fundamentally and diametrically opposed Mao's and Deng's visions have been. Conscious that he had reunified China for the first time in more than a century, and believing he had won power by forced marches of sheer human will, Mao set out after 1949 to use his new power and his mobilization techniques to do nothing less than change human nature itself. He was determined that his would be the country that would give life to the New Socialist Man, who, in most official Chinese views, had been stillborn in the Soviet Union. It was toward this end that Mao drafted all he could of the countryside into vast collective farming "communes" and drove the simplest biscuit and noodle vendors from the city streets as "tails of capitalism."

As he rose to power in the late 1970s after the Great Helmsman's death, Deng's approach to governance was 180 degrees opposite Mao's. Without giving up his often-stated insistence that the new way must still be Marxist and socialist, Deng nevertheless set out, as he gathered power after Mao's death, not to rewrite human nature, but to put human nature to use as he found it. Thus, he sought to turn ordinary, day-to-day human self-interest—even greed and avarice, within limits, and the limits are not always well defined—into motivations for human labor. He summarizes his program as the "Four modernizations"—of industry, agriculture, science and technology, and the military. This vision of Marxism calls for reducing state control of the economy, for opening the way to diplomacy and trade with the rest of the world, and for replacing mass mobilization with personal incentive as the chief motivator of human effort. It is making room for small-scale private businesses and for medium-scale, cooperatively owned factories to operate wholly outside the state plan; for farmers to raise pigs and chickens for profit; for foreigners to invest in restaurants and even railroads; even for foreign-style management schools and for a modest degree of carefully controlled shareholding in some state factories.

That difference is so fundamental that for millions of people it is changing the events of daily life, the ways people choose their friends and spouses, the shapes and sizes of their houses and the furniture inside them, the systems of education and health care, the places and ways people work and earn livings. These changes have brought a vigor to farms that has ended perennial rationing of agricultural products ranging from foodgrains to cotton. They have restored to the city dweller's routine the commonplace convenience of being able to buy a breakfast bun from a street vendor on the way to work, or to find a shoe repairman in the neighborhood. They have also resulted in small steps toward knitting together a single national economy, rather than a collection of economic fiefdoms. In less than a decade, the country has gone from being chronically unable to meet the scant cloth rations it promised its own billion people, to being a major textile and clothing exporter, one of the leading competitors in the United States market. Though many of its major state factories fall far short of the

Beijing motorcyclist riding with a girlfriend. Sunglasses, baseball caps and
girlfriends were badges of modernity among under-30 Chinese throughout the
1980s. For many, a motorcycle was the ultimate status symbol.

A stylish young socialist consumer uses an umbrella for protection from the sun, to preserve the light complexion many Chinese treasure, as she rides home on the delivery tricycle that carries her family's new apartment-sized refrigerator.

This security guard at the Beijing Hotel sports the new white summer uniform that in 1985 replaced the faded, baggy blue cotton jackets of the Maoist years. Fashions changed throughout the 1980s, not only for trendy young singles and couples but for many uniformed personnel.

Left: A new plastic-upholstered sofa heads home on a delivery tricycle. Young city Chinese often sell old, even antique, mahogany furniture they have inherited, often to government shops for a fraction of their market value, in order to buy modern plastic pieces at much higher prices. Then the government sells the antiques to foreigners for hard currency at big markups.

Young workers at a new hotel site in Beijing pose for a foreigner with a camera during a break in 1986. The straw hat worn by the worker on the right is the standard-issue Chinese equivalent of a hard hat, a commonplace at many urban construction sites.

Photo by John Schidlovsky, courtesy of The Baltimore Sun

The author, beside a sign that says "Out of bounds for foreigners without special permits." Signs like these, in Chinese, Russian and English, are posted a few kilometers out of town on roads leading out of most major cities. They are sometimes enforced, as in the 1986 expulsion of John Burns, *The New York Times* correspondent.

Left: In Chinese, these signs say "Please don't spit on the ground" and "Protect public hygiene." Molded plastic signs appeared in residential projects and lanes all over Beijing in the mid-1980s, part of the Communist party's periodic public hygiene campaigns. City people are urged to use long-handled, covered spittoons, like the one pictured on the spitting sign. The spittoons are available in many public places.

In the Valley of the Ming Tombs, a peasant girl from a nearby village, hooded to prevent a suntan that would bring her disgrace, serves as caddy for Japanese golfers on North China's first course. The course was built with Japanese funds and serves an almost exclusively Japanese clientele.

Right: The Jianguomenwai diplomatic housing complex, home to the author for four years and ten months. This government-operated complex, at one of Beijing's key intersections, went up in the 1980s, after Deng Xiaoping's open policy greatly expanded China's diplomacy and the overall presence of foreigners. Most foreign correspondents are required to live in such compounds.

Contrasting eras of foreign presence. On Shamian Island, in Guangzhou, an old church, built when the island was a reservation for foreigners, now serves as a warehouse, factory, and bicycle repair shop. At right, the new Hong Kong–owned White Swan Hotel, one of China's handful meeting top international standards, makes the island again a center of foreign presence.

A boatyard in Fujian Province turns out international-quality yachts with fiberglass hulls. But first the American manager had to go to the top officials of the province to force the retirement of an old boatyard official who deliberately undermined his attempts to install a system of rewards and penalties for workers.

contributions they could make, the country's industrial growth, often led by small, privately owned plants and all-but-private "cooperatives," now ranks among the fastest of any large country in the world. Shortages remain in broad ranges of consumer goods, and quality is so questionable that many people still routinely pay severalfold to buy imported refrigerators or television sets, but the past ten years have seen item after item go off ration coupons. In my years in Beijing, an item as simple as the tomato went from being a rarity to being a commonplace in the free markets for nine or ten months of the year. The hand wrench went from being sold only in hardware shops, and only to work units, to being a staple of most department stores, available to anyone who could pay.

At the same time, it is true that the changes often encompass steps backward into ancient ways Mao had sought with good reason to destroy. They also often lead into totally uncharted territory, down roads that Deng and his allies sometimes seem neither to foresee nor to comprehend, and to unwanted results like a seemingly endemic corruption and occasional bouts with prostitution. But change under Deng is based on acceptance rather than rejection of the basic conditions of human nature, and it is aimed at bringing his countrymen into the mainstream of modern life rather than making the country the inventor of a whole new world. For those reasons, change under Deng is in many ways more dramatic and, for better or worse, may have far greater chances of enduring, than all the monumental change Mao himself accomplished through the revolutionary mayhem of his twenty-seven years in power.

After more than a year of retooling to fit newly devised official versions of reality, the pink marble Mao Zedong Memorial Hall, just south of the center of Tiananmen Square, reopened to the public on Mao's birthday, December 26, 1983. The hall had been rushed into existence—in an appropriately Maoist forced march—upon the Great Helmsman's death in 1976. It was placed prominently in the same square where Mao had declared the founding of the People's Republic of China on October 1, 1949, which then became the new National Day. Breaking an ancient rule of Chinese architecture, the hall was built with a main entrance facing north, so that visitors could enter within sight of the heroic-sized portrait of the chairman. The portrait still dominates the Gate of Heavenly Peace, the main entrance to the ancient emperors' Forbidden City, where Mao stood in 1949 to proclaim the new People's Republic and again in 1966 to review hundreds of thousands of teen-aged Red Guards and to declare the opening of the Cultural Revolution.

For its first six years, the mausoleum housed only the public display of Chairman Mao's memorabilia and, under glass, his refrigerated and chemically preserved corpse, draped with a bright red Communist party flag with yellow hammer and sickle. But when it reopened on Mao's birthday in 1983, it had major new displays. These new exhibitions were memorials to three more dead heroes of the Communist revolution, each of whom had been in some way Mao's victim in the Cultural Revolution. The newly opened rooms now restored full honor as revolutionary heroes upon Liu Shaoqi, once the official heir-apparent as president of the People's Republic but vilified as "China's Khrushchev" after Mao turned on him at the start of the Cultural Revolution in 1966; to Premier Zhou Enlai, Mao's loyal right hand through most of the guerrilla years but denounced as a latter-day "Confucius" near the end of the Cultural Revolution; and Marshal Zhu De, the cofounder of the People's Liberation Army, whom the Cultural Revolutionaries had stripped of top honors in the late 1960s as they rewrote the script of the revolution to make Mao the singular military genius of the epoch. On the hall's reopening day, a contingent of China's ubiquitous professional welcomers stood on the north steps, ready with professional smiles and handshakes to lead a contingent of foreign reporters for an advance look at the revised standard version of the revolution. "It is indeed a rare privilege," Christopher S. Wren, then *The New York Times* correspondent in Beijing, said, "to be present as history is rewritten." Chris gave the welcomers a grin that was half mischief and half self-satisfaction.

Rewriting history is a solemn undertaking within the Chinese Communist party, and the reopening of the revised Mao mausoleum was nothing less than the most prominent single tangible expression of the most radical rewriting history had undergone since the beginning of the Cultural Revolution itself some seventeen years earlier. The rewriting had become indispensable, for there was no way to leave the

Mao cult intact while dismantling so much of what Mao had done in more than two and a half decades in power. So the rewriting began while Deng was still consolidating his power at the end of the 1970s, and the first attempt at codification came in a resolution approved by the Communist party Central Committee in 1981. That resolution effectively made official doctrine of Deng's own version of the revolution. The new version not only restores revolutionary hero status to Liu Shaoqi, Zhou Enlai, Zhu De, and other Cultural Revolution victims but, more important, it cuts Mao back down from godlike status to that of a mere human superhero. Mao was the greatest of the revolutionaries, the resolution said, and without him there would have been no New China. But after he won power in 1949, he made major mistakes, chief among them the Cultural Revolution. After that, in the party-controlled newspapers the very words "Cultural Revolution" would have to appear in quotation marks, and the events would increasingly be mentioned in pejoratives as "the ten years of chaos" or "the ten-year calamity."

This massive rewriting of history continues today. By 1986 Deng Xiaoping himself had extended the definition of Mao's "mistakes" years earlier into the chairman's decades in power, adding to the list two formative events of the 1950s, the Anti-Rightist Campaign and the Great Leap Forward. The new version thus holds that Mao's entire twenty-seven years in power were overwhelmingly dominated by blunders that cost the country priceless time and resources in its attempts to move from the Third World into the developing world. Multiple-volume, officially vetted "Collected Works" by Deng Xiaoping and many others whose writings had long been banned or left unpublished are now regular offerings of the Communist party–controlled printing houses. But the party conducts this rewriting in gingerly fashion. On the one hand, its new policies require a version of history that explains why some of Mao's proudest achievements—the vast agricultural communes, repression of the scantest shreds of private profit—must now be reversed. On the other hand, the Communist party is still the instrument by which Deng and his allies propose to rule and remake society. Any rejection of Mao's revolutionary years would directly raise unanswerable questions about the Communist party itself, and about the ways it won and used its power. So Mao must remain the greatest of the great among revolutionaries, even as the cult is dismantled.

The new official version gets much closer than any previous one did to what foreign historians and political scientists think they understand about China's history, though it greatly overstates the Cultural Revolution's impact on industry after the initial chaos of 1966, 1967 and 1968. It has also brought forth reams of information, adding to the world's knowledge of tumultuous and little-understood times. But those are not its purposes. Its purpose is to provide a context for China's masses to understand the new party line. The Deng Xiaoping leadership is betting that that purpose will be adequately served without dwelling on some of the most telling questions about history under the Communist party. The Liu Shaoqi room that opens a few yards off Mao's right hand in the mausoleum makes no mention, for example, of how Liu died, though many people are aware of an officially sanctioned account that says he died of pneumonia, unattended and ill-clothed, in Cultural Revolution confinement. As to Mao's own life, the revised exhibitions simply leave blank the later years, the years of his most colossal "mistakes." The mausoleum stands athwart the south end of the same square where Mao reviewed huge rallies of some of the millions of armband-wearing Red Guard teen-agers he sent out to bash professors and all but dismantle the Communist party itself. But the displays inside offer only eery silence as to what went on in that square—and in Mao's life and in China—during the ten years from 1966 to his death, the years when Mao personally led his people into the tumultuous upheaval that most marks the political consciousness of millions today. And the displays leave room for future rewriting of history. The Chou Enlai paraphernalia on display in the room that opens a few yards from Mao's left hand spills over for the moment into a smaller hall not unlike the one given over to Zhu De. When I asked Chinese friends whether they thought Chou Enlai's memorabilia would always need so much space, some suggested that the smaller room might one day be filled by tributes to Deng Xiaoping.

Located deep in South China, Guangzhou has much in common with cities of Southeast Asia. For blocks along its streets, commercial buildings have porticos and overhangs to ensure that pedestrians will be able to shop even in the sudden and furious rainstorms that are seasonal throughout the region. The city's streets are narrow and winding, consistent with the riverine setting near the apex of the Pearl River Delta. It was on these convoluted streets, two and a half years into my assignment, that I got my first taste of another characteristic Guangzhou was beginning to share with the metropolises of Southeast Asia—a bona fide traffic jam. Riding to an appointment in a newly imported, blue Toyota Crown taxi, air-conditioned and with the back-seat windows peek-proofed by white lace after the manner of the typical Communist party official, I saw my watch tick away the minutes as we sat in locked traffic, moving a few car lengths at a time only to come again to a dead stop.

I was being led to the interview by a local guide from the Guangdong Province Foreign Affairs Office. Every province, city, county, township and village has its foreign affairs office, as does every university, factory, temple, oil field, museum and almost any other organized entity. The staffs of these offices are expected to ensure that foreign scholars, politicians, journalists and other visitors get the best possible impression and see as little ugliness as possible in local life. They must also make the foreigner's visit as smooth as they can in the often-difficult circumstances of a Third World country. In many places, the ubiquitous China International Travel Service guides who lead tourists from shrine to banquet to Friendship Store work for a branch that reports to this local foreign affairs office. Many foreign residents call these professional hosts and guides "barbarian handlers," in reference to the centuries when emperors maintained similar staffs to keep the headmen of the surrounding Mongols, Manchus, Tibetans and other borderland peoples in line. On the second day of our visit, as time grew long and the traffic relentlessly blocked our movement, our handler repeatedly jumped out of the car and walked ahead, as if hoping to break the jam singlehandedly. It was a nervous gesture, reflecting his knowledge that he, and not the foreigner, would be blamed for this unforgivable tardiness, which eventually stretched into an hour and a quarter. We had allowed twenty-five minutes to go a bit over two miles to the interview. It took us an hour and forty minutes.

In traffic, too, then, the contrast with my 1972 visit to Guangzhou was complete. In that earlier stay, the main traffic problem had been the fact that most bicyclists, pedestrians and handcart haulers were not in the habit of making way for the few cars on the streets. As we sat locked in place in 1985, the driver said traffic jams had been common in Guangzhou for more than a year, since the flow of imported luxury cars had reached flood tide as a little-anticipated but visually very striking by-product of opening the economy under Deng Xiaoping's reforms. In Guangzhou, I would experience many more such traffic jams, which made it as hard to plan a day's appointments in that once-somnolent city as it has been for decades in, say, Bangkok or Manila. Before leaving China, I would be caught in similar traffic snarls several times in Shanghai and would begin to feel the pressure of mounting numbers of cars even on Beijing's six-lane-wide main thoroughfare, Chang An Dajie, the Avenue of Eternal Peace. Any visitor can see these mounting traffic problems. For me, the car came to symbolize both how much life is changing and how much it is staying the same under Deng Xiaoping's reforms. During my five years in China, nothing more clearly summarized the currents and crosscurrents of change than the role of the automobile in urban society.

———————

After 1949, through all the unchartable power struggles and all the manmade catastrophes of Maoist movements like the Great Leap Forward and the Cultural Revolution, one fact of life had remained stable for more than two decades. You knew who was who by looking at the cars. Access to an automobile began only with the upper-middle levels of the Communist party, the People's Liberation Army or the government bureaucracy. At that level, the state was most likely to assign a clanking Shanghai-brand sedan, with a driver, doilies on the felt upholstery, and lace curtains on the rear windows so that the common folk couldn't see too much. During my Guangzhou visit of 1972, a rusting, cream-colored Shanghai sedan was my daily transportation. The shock absorbers had long since given out, giving each day's outing a feel that resembled a rowboat ride on a breezy day, and the car frequently wheezed and sighed and slowed down on the few uphill pulls. But it got us there and back every day, including two days of driving to communes more than an hour's ride outside the city. In the army, sedans were in such short supply that more than a few generals had to make do with Beijing-made jeeps, a cumbersome and under-powered version copied from the Russians about the time of the Korean War.

At the highest levels of power, a few provincial and big-city officials, top-ranking Communists in Beijing, and the highest ranks of the army could navigate the cities in the flagship of the Chinese auto industry, the Red Flag limousine. This dinosaur has tires big enough for a hefty pickup truck, leather upholstery, interior wood paneling, and rear leg room and head room for a pair of young giraffes. It also has a reputation for burning gasoline at a pace unequalled by most racing cars.

In Mao's Socialist system, especially in the years of purported Maoist egalitarianisn, these scarce few hundreds of thousands of sedans and limousines were in one sense much what a car is in any capitalist society—the ultimate combination of convenience and status. But there was a vast gulf between the social role of the car under Mao and the social role of the car in the West. The car in Mao's society was, to begin with, a carefully allocated political perquisite of high position, a sign of rank rather than of wealth, a reward for decades, at least, of political loyalty. There was scarcely such a thing as private car ownership. As late as 1984, a friend who had managed to buy a broken-down car smiled slyly as he showed me his registration card, which he said showed that his was the 357th automobile privately registered by a Chinese in Beijing since 1949. A peculiarity of the system was that virtually none of the top officials to whom a car was assigned had a driver's license or any inclination to drive, for the state or the party assigned a driver along with the car.

For many of those privileged to have one of these China-made vehicles, one of the most searing experiences of opening the country to the outside world, and beginning to send delegations to capitalist countries, appears to have been what they learned about their cars. These coveted status symbols, earned by a lifetime of loyalty to the Communist party, emblems of personal rank and of the country's productive advancement, quickly proved to be out-of-date junkers that wouldn't have passed air-pollution, mileage, or safety checkups in much of the world. Many had ordinary window glass that splintered if broken, not safety glass. When I arrived in October 1982, the streets were still dominated by these sagging Shanghai sedans and shambling black Red Flag limousines, but both were already scheduled to go out of production. A few Mercedes had begun to supplant the Red Flags, and Toyotas were already becoming commonplace, especially in Beijing, the capital.

By May 1984, China-made vehicles were rapidly going out of style among officials. When the late Gary Black, Sr., then chairman of the board of my newspaper, and Reg Murphy, the publisher, came to Beijing, I thought I would treat them to a Red Flag while it was still possible to rent one. I booked the car weeks in advance, as had to be done with most matters of any logistical importance in Beijing. By the time my bosses arrived, Beijing was prematurely into the year's first major heat wave. With temperatures daily reaching well into the 90s, it turned out that the car's air conditioner worked only if we drove at over thirty kilometers an hour, a speed seldom reached on Beijing streets. Even then it was only partially effective. The driver jumped out to open the hood and let the engine cool every time we stopped for an interview, a meal, or a tourist site, but I was not yet good enough in Chinese to persuade him to park in the shade for the benefit of his human cargo. The sweat stains spread until our shirts were almost completely soaked. But the two top officers of *The Baltimore Sun* succeeded somehow in remaining civil to the Beijing correspondent who was giving them this unplanned object lesson in why ranking officials were so rapidly abandoning the products of their own country's automobile factories. On the second day, my guests from the capitalist world joined me in the trend set by thousands of high-level Communists. We switched away from this symbol of local industrial self-reliance in favor of an air-conditioned black Toyota Crown, also equipped with the requisite white doilies and rear curtains.

The flood of imported cars has crowded the city streets, offering not only more and newer cars than have ever before been seen but also a much greater variety of makes and models, as if to reflect a society that is rapidly becoming more complex as new forms of economic organizations arise alongside the limited range of state enterprises the Maoist system favored. It has not changed the basic fact that car ownership is part of the socialist system, for the overwhelming majority of these new sedans are still owned by the "work unit" and are supposed to be assigned according to rank and business need. But the role of the car in political patronage has taken unexpected new turns. The ability to have a car assigned has percolated much farther down into the middle ranks than was ever previously imagined. Foreign businessmen have increasingly reported that they must disguise the cost of a car, or sometimes several cars, in the prices they offer to the local companies or ministries with which they deal, as a prerequisite to getting a contract. The rank system often seems on the verge of breaking down, as business connections frequently enable lower unit officials either to obtain cars long before higher-ranking government officials who are still at least nominally their superiors, or to get much better cars than do their superiors.

By 1986, Hong Kong newspapers with good sources high in the Communist party were reporting a series of rifts over cars. A typical instance began in 1985, when the Chinese Academy of Sciences caught the attention of top-level Communists by importing a fleet of deluxe cars for its ranking officers.[1] Top Communists whose own Toyota Crown sedans did not match the academy's new imports began to lean on the academy officials to exchange cars, which in turn fueled envy among senior comrades who could not get access to the new luxury cars. The resultant jealousies led inexorably to a series of reports to the Communist party Politburo, and eventually the case drew the attention of the prickly octogenarian Chen Yun. As a member of the Politburo's Standing Committee, Chen Yun was at that time officially one of the five most powerful men in the country and the head of the party's Central Discipline and Inspection Commission. Chen ordered that everyone who got a new car from the Academy of Sciences return it posthaste. Then he ordered the disciplinary commission to punish the offenders under party rules. Comparable crackdowns on comparably convoluted car dealings have been reported in most provinces, in many cities and at virtually every middling and upper level of the Communist party. For several months in 1985 and 1986, ranking local Communists in a series of major cities thought it useful, when facing investigation, to make the grand gesture of returning cars they had commandeered from levels below them.

———————

The automobile also has become a daily target of thieves—423 thefts in 1985 in Beijing, police officials reported—as rising crime rates have inevitably accompanied the relaxation of social controls that is a central part of the reforms. Most of these thefts have been for joy rides, but a few have been by serious criminals who have used the cars in murders and robberies. The car has also become a recurrent focus of corruption, including the biggest single money scam in Chinese Communist party history. That scam took place on Hainan Island, off Guangdong Province in the south, when local officials discovered ways to take advantage of the island's status as a duty-free zone. They imported tens of thousands of Japanese cars, then sold them at huge markups to places in the interior that would otherwise have had to pay duties amounting to more than 100 percent of the purchase price. By the time the Hainan Island scam was broken, it had extended to imported televisions and tape recorders and had involved government agencies ranging from the customs service to the navy, whose ships were used to deliver thousands of the cars from the island to the mainland.

The Hainan Island scam was one of many ways in which the automobile made major contributions to a massive drain on carefully husbanded foreign currency reserves in 1985, when the government sought to expedite development by relaxing its exchange regulations. Instead of the hoped-for surge in imported machinery and technology, the relaxation produced a massive leap in automobile, electronic, and other consumer imports. It apparently proved much easier to form a taxicab company and import a few dozen cars than to steer blueprints for new production equipment through a sluggish bureaucracy. By the time the government decided to crack down and recentralize control of foreign currency purchases, reserves had plunged by several billion dollars, to about $11 billion. In the meantime, hundreds of foreign companies had negotiated contracts based on the relaxed rules, only to discover that goods already delivered could not legally be paid for in hard currency or that payment would be delayed for months. Aside from tens of thousands of imported cars that suddenly became available to officials, Beijing, Guangzhou and several other cities acquired the distinction of ranking among the few places in the world with taxi fleets dominated by brand-new Toyota Crowns, Nissan Cedrics, Volvos and Citröens. In many parts of the countryside, the numbers of trucks and tractors on the road increased comparably, adding to a growing impression of ceaseless motor traffic against a backdrop of Third World agriculture and architecture.

For the overwhelming majority of China's one billion people, the automobile remains such a remote prospect that few ever contemplate what it might be like to have one. Only a small minority have ever taken a ride in a car, and even among city people, personal experience of the inside of an automobile seldom extends beyond the occasional taxi trip. Several times I parked *The Baltimore Sun*'s green Toyota Cressida station wagon near a tourist site and later came back to find a family gathered beside it to pose for pictures. When I had time, I sometimes suggested that they take pictures of one another actually sitting in the car, an invitation usually accepted with nervous laughter that seemed to betray awe and delight all at once. At the Forbidden City and some other tourist sites, photographers do a thriving business taking pictures of visitors posed with old Shanghai sedans.

But most people have not needed much contact with the automobile to feel dramatic differences in their lives in the past eight or ten years. The car is only one of the more visible indexes of what is going on in the economy, society and polity as Deng Xiaoping and his reformers grope for a Chinese way into the modern world. The new economic life that the automobile brings so dramatically to the foreign visitor's attention on city streets is part of a broader and rapidly growing emphasis on convenience and comfort, an expanding personal mobility and freedom. It has led to a substantial growth in personal incomes and a rapidly improving availability of goods and services, as well as to a stretching and evasion of old and new rules and a growth of corruption and crime. All these changes are taking place, in ways both visible and harder to see, in the daily lives of millions of people.

Chinese friends in Beijing loved to talk about these changes, delighting in newly available tape recorders or vegetables but bemoaning price increases that have accompanied the reforms. These conversations often provided glimpses of how the reforms were working, how the incentives Deng Xiaoping has introduced were creating both improvements and new sources of dissatisfaction in people's daily lives. To a significant extent, the dissatisfactions had to do with China's belated entry into the world of rising expectations, after decades of simply being so isolated that few people had any real idea how far the rest of the world had moved since 1949. Today, millions are aware of products and ways of living that had been kept from them for years.

One recurring conversation with Chinese friends taught me how the same changes that improve lives can simultaneously breed discontent. That conversation usually began with complaints by a friend about the latest round of increases in the price of lean pork. Pork is the principal meat but is still reserved mainly for special occasions in a lifestyle that affords little animal protein. Many cities had taken lean pork off the controlled list, and many others had allowed its price to rise several-fold during the 1980s. Shoppers were often shocked to find another major price increase when they went to get meat for a special meal. I would usually agree sympathetically that the price had gone up dizzily, and I would ask my friend how often his family had served lean pork in the past year. The reply might typically be six or eight times, and I would agree that this didn't seem very often. "You must have been able to afford lean pork much more often when the price was so much lower," I would comment, knowing that the truth was the opposite. "Well," my friends would reply, "not really—in fact, at the old prices, only at Chinese New Year." "If the price was so low before the reforms," I would ask, knowing what the answer would be, "why so seldom?" "There wasn't any in the markets," my friends would acknowledge. The controlled prices had been so low for so long that, through most of the Maoist years, farmers would not even attempt to raise the number of hogs the market demanded. Supplies were only somewhat less short even by 1986, and the new high prices made pork still an item to be eaten only on special occasions. But many urban families are now eating pork at the higher prices far more often than they did at the lower, because now more farmers raise hogs.

These changes in the economy, polity and daily life are broad and dramatic, but their roots will remain shallow and vulnerable to political change for years. This reality impressed itself on me one morning during my 1985 visit to Guangzhou, as a fiftyish man named Chen Sinchang squeezed his well-fed and well-clothed frame through narrow staircases, leading me from one tiny loft to another. Mr. Chen was showing me small rooms where young Cantonese women sat at sewing machines, all placed near windows to get enough light to stitch dresses, skirts, and blouses. "They say I am becoming the richest man in Guangzhou," Mr. Chen said with a broad smile after we had passed a cramped stairwell landing that he and his wife used as their bedroom. In the downtown row house he has turned into an improvised factory building, he explained, he couldn't spare a room for sleeping quarters because every room with a window was in use for production. Rooms without windows were crammed full of pre-cut pieces or dresses waiting to be shipped. Mr. Chen and seven family members had joined forces in 1979 to start the dress factory with two treadle-powered sewing machines. By the time I visited six years later, he had hired thirty additional workers and owned nine new electric sewing machines, ten foot-powered ones, seven electric hemming machines, three electric cutting machines, a $40,000 savings account, and a $50,000 share in a nearby government building, purchased for space to expand his ever-growing dress factory. He estimated that his monthly orders ran to about 9,000 frocks and blouses, worth about $16,000.

In most of the world, Mr. Chen would have been called a small businessman. But in a land still groping to define what Deng Xiaoping means when he speaks of "socialism with a Chinese face," officials were still shy in 1985 about admitting that any creature so recently reviled and persecuted as the businessman could now be permitted to flourish. Mr. Chen himself, in fact, had been beaten and paraded through Guangzhou's streets in 1966, wearing a dunce cap and a signboard labeling him an "illegal capitalist" because he owned four sewing machines and worked as a private dressmaker. Now Mr. Chen was running a small factory that employed thirty young women who, a few years earlier, might have been "job-awaiting youths," the official euphemism for unemployed school graduates. He was selling dresses to every province, a fact that by itself spoke volumes, both about improvements in the country's transportation system and about the rapid erosion of Mao's dictum that every region, province, county, town, and commune must be as "self-reliant" as possible. Mr. Chen thus was owner of a modest factory, employer of dozens of workers and a small-scale pioneer in China's attempts to knit together a national economy to replace Mao's deeply compartmentalized system. If such a man was not a businessman, then what was he? "We call him an individual laborer," a guide from the government foreign affairs office replied when I asked. "Individual laborer" was a new economic category permitting labor for personal profit under the new rules established as part of the reforms. As formulated, the category applied mainly to neighborhood service people, shoe repairmen, biscuit vendors and the like. A complex system of rules was supposed to put very strict limits on the number of employees that "individual laborers" could hire from outside their families.

Mr. Chen's shipments to other provinces went far beyond the neighborhood concept, and thirty was far more than any number of non-family workers permitted by the published rules. One reason Guangzhou's economic growth was ahead of most other places seemed to be a willingness to stretch the new rules, making them fit whatever worked rather than restraining successful ventures to make them fit the rules. This principle was working well in Mr. Chen's factory, but what might a change in China's volatile political climate do to some of the ventures spawned by Deng's reforms?

Mr. Chen said he felt confident that his position was secure, and it seemed so the day I visited his factory. He had been named a delegate to the Guangdong Provincial People's Political Consultative Conference, an adjunct to the provincial legislature, shortly before I visited. That kind of political insurance might well insulate him against any minor or short-term changes in the climate. But the government's inability to find within the new reform system a category that really fit what he was doing also was an index of how fragile some of the most successful undertakings remained under the reform. A less hospitable administration, in Beijing or in Guangzhou, would have little trouble finding grounds to harass Mr. Chen, perhaps even to hound him out of business, all the while sticking well within the rules outlined by the reforms. Even as I read articles in which newspapers and officials of other provinces pointed to Guangzhou as a place to emulate, I could not shake off the feeling that the roots of some of the most successful undertakings remained fragile, that important parts of what was so dramatically changing could be shredded by any strong or long-lasting change in the political winds out of Beijing or the provincial headquarters.

That fragility stems not only from China's long history of political volatility but also from the tangle of hopes and successes, frustrations and difficulties, that have accompanied rapid economic growth. The Chinese people have experienced both the delights and the unintended fallouts of new relative riches, new relative freedoms, many promising beginnings, some successes and some disappointments in these years of searching for something to replace the discarded Maoist dream. Their story is the story of a nation in search of its own future. A look at that search in terms of what it suggests about how far the world's most populous country has come since Mao Zedong died, and how much farther it still has to go, and some of my own thoughts on the long-term prospects for Deng Xiaoping's reforms, will be the grist of the chapters that follow.

2

Starting
in the Countryside

In the fields around Jinan, the capital of East China's Shandong Province, spring can seem harsher than winter. Northern winds still rake this eastern edge of the North China Plain well into April, long after the last snows have ceased to cover the powdery yellow earth, and the land dries so quickly the frost seems to evanesce rather than thaw. The chill air begins to fill with fine dust even before the first farmers pile on padded blue overcoats, wrap themselves in scarves, jam hats down over heavy bandannas, and grip the crooked wooden shafts that will bear steel-tipped hoes back into the annual struggle to extract human subsistence from the reluctant soil. As the hoes begin to rise and fall, the winter crust gives way, six or eight inches at each stroke in tens of thousands of tiny farm patches, releasing more and more of Shandong's surface into the winds. For days at a time, repeatedly until planting season ends and crops shoot up their first sprouts, the counties around Jinan become home to thousands of small, manmade dust storms.

In March 1985 I spent three days with a translator, a driver, and the usual squadrons of government-assigned barbarian handlers, driving north and west from Jinan into this chill, sandpapery wind to visit farmers and villagers. Wherever we went, the first impression was of the starkest imaginable contrast with the propaganda pictures that had dominated the decades of the late Chairman Mao Zedong's radical collectivizing. Those photos from the 1960s and early 1970s, published by the tens of millions, showed long ranks of peasants, rosy cheeked and joyously inching their collective way across the sun-drenched fields of a commune, often accompanied by a big red tractor or even a row of tractors, usually raising and driving their hoes in unison for the common prosperity. In 1985, what I watched through the dust haze of the Shandong spring, and dozens of other times wherever I went in China, was the precise opposite—mile after mile of tiny plots, each being laboriously broken open by a solitary farmer with a hoe. In Shandong that spring, I seldom saw as many as three or four people working together in the same field. The People's Communes, the vast farming collectives that had been the proudest single achievement of Mao's decades in power, were gone.

After Mao's death in 1976 made the concept of life without a Cultural Revolution mentionable, the men who were rising to power with Deng Xiaoping confronted compelling reasons to dismantle the Great Helmsman's work first in the countryside, rather than in the cities. Foremost among these reasons was the arithmetic of the Chinese people, whose numbers were approaching a billion in the late 1970s. Nearly eight of every ten Chinese were listed as rural residents at that time, well over a sixth of the human race. A population both so huge and so overwhelmingly rural made it plain that, in economics and in politics, success for China had to come first in the countryside. Only a prospering countryside could provide the economic foundation and hinterland, as well as the political stability, to make overall modernization possible. In political terms, Deng and his allies also had to deal with the ideological legacies of Maoism as they peeled away layers of the late chairman's work. One critical legacy was Mao's long-standing distrust of the city. By encouraging some farmers to prosper before city folk, the reformers could take away at least one of the arguments surest to be raised against discarding so much of what the chairman had built. And it was, quite simply, possible to move ahead in the countryside more quickly than in the cities. China's countryside, big and populous though it is, houses a much simpler economy and society than the cities, with their factories and universities, department stores and government ministries. Reform of the cities would have to wait, not only because the countryside's vastly bigger population demanded attention first but, perhaps almost equally, because of the unpredictable complexity of any tinkering with the urban economy's arbitrary prices, state-run job assignments, egalitarian wages, subsidies, allowances and outright welfare plans—the Rube Goldberg contraption the Communist party had pieced haphazardly together during its first three decades in power.

Beginning in Sichuan, the traditional breadbasket and rice bowl in the southwest, and spreading across the country as rapidly as the Communist party could reorganize, the changes of the late 1970s reversed virtually everything Mao had stood for in China's countryside. Villages divided their land into family-sized parcels and put these parcels out on "contracts" that required each household to deliver a grain quota to the state at fixed prices. Once the farmers met their quotas, the contracts left each family free to choose among a variety of crops, even to sell any surplus grain privately if the family could find a buyer willing to pay more than the state. The economics of grain farming was reversed, at least for a few years, by a series of major increases in the price the government paid for any grain a family delivered over and above the quota. For the first time in years, it suddenly became attractive to exceed the grain quota. Not only land but also the brigade and commune tractors and work animals, often even the irrigation reservoirs and small hydropower stations, were put out on contract.

Almost as abruptly as Mao had ordered the countryside to form communes, and all but give up private gardening, government policy now decreed that the family would be the basic farming unit—and that farmers would be encouraged to raise the household chickens and ducks Mao had once denounced as "remnants of the bourgeois lifestyle." Peasants were invited anew to take vegetables and home-made brooms into the nearest city to sell at the same free markets that had been banned under Mao. In many cities, the free markets simply reopened in the same places they had occupied before Mao banned them. Or they sprang up, with or without official permission, next to state vegetable markets. One such juxtaposition was less than half a block from *The Baltimore Sun*'s office in Beijing, and for nearly five years I watched a "laboratory study" in contrasts. Onions, cabbages and the occasional apples arrived at the state market in the state way, by the big gray or green truckload. They were delivered to the market in the state manner, by lowering one side of the parked truck and dumping them into piles on the concrete. They then went on display in the usual state condition, filthy, bruised, sometimes broken or crushed, rotting, if that was the way they had arrived. At the peasant- and vendor-run stalls next door in the free market, onions, carrots and tomatoes usually arrived carefully arranged in bags on the backs of bicycles, or on flatbed tricycles. They went on sale looking less appetizing than Americans would expect at a typical supermarket or vegetable stand, but cleaner and much less battered than those in the state market.

As relative prosperity spread during my years in Beijing, a slowly but steadily growing minority of customers seemed to give up on the state market and go directly to the free market stalls, though the farmers always charged more than the state. Most of the cities I visited in nearly five years in China offered comparable studies in contrast wherever a state market and a free market coexisted as next-door neighbors. I sometimes asked the state clerks why things looked so much better next door, and they usually answered that the peasants always hold back their best goods to sell for the best price. There is no reason to doubt that the peasants took every advantage they could find in the dual system. But when I visited state purchasing stations in the countryside, I found them taking in reasonably presentable produce. I concluded that an important part of the contrast had to do with the fact that the peasants could get their produce to market faster, and therefore fresher, than the state bureaucrats, and that the peasant vendors had better reason than the state workers to take care of what they handled between farm and market.

As Deng Xiaoping began his rise to power in the late 1970s, he and his allies set out to use this self-interest of the Chinese farmer to breathe life into an agriculture that had grown stagnant after the first rush of enthusiasm for Mao's collectivization. By the time Mao died in

1976, it had become self-evident how abysmally his great experiments had failed. Even many farmers who had enthusiastically joined the communes nearly two decades earlier were deeply demoralized across much of China. They had gradually adjusted to the reality that communal farming meant communal rewards. Once it became clear that the shirker got much the same as the worker, it became harder and harder in many places to get farmers to work. By 1971 I could look across the border from Hong Kong and see men from the People's Liberation Army in the fields of Guangdong Province at planting and harvest time. Newspapers and provincial radio broadcasts made clear that this had become national practice, to send soldiers to "join the peasants in the harvest." Over the seasons, Chinese friends would tell me more than a decade later, the soldiers joined less and less in laboring alongside the peasants, more and more in enforcing labor discipline on reluctant workers.

By the time I arrived in China in October 1982, much of the first big rush away from Mao's rural collectivization had been accomplished. The 1982 grain crop was one in a string of all-time records or near records. The importance of a string of record-breaking grain crops is immense any time in a country that struggles to feed over a fifth of the world's people on barely a sixteenth of the world's arable land. But to Chinese in those years, the deeper importance lay in the tangible contrast the record harvests formed with the agricultural stagnation of the late years of Mao's communes. The contrast was further underscored by the importance Mao's own policies had given to grain. "Take grain as the key link," the Great Helmsman had declared, and Communist party secretaries across the countryside had put the axe to hillside orchards in order to carve out tiny grain terraces on slopes too steep and rocky to give respectable yields. Vegetable plots had been switched to grain, further impoverishing a diet already seriously lacking in protein. Essentials like oilseeds and cotton took hind place and fell into chronic shortage, regularly failing to supply even the country's extremely tight rations of cloth and cooking oil. In the high plateaus of Tibet and Qinghai Province, Han Chinese secretaries of local Communist party branches had been sent to teach the illiterate locals how to get things done. They were determined to show their superiors they could increase grain production. Tibetans told correspondents who visited Lhasa in 1983 that their Han Chinese party overlords had pressured Tibetans to switch barley fields to wheat, which they thought might yield more bushels per acre. The yields had increased in some places and not in others, as the party secretaries had struggled to teach a tradition-bound people new planting, thinning, tending and harvesting techniques. Regardless of yields, Tibetans went hungry. It had not occurred to the party secretaries, themselves often barely literate and frequently as ignorant as they are contemptuous of customs among China's ethnic minorities, that bakeries were scarcely known outside Lhasa, the capital, or that wheat is wholly unsuited to the tsampa barley-flour paste that has been the staple for longer than Tibet's recorded history.

The product of Mao's exhortations to raise grain output by the sheer enthusiasm and willpower of his People's Communes had been across-the-board stagnation in grain and chronic shortages in the rest of China's agriculture. But by the time I arrived in China in 1982, some areas of the countryside appeared to be in something resembling boom conditions, though it was clear that China was still a deeply poor and backward country. It remains true to this day, and seems likely to be so for the foreseeable future, that a train headed north or west out of Beijing rolls first through the capital's prosperous suburban communes with their big red tractors and lucrative vegetable plots, then through long stretches where farmers use small hand-tractors, and then draft animals. Finally—near the steam locomotive manufacturing center of Datong, for example—the train passes through miles of fields where peasants in patched and repatched clothing hitch one another up to pull the wagons and the plows. But any train ride virtually anywhere I went revealed extraordinary numbers of new houses going up in village after village. Roads and byways were lined with endless streams of hand-tractors and animals pulling loads of brick, stone, grain, and vegetables. There were no signs of unusual numbers of tractors or other vehicles sitting idle for lack of fuel or maintenance. Town and city markets that my foreign and Chinese friends had warned me would be barren were beginning to have modest, even respectable, stocks.

In strictly economic terms, what gave the impression of a boom probably could better be described as recovery from an extended period of manmade disaster. Grain outputs jumped and other agricultural commodities soared as land was put back into uses that suited it.

Production of cotton, long a deficit item that China had had to import even to meet its skimpy rations, doubled between 1980 and 1984. It finally glutted the market, and cotton acreage had to be cut back in 1985 as an urgent matter of national policy. China's 1984 cotton crop may have been one of history's least-noticed landmarks. Except for years between the two world wars, when the international market for Chinese export silk sometimes collapsed, the 1984 cotton crop was the first case I've been able to find where China's modern economic history has recorded a severe oversupply of a major agricultural commodity.

In the late spring of 1983, a bit over half a year after getting back to Asia, I joined a planeload of my Beijing-based colleagues on a trip into Southwestern China. The trip was organized by the Foreign Ministry's Information Department, the principal body of professional barbarian handlers assigned to deal with the foreign press. Its purpose was to look at some of the places along the border with Vietnam, where both countries had now and then reported troop buildups and shots fired in anger. But the trip entailed several days of riding in a caravan of minibuses out of Nanning, through the limestone karst outcroppings and rolling countryside of Guangxi Province. Huge white clouds billowed in blue skies above the jutting limestone, and we joked and listened to walkmans as our handful of air-conditioned Toyota vans rolled through some of China's most spectacular scenery.

In the seat in front of me for much of the trip was a colleague and friend who was also based in Beijing. Wearing red nylon gym shorts and white polyester-cotton tank top, he traveled through Guangxi wired for sound, with a two-headset tape player that let him and his wife jointly indulge their shared taste for American and British rock music. My friend's name is not essential to this account, but he was known to reserve his skepticism about China for use to help him through the rare moments when his cynicism failed him. From our minibus windows, we looked out across paddies where peasants in dark shorts and broad straw hats stood up to their calves in mucky water, bending themselves in half to transplant rice. They worked tiny green seedlings into land punctuated by huge gray towers of limestone karst that had been carved by undersea currents millions of years ago when this part of Southeast Asia was covered by a prehistoric ocean. My friend commented several times on the scene's timelessness. He meant not mainly the topography but the lives of the people. "Nothing has changed for them in hundreds of years," he said at one point. "It's all the same; they still live the way they did in the fourteenth century."

As he put his headset back on to rejoin his wife and the Grateful Dead, I wondered how many times all of us, myself included, had commented on the changelessness of Chinese life, especially rural life. But most of our driving on this trip was on a paved road, and thousands of the peasants we passed on it were riding bicycles. A favorite complaint we all shared on the trip was that so many of our best scenic photos were spoiled by the ubiquitous electric lines and poles that extend even into this remote corner of the Chinese countryside. In this and many other parts of China, electric lines mean that pumps now make it possible for new generations of Chinese to grow up with no knowledge of work men, women and animals did until twenty or thirty years ago, walking endless hours on treadmills to lift water into some of the grain fields.

Wherever a big city is close enough to provide a television signal, the electric lines also mean that country Chinese can gather around a tube in the village center and see for themselves more than their grandparents could have dreamed about the world outside their village. Many of the same dams that provide the low-wattage rural electricity also have expanded the land area served by irrigation, thereby increasing the amount the land can produce. Our minibus caravan passed hundreds of small schools, where girls and boys learn at least some rudimentary reading and writing, in a countryside where until the 1950s literacy was a luxury and a route to local power, available only to an almost exclusively male elite. We passed thousands of small hand-tractors hauling minuscule wagonloads of bricks and crops, a few of which might have been moved by muscle power a few decades ago but most of which would not have gone on the road at all. New peasant houses seemed nearly as many as old in some of the villages we passed. The countryside was dotted, as is most of China, by public latrines, usually small brick sheds with separate entrances marked for men and women. These tiny outhouses had dramatically changed both rural santitation and the fertilizer supply.

It is beyond both the scope of this volume and the competence of this author to calculate how far these changes are the handiwork of the Communist party and how far simply the product of political stability itself—of the sheer fact that somebody, anybody, finally won the civil war and at last reunified China's mainland in 1949, making it physically possible to get on with daily life and a peacetime economy. Even that achievement, reunifying the country under a single government after nearly two centuries of progressive disintegration, makes the Communist party a unique force in today's China. And some of the subsequent changes in daily life clearly have to do with how the party has used the power it won in 1949. Universal education, still a goal that eludes many parts of the country, became significantly effective as national policy only after 1949. Rudimentary sanitation and health care in the countryside were major campaigns of the Maoist years that markedly distinguish China from most Third World countries. Such changes go far to account for dramatic advances in life expectancy, from somewhere in the late thirties or early forties before the revolution to more than sixty years of age today. For country Chinese, these are palpable changes in both daily life and the seasons of life.

Still, the foreigner is not wrong, as he rides by air-conditioned minibus from show township to model family, to wonder whether China's agriculture may be decades, rather than years, behind the modern world. Neither is he wrong to wonder whether the decades since 1949 might have been more productively used had the Communist party had the vision and found the will and the means to deter its Great Helmsman from steering exclusively toward the left. Muscle power, of humans and animals, still dominates the work that is directly applied to the land in many areas. Human and animal excrement are still principal fertilizers, not only of grains that reach maturity atop high stalks but also of celery and cabbages that grow on the ground in their fertilizer. Archeologists have found numberless remains of crooked wooden hoe handles, like the ones I saw rising and falling in 1985 in Jinan, and at countless other times in countless other parts of China. Six thousand years ago the handles were fitted with sharpened stone blades at the working end. Over the eons, stone has given way to bronze, and bronze to iron, and iron to steel. But the power source that has raised the hoe and driven it into the earth has not changed. It is human muscle. An irony of Deng Xiaoping's Four Modernizations is that, because the scale of agriculture has again been cut back to the family patch, in some parts of the countryside more work is done today by human muscle, and less by tractor and communally owned animal, than was so a decade ago. That, today's Chinese leadership argues, was the necessary first step to get farming back to a rational starting point.

———————

I ventured into the gritty spring winds of Jinan in 1985 because, at that time, China's top agricultural thinkers in Beijing were talking of new and much bigger changes in the lives of rural Chinese. In late February, Du Runsheng, the chief rural planner for the Chinese Communist party, told a Beijing press conference that China was now making it national policy to attract farmers off the overcrowded land as fast as new jobs could be created for them. He estimated that tens of millions of rural Chinese had already come off the land in the first half of the 1980s, and that as many as a third of the 800 million people then officially listed as "rural" would be out of farming by the end of the century. What Du Runsheng said struck me as a prescription for one of the most massive social changes in human history. China's rural population alone numbers nearly a sixth of the human beings on earth. Du was describing a national policy intended to alter profoundly the daily lives of the vast majority of this huge population, to shift hundreds of millions from farming into commerce, industry and transportation in a matter of a few decades. His argument for the policy was essentially simple. Everyone, he said, foreigner and Chinese alike, has known for more than a century that there are far more people laboring over China's soil than can possibly prosper. The logical course, he said, is to permit and encourage the growth of precisely those rural commercial, transportation and industrial enterprises that were banned under Mao. This would not only relieve the pressure on the land but also enrich rural Chinese and turn the countryside into a vast marketplace that could absorb industrial products and speed China's modernization by stimulating the cities and their factories.

To get a first impression of the pressure 700 or 800 million rural dwellers create on China's scarce arable land, it is sufficient to look down from an airplane on a flight from, say, Shanghai to Beijing, a trip of some two and a half hours. Wherever there are not mountains or lakes, there are clusters of perhaps fifty to a thousand adobe or brick houses, with tiled or thatched roofs, never more than a kilometer from the edge of one cluster to the edge of the next, often little more than the length of a few football fields. Trees scarcely exist, except along roads and canal banks, or in places too steep or too high on the hills to be used for anything else. The scene is one of whole communities jammed much closer to one another than are individual farmhouses in the American Midwest.

To walk through this same scene on the ground is to enter a world where the typical farm consists of two or three patches too tiny for most American farmers to imagine how they might be made to support a family. In most places, a family typically gets a few hundred square yards of "good grade" land, a similar patch of "middle grade," and one of "difficult grade." Theodore S. White and Annalee Jacoby wrote, in *Thunder Out of China,* that the typical Chinese farmer in the 1940s had such a small patch he could not really farm, but only gardened. Since then, thanks in part to the decades when Mao still believed that China's greatest strength was the ballooning numbers of the Chinese, the country's population has more than doubled. If large numbers of rural people could be encouraged to come off the land and into other ways of making a living, Du Runsheng argued, it might become possible to accomplish naturally and voluntarily the consolidation of farm lands Mao had attempted by regimentation and exhortation through the communes. That, in turn, would pave the way for gradual increases in mechanization, a goal the communes had sought but had glaringly failed to reach by forced march, a goal that must be reached if China's diminishing arable land is to yield improving sustenance for her nearly one billion people.

My three days in Shandong included an officially escorted afternoon with the Su brothers, three sturdy men in their late twenties and early thirties. They were brought forth as examples because the three of them had parlayed one brother's former job as commune tractor driver into a private transportation business that was netting them an unheard-of income, equal to about $500 a month at the official exchange rates of the time. This meant that each of them, living in a part of China that was still in the early stages of the conversion from paying peasants in grain to paying them in cash, was making about four times the total income, including bonuses and all subsidies, of workers their ages in one of the big state-owned factories, the dream jobs of many urban Chinese. The key to their newfound prosperity, they said, was the fact that Su Tongxiang, the eldest, had been a tractor driver for Sunrise Production Brigade when it was liquidated, along with all the other parts of Mao's communes. The Sunrise Brigade gave way to what is now called Sunrise Township. In the first year after the land was parceled out into peasant contracts, Su Tongxiang found that few of his neighbors now had any interest in hiring him to come with his tractor to plow their tiny patches of land. But he also discovered that brickyards, limestone quarries and a whole range of other new or expanding enterprises now had rapidly growing need for cheap local transportation to get products to their customers or to rail yards. In his first year under contract to the commune, he earned more than $490—well over three times what a Shandong peasant might have earned farming that year—most of it by hauling brick, limestone, and machinery parts.

Su Tongxiang and his brothers pooled their savings, borrowed from friends and relatives and put together a total of $6,500 to buy a bright yellow, two-year-old Shanghai-brand tractor and a steel-bed wagon, bigger, newer and more powerful than anything the brigade had owned. By the time I met them, they had been using the new tractor and wagon for about two years to haul uncounted thousands of tons of bricks from a nearby brickyard to the railyard, a bit over an hour away in Jinan. At about a cent and a half a brick, they said, they were making about $20 a load after paying for their gasoline. They could usually make two trips, or about $40, in a day when there were that many bricks to haul.

In my interviews with township officials, I was told that as recently as 1980, more than 1,100 of Sunrise's 4,500 residents had been employed principally in working the scarce land of what was then called Sunrise Production Brigade. By the end of 1983, the last year for which local figures were complete by the time I arrived in March 1985, about 600 people worked mainly on the land. In that sense,

Sunrise Township had already fulfilled the goals Du Runsheng, the Communist party's top rural planner in Beijing, had set for the end of the century. But the officials at Sunrise Township seemed to feel much more was needed. Assuming the existing technology levels—farming mainly with hoes and shovels and helped sometimes by donkeys but rarely by tractors—I asked how many would be the ideal number of people to work the township's farmlands. They guessed that the right number would be somewhere near 150. By their standards, it appeared that even the massive social change Du was prescribing would not get within reaching distance of the relief the land needed.

Officials of Sunrise Township estimated that some 1,500 residents by that time were earning the major parts of their incomes by livestock breeding, small commercial enterprises, handicrafts, factory or construction work and a wide range of other nonfarm lines.

The officials took me to visit a Mrs. Dou, a woman in her forties who had worked the land every day since her teen years until 1981. That year, she switched to stitching pants. Every day, she loaded her bicycle with trousers she had stitched the day before, sewing by window light on a treadle machine in a bedroom of her low brick farmhouse. She walked her bikeload of yesterday's pants about half a mile to the local cutting center and turned them in for a new stack of unstitched britches, which she then took home on her bicycle to start a new day's work. By doing this, Mrs. Dou earned about $750 in 1984, nearly four times what the average Shandong peasant had seen by the end of that year working in the fields. And she could tend her granddaughter at home while her daughter-in-law worked the family patch.

Officials in Shandong have praised this piecework plan as a creative way of extending into rural industry the "contract system" that had been the basis of agricultural reform. Economic historians would be forgiven if they also found in it overtones of the "putting-out system," a feature of the early industrial revolution in England that eventually was banned because it left workers helplessly vulnerable to exploitation. As new kinds of work come to China's countryside, these shadows of the early industrial revolution fall farther and farther beyond the urban factories, where they are already heavy in many Chinese cities. That is especially true of working conditions in rural factories. In Sunrise Township, I was guided to a low brick building that is little more than an oversized shed. There, a few dozen workers man a room that is somewhere between a large blacksmith shop and a small foundry, turning out a few dozen ball joints every day for shipment to a truck factory in Jinan. Charles Dickens would have been hard put to describe their work place. Flames billow from the unprotected sides of a furnace where workers stand wearing cotton farm clothing as they reach in with yard-long tongs to pull out white-hot disks of steel. In other rural factories, I saw workers assigned to stools directly under small overhead cranes that carried heavy steel boxes that were held to the crane only by an electromagnet; workers melting plastic sandals' for reprocessing in vats that gave off acrid fumes directly into the workshop; men sitting on stools wielding hammers as fellow workers with tongs carried red-hot ingots within a foot or two of their heads.

I had chosen the Jinan area partly because it was convenient, an overnight or one-day train ride some 220 miles from Beijing, and partly because the Shandong segments of the Yellow River area had a reputation for having moved more or less in pace with, not faster than, the general rate of change in China's rural heartlands. For a look on the ground at some of the questions Du Runsheng had raised, I did not want to go to an area famous for being either far ahead of things or far behind. Du and the visit to Shandong had added a whole section to the list of questions I regularly asked whenever I traveled in the countryside. China's farmlands cover big and immensely varied territories, from the treeless and powdery expanses of yellow loess on the fringes of the North China Plain to the subtropical palms and watery green rice paddies in the Pearl River Delta near Hong Kong. But in my two and a half remaining years in China, I found that most places I visited were going through changes much like those I had found around Jinan. The proportions of people already off the land varied greatly, and the stages of reform and development were never identical, but the rush to rural brickyards, construction and transportation companies, factories and commerce was palpable wherever I went.

So were new social and economic forces, being set free by the rapid pace of change, but only dimly understood or, in many cases, unnoticed by the county and township leaders. In Sunrise Township, I visited a newly built "Home of Respect for the Aged," for elderly people who have no family to care for them and who no longer can care for themselves. The township was still struggling with the question of how to raise money for the home's operating costs now that there was no longer a commune or a production brigade. The township had followed Beijing's order to separate economics and government, after the two decades in which Mao's communes had combined them into one. Now, local officials were finding that welfare—and a broad range of other areas where economics and government intersect—needed whole new sets of institutional arrangements that had not been thought out as Beijing ordered the rush to reform.

One example that would prove important before the end of that year was maintenance of vitally important public works. Human life in China is deeply dependent on hundreds of thousands of miles of dikes that stave off flood disasters that would otherwise be at least annual events, and on tens of thousands of reservoirs and literally millions of miles of canals that distribute the water without which the land has no prospect of feeding its billion people. On the positive side of the ledger of Mao's commune movement had stood the effectiveness of the huge collectives in raising corvee labor to expand and improve these life-sustaining earthworks. By the time I went to Shandong, officials both in Beijing and in the countryside were still trying to deny reports that peasants in many areas were neglecting or even vandalizing the dams and dikes. But in 1985, the grain harvest declined by 28 million tons, the first drop since the reforms began and one of the biggest in modern Chinese history. At first, officials both in Beijing and in the countryside sought to blame the weather, the culprit reflexively cited whenever China's agriculture meets problems. But by the spring of 1986, they were acknowledging that in many areas some of the problems were not only manmade but directly attributable to the reforms. Television and newspaper accounts began to report that droughts in some areas had been intensified because dams and the canals leading from them had been ill maintained or even drained by peasants seeking private advantage, that flooding had been worse than necessary because dikes had not been maintained and because illegal fisheries and docks had been allowed to obstruct major drainage routes.

In April of 1986, I spent eighteen days visiting twenty-one townships in Sichuan and Yunnan Provinces in the southwest and Guang-dong Province in the far south. Liao Jie, deputy director of the Sichuan Province Water Conservancy Bureau, acknowledged that surveys in 1983 and 1985 had turned up tens of thousands of places where reservoirs, canals and dikes throughout the province had been dam-aged by neglect, misuse, vandalism or theft of building materials. He estimated that each survey disclosed damage that would affect the farming potential of about 1 percent of the irrigated land in China's most productive farming province. "There has been some economic loss," Liao acknowledged, "because under the contract system some peasants have served their own interests more than the interests of all. Also, at the beginning of the reforms, the management of some of the projects became lax for a period."

Like the home for the elderly in Shandong, the support and man-agement of the life-sustaining waterworks seemed in many places to have become an afterthought of the township and village officials, rather than the prime concern it had been under the commune system. As I traveled from county to county and from province to province, I discovered that, to a considerable extent, local officials were left on their own to figure out how to get money and labor for these essential public works. There was no consistency in the plans being followed from place to place, no unifying theme to suggest that the central government had offered any but the vaguest instructions on how to make small rural dams, dikes and canals fit into the economic theories now coming down from Beijing. In Shandong and in some parts of Sichuan and Guangdong, I sometimes found townships that were op-erating their earthworks out of the local welfare fund. But who was to pay into the local welfare fund—whether, for example, it would be supported mainly by levies on the peasants, or mainly by funds from the township-run businesses, or mainly by exactions from the new private and cooperative enterprises now springing up everywhere— was a question each place seemed to resolve differently. And in some parts of each of the three provinces, I found places that were actually trying to find ways to put mud-banked irrigation canals out on a "contract system," like pieces of farmland, in effect making them a form of government-franchised private enterprise.

Among the gray heads of orthodox Leninist conservatism, whose voices can still be heard both at the center of the Chinese Communist party and at many provincial and lower levels, China's need to be self-sufficient in grain is not a political or economic question but an article of faith. It takes on a mystique that is religious in its tone and metaphysical in its logic. Chen Yun, the octogenarian spiritual leader of the orthodox, summarized this fundamentalist approach in a much-quoted speech in which he laid out his objections to the course of reform on the closing day of the October 1985 Communist Party Conference. If the party failed to pay more attention to grain production, Chen warned, there could be production shortfalls that would "lead to social disorder."[1] In Mao's decades in power, the Great Helmsman had extended this demand for grain self-sufficiency to the ultimate, ordering every province, every county, every township and, where possible, every village to meet its own grain needs from the local land.

My April 1986 visit to Guangdong Province included a day in Shunde County that suggested how far the new leadership was prepared to go in at least some places in reversing the demand for grain self-sufficiency. My government-assigned hosts from Guangzhou (Canton) city escorted me on a visit to the four-story, $7,000 home of Wang Ming, who had made $8,000 the previous year by raising flowers and shrubs for export to nearby Hong Kong. A family income of $8,000 a year is as hard for most Chinese to grasp as the Department of Defense budget is for an American—numbers like that simply don't relate to real-life experience. But it was clear that the idea had its attractions. Not only Wang Ming, but virtually all of his neighbors as far as the eye could see, had taken their land wholly out of agriculture and had put it into nursery stock. Rice farming, the staple support of South China for thousands of years, had simply gone out of style.

Rice farming's passage from the scene has had the active support of the local government. Legally, local farmers still have been required to meet a "grain quota" for the land they farm. But they meet their grain quota by delivering cash, rather than rice, to the district grain office. Then, as if to underscore the complete rejection of Chairman Mao's demand for local grain self-sufficiency, the grain office buys rice and hauls it in by truck or by train from other districts, even from other provinces.

A singer practices Beijing Opera songs in a Beijing park early on a Sunday morning, while an accompanist plays the *er hu*, a two-stringed traditional instrument that often accompanies traditional opera solos. Sunday morning practice sessions are common in Beijing's parks, often drawing small but loyal audiences. Sometimes the singer turns out to be a well-known performer, working without makeup for his own pleasure.

Unless otherwise indicated, all photos are by John Woodruff, courtesy of The Baltimore Sun

A group practices martial arts with swords in a sunrise session in Beijing's Sun Altar Park. Most Beijing parks are crammed with large and small groups of martial arts practicers soon after sunrise. Recreational space is at such a premium that each group arrives early to stake out its patch. Many of the city's highway divider strips and tree belts also are the scenes of early morning taijiquan and other martial arts sessions.

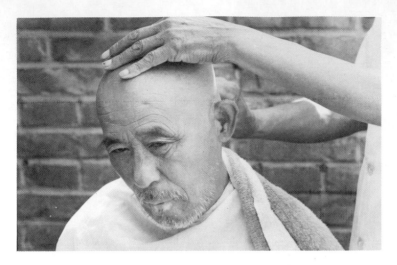

An old man gets his head shaved, a favorite defense against Beijing's summer heat, at an outdoor barber shop. Such streetside shops were banned in Mao's later years as "tails of capitalism." Residents of many cities found themselves traveling miles to state barber shops once these small neighborhood places were closed.

Capitalist tools. These barber tools, plus a folding chair and a sheet to spread over the customer, constitute the capital that once got the neighborhood barber banned from the streets.

Capitalism's comeback. This small shop, now being renovated, will open as a private enterprise. Family-scale and individual private enterprises became legal under the reforms, after being banned for decades. Here, neighbors have drawn up chairs to spend the day watching. Entertainment is still scarce in Beijing, and simple events like this, or a policeman giving a parking ticket to a foreigner, can attract audiences, often far larger than this one.

Sidewalk shoe repairmen break for a snack on a Beijing street. Repair stalls like these, and curbside biscuit and noodle vendors, were driven from the streets in the Cultural Revolution. They came back in large numbers under Deng Xiaoping in the 1980s.

Men gossipping outside a house in a Beijing lane show their amusement at the idea of a foreigner wanting to take a picture of life in the lanes. For many, the lane itself is the living room, especially in summer.

This small private barber shop entrance is typical of the bits of commercial life that have come back to Beijing's urban lanes now that private craftsmen and vendors are again legally permitted.

Piles of coal, used for keeping warm against Beijing's bitter winters, are a standard sight at the entrances of houses along Beijing's residential lanes. A supply of tires and waiting bicycles identify this house as one that doubles as a privately run bike repair shop.

In strictly economic terms, Shunde County has been doing what comes naturally—using its land and other resources to produce whatever would make it the most money, and using the money to buy the grain that other places could produce more efficiently. It is arguable that the Asian economies that have grown rich fastest in this century— Japan, Hong Kong, Singapore, Taiwan—have been the ones that have worried least about full self-sufficiency in staple grains and instead have produced what would sell. Shunde County is a corner of China that was already learning from those examples when the reforms made its activities a sure route to riches for some farmers.

But the article of faith that says China must be self-sufficient in grain runs deep among some true Leninist believers at the Communist party center, and not all of the men at the top of the Chinese Communist party can be expected to approve of the way Wang Ming and his neighbors earn their keep. Shunde County, moreover, is close enough to Hong Kong that it can race ahead of other parts of China. But it is unique only in degree. Every one of the eleven South and Southwest China townships I visited in April 1986 reported significant reductions in the amount of land planted to grain in recent years. In most areas, grain land was converted to cotton, vegetables, oilseeds and other more profitable cash crops.

Officials in most of the places I visited confidently predicted that they could switch land back to grain production fast enough to offset the losses of the 1985 crop, but in fact, the 1986 and 1987 grain crops never did get back up to the 1984 record level. And in many cases, the loss of grain land is not merely a matter of deciding which other crop to raise. It is a permanent loss of land from any form of agriculture. The movement of millions of Chinese from the land into rural brickyards, factories and repair shops has inevitably been accompanied by a transfer of significant portions of China's scarce farmlands out of farm uses. The rural housing boom has further encroached on the arable land. Du Runsheng estimated that the country was losing about 1 percent of its arable land to other rural and suburban uses each year. This steady loss of farmland to nonfarm uses has become a subject of official alarm in Beijing. Vice-premier Tian Jiyun, a leading advocate of the rural reforms and a close associate of Premier Zhao Ziyang, told a leadership meeting in Beijing in January 1985 that China must stem this trend or "face grave consequences and visit untold troubles on our descendants."[2] In March 1985, the Communist party Central Committee and the State Council, China's equivalent of a cabinet, followed up Tian's warning by jointly issuing a circular ordering strict punishment for anyone appropriating farmland to other uses. The National People's Congress, China's legislature, backed this order by passing a new land-management law aimed at strict control of any conversions of arable land away from farm use. But everything I saw in my travels by the time I left China more than two years later suggested that farmland was being nibbled away at an accelerating pace.

Beekeepers were the first to make official complaints about what the policy of bringing farmers off the land was doing to Nanping County, outside Kunming, the "City of Eternal Spring" that is the capital of Yunnan Province in Southwest China. They told the county environmental officer in December 1985 that fumes from the county's new lead smelting plant were killing their bees. Bees are not naturally abundant in most of China, so beekeepers play a critical role in pollinating a broad range of crops. When beekeepers complained, the environmental officer knew he had better listen. But it took him until March 1986 to get papers ready to order the plant out of business. By then, angry villagers had already done the job for him. They had cut off the plant's electric lines and smashed enough equipment that it could no longer operate.

Xiong Limin, deputy director of the Kunming City Environmental Protection Bureau, told me the story of the Nanping County lead smelting plant when I visited him in April 1986. This was one among hundreds of thousands of vignettes being played out across the Chinese countryside as residents and officials began to struggle with the environmental effects of a rural industrialization intended to go faster and farther than any seen anywhere else on earth. In the two suburban farming districts and eight rural counties under Kunming city's jurisdiction, Xiong said, some 30,000 enterprises had been built or substantially expanded since the reforms had gathered momentum in the early 1980s. Of these, some 3,000 were officially known to have violated China's still rudimentary pollution standards, about 900 of them in ways Xiong defined as "serious."

For decades, China did not officially acknowledge environmental problems. When I visited Guangzhou in 1972, I asked a deputy mayor about soot pouring out of the smokestacks of dozens of factories visible from my window at the Oriental Hotel. He smiled smugly and explained that pollution was a product of rapacious capitalists who didn't care what they did to the environment. Since socialist China no longer had rapacious capitalists, he said, the Chinese people no longer needed to fear pollution. Only one more year would pass before the late Premier Zhou Enlai would begin to call a series of nationwide conferences to deal with mounting complaints from city residents against massive fouling of the air and water. But political chaos stretched on into the 1970s. Local environmental offices, even in most of the country's biggest cities, were set up only in the early 1980s. Environmental protection was not available as a major at a single college-level institution by the time I left China in the summer of 1987. Environmental officials in most places I visited acknowledged that their skills and equipment were far too backward and their staffs already stretched much too thin to do an adequate job of policing any but the most blatant urban problems. For the most part, the battle to protect the air and water remained a losing one in the cities even as national policy began to embrace active industrialization of the countryside.

No one pretends to know, and hardly anyone shows any sign of caring much, what the massive experiment in rural industrialization will do to the environment. That is not unique to the current experiment. One of the biggest and fastest degradations ever known in a rural environment surely was Mao's Great Leap Forward. That experiment consumed so much coal for its mainly worthless backyard forges and foundries that peasants stripped the countryside of its few trees, bushes, and even orchards to survive the winter with fuel for cooking and heating. In a country where rivers run richly yellow with eroded soil, and the Yangtze River alone deposits enough silt to move the East China coast almost a foot closer to Japan every year, national policy for those few years in the 1950s led to massive increases in already formidable erosion problems. Today's Chinese leadership seems to have some corporate memory of that manmade calamity and has ordered appointment of environmental officers in every rural county and at least a part-time environmental officer in each township. But they are given insignificant budgets and effectively no training. By the time I left China, many townships and counties I visited had not met even these formalities. In many that had appointed someone to look after the environment, it was the same person whose main responsibility was to develop rural industry. Xiong Limin and environmental officers in other cities acknowledged that these situations were commonplace. In most places, the handful of environmental officers who have the competence to detect problems are spread so thinly that no one even talks of making regular inspection rounds. Instead, officers usually are hard pressed to keep track of complaints that come in from the communities. What happens when pollution is not palpable to the layman—heavy metal discharges into rivers, invisible and odorless poisons in the air—no official could say. "It is much harder in the countryside," Lai Guangci, the deputy director of the Guangzhou Environmental Protection Office, acknowledged when I visited him in April 1986. "The areas are so much bigger than in the cities, and everything is so much farther apart."

Physical effects—on the environment, on scarce farmland, and on life-sustaining rural waterworks—are only one face of the powerful and unpredictable forces set loose by the massive policy changes in the countryside. Equally powerful and equally unpredictable forces are now loose within the rural society and polity. Mrs. Dou's personal decision to take care of her granddaughter at home while she stitches trousers on her treadle sewing machine has a broader significance within this context. Wherever I traveled, I saw more and more babies being tended at home, carried into the family field, even taken to construction sites on the backs of working mothers. My own travels gave me frequent glimpses of these changes, but it was in conversations with health professionals from international agencies that I began to understand how profoundly such policies were affecting rural life. The work of these health professionals keeps them constantly in the countryside and gives them broad access to areas normally closed to foreigners. Dr. Carl Taylor of the Johns Hopkins Medical Institutions in Baltimore, was the UNICEF representative in China during much of the same time I was there. He described changes that he summarized as "the collapse of the rural health and child care system."

Modern health care never existed in most of China's countryside before 1949. One of the Communist party's clearest claims to achievement was the extension of some rudiments of modern hygiene, first aid and primary health care to a rural population that had never known any such luxury. But this system had grown up as part of Mao's collectivization of the countryside, and it was geared to the massive farming communes and the "production brigades" that were their components. Now, as the communes were disbanded and income came to depend on labor and enterprise, Taylor explained, the health care system that had grown up in the communes did not readily adapt to the new circumstances.

One case in point that was affecting daily life for millions of country people was the "barefoot doctor" network, which had always seemed to me to be one instance among Mao's many social experiments that deserved some of the worldwide praise it had received. Usually trained for little more than a few weeks or months, often at People's Liberation Army medic schools, these rural practitioners, despite their scant training, gave hundreds of millions of Chinese peasants their first rudimentary experiences of modern first aid and primary medical care. But their place in the new incentive-based countryside was unclear and uncertain. Most found that their tiny cash stipends ended with the dissolution of the communes, and most were now required to contract for farmland along with anyone else who was classified as a "rural" resident. Some had switched to charging a fee for services or to taking a profit on medicines they dispensed. That change, Carl Taylor observed, was now leading to a subtle shift in emphasis in their work, away from prevention of illness and toward treatment after the patient became ill. Much less subtle was the fact that hundreds of thousands of barefoot doctors were simply leaving medical work altogether, and hundreds of thousands more were taking up second occupations that ate up large chunks of time previously devoted to treatment. In the five years from 1981 through 1985, Carl estimated, the number of barefoot doctors had declined from about 2,000,000 to about 1,250,000. Many had gone back to full-time farming now that there was a chance to make a living on the land, and many others had found new places in the growing rural economy.

Now that mothers and grandmothers can work at home or in the family field, parents and grandparents like Mrs. Dou are returning to timeless ways of taking care of their own children and grandchildren. The return to child care at home, Carl said, has not been without a costly trade-off—much less regimentation and much more familial affection in the way children are brought up in some parts of the countryside, but major complications in the way China takes care of rural children's health. In the decades when both parents were required to join the long lines of peasants working for the production brigade, children of some localities were gathered daily at day-care centers. There, they could be lined up conveniently for inoculations and checkups. But now the spreading return to family child care and the closing of thousands of day-care centers have created a health-care void that has yet to be filled, Carl said.

At the same time, the return to farming for profit has made it economically attractive to apply human and animal manure directly to the fields, so local experiments with family biogas fertilizer treatment plants that once won some parts of China much publicity are being abandoned in many places. There is not as much fertilizer left after the biogas treatment, Carl continued, so once farmers were freed of regimentation in the communes, they started going back to old ways to get more use out of the manure. For children, one price of this reversion to older ways has been abrupt increases in medical conditions that had once been under some degree of control. "In some of these areas," said Carl, "we're now back to a situation where the incidence of worm infestation in children has soared back up to 80 or 90 percent."

Carl Taylor and UNICEF were at work on plans to deal with some of the health-care problems that had grown out of the rural reforms. A series of "model counties" was being established to show provincial governments what could be done by combining what remained of China's rural health system with methods UNICEF and other international organizations had developed in other Third World countries. While the leadership in Beijing seemed patently to have failed to foresee the effect the rural reforms would have on health care in some of these parts of the countryside, Carl said, "to their credit, once the depth of the collapse became clear, they set to work to rebuild a system, and this time they will have the help of the international agencies that China did not welcome in the past."

Other social forces set loose by the reforms are even harder to measure and even harder to predict. The return to older ways has encompassed a rebirth of a broad range of ancient superstitions and native religious practices that had only been repressed, not genuinely replaced or supplanted, in the Maoist decades. As prosperity has risen, rural Chinese have used some of their income to hire geomancers to tell them how to locate and orient houses, soothsayers to tell them when and to whom to marry their sons and daughters and fortune-tellers to help them see their futures. Infanticide, long one of the countryside's darker traditions, seems to have surged significantly in the early 1980s as farmers have realized the economic burden that would be represented by defective babies, or even by daughters. Envy—known in Chinese as "red-eye disease"—has become an increasing source of crime and passion, with myriad negative examples reported in the national and provincial newspapers, as a few farmers begin to "lead the way in becoming rich" while an increasingly visible minority lags behind in poverty.

At the same time, persisting inability to reproduce the grain records of the early 1980s suggests that, in economic terms, the government has now used up the rapid agricultural growth it can expect to get out of recovery from the manmade disasters of the Maoist years. From now on, it seems likely that agricultural growth will be less spectacular and harder to get. It will now have to come through steady modernization and increased use of modern seed strains, chemicals and techniques. China's record, under Mao and under Deng, offers no evidence that the country has yet solved the problem of how to produce and distribute any of those necessities in anything like the quantities that will be needed. And as economic inequality returns to the Chinese countryside, it is not yet clear what kind of political force the farmer who lags behind may become. There is good reason to speculate that, as some farmers "lead the way in becoming rich," their riches will be socially tolerable only in a context of generally rising prosperity. If that rising prosperity bogs down now that the "recovery effect" has been used up, the social chemistry of China's countryside will be anybody's guess. My own guess is that, despite the current aura of good feeling, the undercurrents suggest that bouts of social volatility may lie ahead in some rural areas.

And even as peasants come off the land by the millions to work in the growing cash economy, it promises to be a long time before one of the chief modernization goals of the new round of rural reform can be realized. A principal goal, says Du Runsheng, is to encourage peasants who find work elsewhere to give up their land to other peasants, thereby opening the way to farm plots big enough that mechanization and other modern methods will make sense. How urgent that goal is can best be measured by the scarcity of land in China, which has about one fifth as much arable land per person as, for example, India. But in fact, no significant consolidation of landholdings was noticeable in the Jinan area, or in any other places I visited during my last two and a half years. The men and older women of each family are indeed leaving the land for better-paid or easier tasks. But the family plots are small enough that one or two women can do most of the work. So a woman or two in the prime of life stays behind to till the fields. It is rare—and unlikely for years to come, if what I saw is any guide—to meet many peasant families who have trusted the new party line from Beijing enough to give up the last claim to a patch of the earth. To a Chinese peasant, that would be a fateful step away from what has supported the ancestors and symbolized food itself through the generations.

3

Fight for the

Factories

Black tires and black hoses were the staple goods in the glass display cases at the South Seas Rubber Products factory when I arrived in the grimy, charcoal-colored Yangtze River industrial port of Chongqing in the fall of 1985. I had been to Chongqing before, and I did not relish another visit, though the city always produced plenty to write. Sichuan, the Southwest China province that is home to Deng Xiaoping and the place where Zhao Ziyang made his reputation before being called to Beijing to get in line to become premier, is at its best in its fruitful countryside. Farther north, around Chengdu, the provincial capital, rapeseed plants burst into yellow flowers two or three times a year. For those weeks, the brilliant blossoms, known to Chinese by the prosaic name "oil vegetable flowers," share the rolling hillocks with intense-hued rice paddies and wheat and corn fields, turning the landscape into a yellow and green patchwork.

In the hills around Chongqing, centuries of human tedium, digging and chipping away at the steep countryside with hand tools, have produced some of Asia's most spectacular rice terraces. But Chongqing itself, the province's biggest and busiest metropolis, stands out as one of Asia's ugliest places. After Chiang Kai-shek's Nationalist government retreated there to relocate the World War II capital behind the militarily impassable Yangtze River gorges, the city was bombed relentlessly for three years whenever the weather permitted Japanese air raids. Today, the city is unique among China's older population centers for the extent to which it had to be rebuilt. Its contemporary ugliness is one of the achievements of the no-frills socialism the Communist party practiced after it came to power in 1949.

Chongqing is located where the Jialing River cuts through to meet the Yangtze, which is still turbulent and falling fast as it struggles against the confines of Sichuan's steep and rocky hills. During the day, the city looks like a vastly enlarged version of the bleak coal and grain ports that stand atop all-but-vertical mud or concrete stairways, carved into the riverbank all along the Sichuan reaches where the Yangtze begins to be navigable on its way from Tibet to the East China Sea. Only after dark, when the scene is dominated by thousands of pinpoints of electric light and the moonlit ribbons of the two rivers, did officials suggest that I take a drive up to the top of one of the hills. Only then is it possible to sense how spectacular the vista might have been.

By daylight, Chongqing reminds the American observer of what Pittsburgh once did to a similar hill-and-confluence setting, in the decades before it began to take its environmental problems to heart. Chongqing's steep and potentially spectacular hillsides are dominated by the grimy appearance created by thousands of five-story walkup flats built after World War II out of charcoal-black bricks. The city often is socked in with industrial haze even when the surrounding countryside is in sunlight. Grime falls copiously from overhead for most of every day. As I took notes during a sidewalk interview on my first visit in the spring of 1983, I repeatedly found myself brushing at my notebook to remove soot that fell steadily from the air. During that visit a young engineer, appointed two years earlier to create a new environmental office, had monotonously reeled off the then-known dimensions of the pollution horrors created by Chongqing's thirty years of "building socialism" with no encumbering burden of rules to protect the air, land and water. Among those dimensions was the fact that Chongqing had China's worst acid rain problem—worse by far, he said, than the fouled air and rain that had long since eaten the glaze off most of the once-gleaming amber tiles of the Forbidden City's former imperial palaces in Beijing.

I had gone to Chongqing because it seemed in many ways a natural place to look at how things were going in the Communist party Central Committee's attempt, then about a year old, to breathe life into the moribund state-owned factories that are the core of the industrial economy. If the countryside is where Deng's reforms must begin, the state factory is where they must advance. With Soviet help in the 1950s, China established a system of socialized factories virtually from scratch. Many of the large factories are impressive to visit, but most are monuments to incompetent management and low-productivity labor. Chinese and foreign economists alike are agreed that there can be no real modernization in China without drastic changes in the country's factories, especially the mid-sized and large state enterprises.

I arrived in China in October 1982 to find a society that seemed eternally frozen in shortages of all kinds of manufactured goods, but especially of consumer durables. The television tube was still in the process of becoming a household object—rather than something to be viewed communally at the factory, park, or rural production brigade—more than thirty years after it had changed the economies and daily lives of most advanced countries. Tourism was becoming popular, but a Chinese tourist with a camera was rare. Most who did own one carried a locally made Seagull brand of a type, then still the staple of the Seagull factory's production line, that had been taken out of production two decades earlier in the rest of the world. The standard 35-millimeter camera, with light metered through the viewfinder, the stock production number for twenty-five years elsewhere in the world and itself already yielding ground to electronic and autofocus models, was still beyond the capability of the Seagull people. They would not offer one as a regular product for two more years.

Foreign and Chinese friends repeatedly promised that a trip to Shanghai would provide glimpses of a more industrially competent and fashion-conscious China. On my first visit, in the spring of 1983, I did indeed see a city where people seemed less regimented, in that fewer wore the rumpled blue Mao jackets and baggy blue or gray pants that dominated Beijing. But it was also a city where the newest look in fashion seemed decades out of date. As the political climate permitted more and more individuality in dress, Shanghai clothing factories seemed to be dusting off the patterns and even the bolts of cloth they had used to produce skirts and dresses at some time well predating 1966, when the late Great Helmsman's Red Guards began to enforce the Maoist dress code with a vengeance. Women seemed as at sea about what clothing should look like in the wearing as factory directors did about what it should look like in the making. A Shanghai woman wearing, say, a bright green plaid skirt and a pink and black polka-dot blouse was still a far more common sight than a woman wearing two pieces that looked as if they had anything to do with each other.

To break through this industrial stultification, Deng Xiaoping's reformist allies had begun in the early 1980s to permit small-scale private and cooperative enterprises. By the mid-1980s, China had the fastest industrial growth rate in the developing world. Economic overheating, especially in small industries, had become a leading concern of planners and top Communists for the first time in the history of the People's Republic. Many goods that had been in shortage for decades were coming into adequate supply, some even into a degree of abundance. In particular, simple light-industrial articles like plastic sandals and cotton or synthetic frocks, long hard to get in many cities and rarely stocked in village markets, were now on display in street markets and even in some village stalls. But the overwhelming impression was that the real action in the industrial sector was the phenomenal growth of small, private, cooperative and village-run factories, now that they were legal again. Many state factories, though showing some stirrings, were far more sluggish. And it is the state factories that dominate China's industry.

I was and am convinced that dramatic improvements are necessary if these state-run factories are to play a role in modernization that justifies the decades of big investments they have required, mostly of state funds painfully accumulated by severe demands on the peasants. By the time of my trip, many ordinary consumer goods had begun to approach adequate supply, though prices of the big-ticket pieces often remained shockingly high. Watch factories were in the process of abandoning the heavy, thick-jeweled models that most Chinese had quit buying and were slowly switching over to more reliable and less cumbersome quartz watches. The black one-speed bicycle, the staple commuting wheels for most workers and long an item most Chinese could get only by waiting years for a ration ticket from the work unit, was gradually being taken off the ration system in many areas, though the top brands, thought by Chinese to last longer and work more reliably, were still rationed in most cities. On a late 1985 visit to Shanghai, I would see—in a hotel display window—my first Chinese-made ten-speed bike.

Television was becoming commonplace in most cities, and on hot nights in the residential lanes, a black-and-white tube at the end of an extension cord was only slightly less ordinary than the ubiquitous cots and chairs as people came out of their houses to get some air until the temperature dropped enough that they could sleep next to a fan. More and more of the sets were color, and in 1984 color TV sets had first surpassed black-and-white in sales. But by late 1985, anyone who brought a color set out for an evening in the lane still was likely to find a circle of his neighbors' chairs and stools forming several rows deep around it. In Beijing in 1985 I began to notice a steady flow of refrigerators, typically about 9 or 10 cubic feet in size, and the great majority of them made in Chinese factories, on the backs of the flatbed tricycles that are the capital's standard home-delivery vehicle. It was visible in any city that something was happening in the factories. I decided to go to Chongqing and Shanghai to try to see if there was any clear linkage between what was visible on the streets and the endless stream of propaganda—in newspapers and magazines and on television and radio—about factory reform.

The idea of the industrial reforms was to attempt in industry some of what Premier Zhao's Sichuan plan had done for many areas of the countryside. Sichuan had been the testing ground of the rural reform, and Chongqing had been authorized to make some of the early tries at factory reform. The city's leadership had close ties with the top of the Central Committee, and on my first visit I had felt that officials in Chongqing seemed less reticent about potentially embarrassing truths than those in other places I had visited. The officially guided stop at the South Seas Rubber Products factory was arranged in response to a request I had made to see a factory that was fairly well along in the new reforms, which by that time had been dominating industrial news for most of a year. The rubber plant apparently was chosen to meet my request because it had been one of thirty factories in Chongqing chosen in May 1984 to lead the industrial reform there. I was given half a day with Liu Maoxing, a forty-six-year-old technical school graduate who was introduced as the plant's deputy director and an example of the younger and better educated people the factory was putting in power in response to orders from Beijing.

Liu Maoxing outlined a familiar list of changes, all of them in line with orders Beijing had sent out fourteen months earlier to get each province to work on industrial reform. Some sixteen older officials had retired to make way for younger blood. A new factory director had come in, he said, and the powers of the factory's Communist party secretary had been drastically reduced. In particular, the factory director now had the final say in all matters directly affecting production, and with it the power, for the first time, to discipline or even dismiss workers who failed or refused to do their jobs. The factory director was responsible for introducing new technology and developing new products. The factory's bonus fund, long used as a kitty to be divided up equally regardless of effort, was now to become the source of rewards for individual performance. The factory would be responsible for its own economic success or failure. Instead of turning over all its profits to the state and waiting for central planners to decide how much money it could have for investment and how much for distribution as bonuses, the factory would pay taxes, retain its after-tax profits and make its own decisions about how to invest. Even decisions on bonuses would be within the factory's local powers, though limits were already being imposed because many factories had simply cut up their profits equally among the workers and had kept little or nothing for investment.

The central idea behind these changes, which were already becoming staples of national news reports, was to give factories some degree of autonomy, to introduce incentives into the work place and to put at least some of the most vital production and fiscal decisions into the hands of managers and technicians who would see the issues as economic rather than political. These factory reform plans were sent down from Beijing, based on experimentation in 1982 and 1983 in a few carefully chosen model plants. They were intended to shake up a moribund system that had turned most of China's state-owned factories into vast welfare operations.

Despite the decades of Marxist and Maoist rhetoric and exhortation about production, it would be possible to make a case that the typical big state-owned factory today is better organized to meet and regulate its workers' needs as consumers than to produce goods. For millions of workers, the state factory exists less as a place to perform work than as a source of subsidies and noncash, daily-life benefits. Many state factories operate the schools their workers' children attend, pass out subsidies to help buy coal and cooking oil, distribute melons and cabbages, run the hospitals their workers' families visit for flu medicines and birth-control pills, and maintain fire and police services not only for their own plants but for their workers' apartments. Most important, tens of millions of Chinese workers look to their factories for relief from the country's desperate housing shortage. It is the work unit that provides the heavily subsidized housing that gives a young married couple—most often after a wait of anywhere from a year to several years of living with the in-laws—a few square yards of cement-floored, cold-water walkup for a rent that rarely equals two-days' pay.

In the new world of Marxist-Leninist-Maoist economics that the Chinese Communist party set out to build after 1949, unemployment was regarded as a peculiarly capitalist evil. China declared it was going to demonstrate that, with proper central planning and abundant socialist compassion, everyone could have a job. In reality, factories never grew at anything like the pace needed to absorb urban population growth, and most have been obliged to overstaff egregiously in order to help the Communist party prove that socialism was making unemployment obsolete. Beginning with the Anti-Rightist Campaign of the late 1950s, and far more so in the ten years of the Cultural Revolution, literally millions of urban and town Chinese were driven out of petty commercial jobs as Mao set out to snip off the remaining "tails of capitalism." The most typical of these "tails of capitalism" was perhaps one of the ubiquitous food vendors, whose "capital" would have amounted to a rusted oil drum converted to use as a cookstove, a few worn wooden stools, and three or four square yards of patched canvas to shelter customers from sun and rain. Aside from making it harder for all urban people to find a quick breakfast, snack or shoe repair, the main consequence of clearing the streets of these hundreds of thousands of tiny scraps of capital was to increase pressure on state enterprises to help make places for the workers thus displaced.

So factories have for decades been under relentless pressure to help prove that socialism could eliminate unemployment. Wherever I went, I asked factory officials what would be the biggest steps they could take to improve their operations. Only a few did not put big staff reductions high on their wish lists. Many said that, even at today's low technological level, the only way to get real efficiency would be to get rid of anywhere from 30 to 60 percent of their workers. Several complained that overstaffing was so severe, it not only left each worker feeling that a few hours a day was a heavy work load but also sometimes meant that extra hands literally got in the way of production.

Virtually every walk I took through a factory turned up comic-opera scenes of overstaffing—workers assigned to gardening in tiny plots outside the offices, or to shopkeeping in embarrassingly understocked factory outlet stores; knots of workers chatting throughout the factory, often outnumbering those doing actual work; two, three or sometimes half a dozen people doing tasks one person would do anywhere else. I sometimes made mental or written notes on the division of labor. At a utensil factory in Shanghai, workers building a temporary shed to house new stamping machines were organized this way: A young man picked up bricks from a pile, one at a time, and handed them to a workmate who put them on a wooden board attached to a rope. Atop the scaffolding, a worker waited until it was time to pull the rope up to lift the bricks to where they were being laid. Once he got the bricks up to the top, he waited while another worker took them off and handed them to a worker who put them in a pile. Then another worker lifted each brick off the pile and handed it to a young man standing next to the bricklayer. On the other side of the bricklayer stood a man holding an easel full of cement, from which the bricklayer now and then replenished his trowel. The easel-holder received deliveries as needed from a man who spent most of his time standing next to a metal trough, where another man now and then stirred the batch of fresh, wet cement. In effect, the one bricklayer was supported by nine young men divvying up the work of a single hod-carrier and a single cement-mixer. Given this environment, it was hardly surprising that the bricklayer himself showed no inclination to hurry the job.

What is true of work and workers is doubly or triply true of supplies, planning, production and distribution. If any idea could be easily grasped as China adopted Soviet-style socialism, it was that central planning should be a critical tool to a poor country that wanted to reduce waste as it industrialized. All the waste inherent in individual decision making would be eliminated. Only the needed numbers of chemists or engineers would be educated; scarce materials like coal and steel would be channeled where they were most needed rather than simply where there was money to pay for them; wrenches and teakettles would be produced according to a plan rather than according to the wasteful competitive instincts of company managers.

The idea has long since proved richer in symmetry than in efficacy. The reality has been a system in which factory administrations have scant control over their own work, either in the planning or in the execution. The typical state factory looks to its higher unit to tell it what to produce, looks to a state-run distribution system to bring in parts or raw materials, looks to a central buying system to sell its products, and looks to a government assignment agency to send it engineers and technicians. So if the products it is assigned to make are no longer salable, that is the fault of the higher unit, not of the factory director. If the parts or raw materials are not available or not on time, there is no turning to an alternate supplier, and no longer any holding the factory administration accountable for its production schedule. If the supplies and components—and, hence, the products—are below grade, that is the fault of the suppliers, not of the factory, and in turn becomes the problem of the state distributor, not of the factory. If a plant that needs a chemist ends up with an electrical engineer, that is the fault of the central assignment agency, not of the factory's hiring system.

The product of this system has been an Alice-through-the-looking-glass economy in which managers rarely are able to assert basic management principles. Bob Davis, who managed a small service staff of Chinese technicians for Perkin-Elmer, a precision-instruments company based in Norwalk, Connecticut, ran head-on into problems like these as soon as he arrived in 1983. "The technicians knew how to do their jobs well," he told me one evening over dinner, "but there was simply no organization at all, so they just assigned themselves willy-nilly to whatever service calls they chose to make. Our installations are all over China, and what I discovered first was that very few Chinese people like to go to the really remote places like Tibet or Xinjiang or Manchuria. So we had places in Tibet that had been out of service and pleading for repairs for a year or two, and we had places Chinese like to visit—Shanghai and Guangzhou—where there might be several service trips a year, with or without any request from the client." Davis dealt with this problem by the simple but quintessentially capitalist device of making it financially attractive to go to remote areas. He put his staff on an incentive system in which days of service work would be the basis of rewards, and travel time would count as days of service work. Before long, technicians were showing special interest in remote assignments.

Bob Davis also found symptoms of the shortage-oriented mentality that pervades many industries. "They are so used to ordering too many of anything they order—so they'll not get caught short next time they need it—that it's as if there's no such thing as the cost of maintaining stock. I found millions of dollars tied up on the shelves in replacement parts that were sure to be obsolete before we could ever use them. We worked on that with the Chinese for a while, but finally I had to put my wife in charge of the stock. It was the only way to get it under control."

Evidence is scarce of any concept that stock—or machinery, or an engineer's education, or any other form of capital—represents earning power that needs to be kept in full use. In my years in China, I visited perhaps a dozen hospitals altogether. All but one sooner or later proudly led the foreign guest to a radiation department that had equipped itself with some kind of multi-million-dollar American, German or Japanese scanner. Except for one that was turned on briefly to give me a routine chest X-ray, I saw only one of these big capital investments actually in use. All of my visits were during normal working hours, but I usually arrived to find these impressive and costly devices still in dust-coated plastic shrouds provided by their foreign manufacturers, or under slipcovers custommade for them by Chinese drapers or upholsterers. In response to the inevitable questions about utilization, most of the radiologists reported that these costly machines either were unused for various reasons or were being used for half a dozen or fewer patients per week.

The highest rate of use I encountered, in Guangzhou, was three or four patients a day. I asked if that was the machine's capacity, and the chief radiologist assured me that it could handle fifteen or twenty patients a day. I asked if that meant there were only three or four patients a day in Guangzhou who needed this kind of attention. Oh, no, I was told, there were more than enough to keep it busy all the time. Why, then, the underutilization? Well, it seemed there were not enough trained personnel to prepare the patients for the scans, and training them would cost several thousand dollars more than the hospital could budget. So the equipment went severely underutilized, and hundreds of patients went without scans that might have helped them, because a hospital that had been able to find nearly two million dollars to buy the latest prestige article could not find a few thousand dollars to train the people needed to keep it in full use.

Much the same was true in varying degrees in many factories I visited. New Japanese textile-making equipment in Chengde, the former Qing Dynasty summer capital, sat idle because it had been bought without checking to make sure the plant would be allotted the added electrical power needed to run it. The same factory director who might point to the saving he had accomplished by assigning idle workers to sort through metal scraps for fragments that could go back into the smelter was likely to respond with a mystified, blank look when asked about the waste of capital represented by idle machinery. Taken in combination with the surplus of labor that was likely to be one of his first complaints, the down time of his machinery would smell of opportunity to any Western factory manager. But the Chinese factory director is very likely right not to strain himself in this direction. The system allows him little or no leeway to take the initiative that would be required to find the materials and supplies, or even the added electrical power and cooling water, that he would need to turn idle machinery and excess workers into an additional shift. In many places, I found factories that were limited to daylight operation simply by the lack of electricity to keep both the lights and the machinery turned on at the same time.

The crippling effect this system has on factories is amplified and reamplified by the extent to which the Chinese Communist party has regarded the factory as a political fiefdom first, and a means of production second. The rhetoric of the Maoist years has based the exaltation of workers and farmers on their roles as producers. According to this argument, the producers have created what Marxists term "social wealth," so they should have the power, and the society should be organized to serve them. Thus runs the logic of the worker's paradise, and the logic plays itself out daily everywhere in the economy. Store clerks sullenly toss goods and change at customers, whom they often seem to regard as interruptions in the daily round of conversations with their workmates. "I know that people all over the world complain about bureaucracy," remarked Wu Qi, a professor of automation at Qinghua University, Beijing's premier engineering school, during one of several interviews. "But in China, we have created a world where the person who sells you an onion or a flashlight is a bureaucrat." The end product of this logic has been a world in which city people spend their forty-four or forty-eight working hours every week in the worker's paradise, and then spend the rest of their hours— that vast majority of adult life that most urban humans spend as consumers—in purgatory.

In the Maoist decades, control of the factory became a critically important expression of the Marxist ideal. It is fundamental to the Leninist political system that the only body able to understand and enforce the true will of the workers and peasants is the Communist party. So if the factory is to be truly under the control of the workers, the faith holds, it must be under the control of the Communist party. In practice, this has usually meant that all significant decisions in a Chinese factory must ultimately be approved, if not actually made, by the factory's Communist party secretary. For most of the decades since the Communist party won power in 1949, this has meant that the party secretary has decided, or at minimum has approved, everything from which direction the production line should flow to who should get a bonus; from who could be promoted out of the ranks to whether to open a commissary; from where to build a warehouse to who would be principal of the factory's elementary school.

For most of those same decades, China's economy was short of both money and goods. So money mattered little, and the one thing that mattered most was what Americans call "connections" and Chinese call *guanxi*. With the right *guanxi*, you could get access to meats that are never available in the markets but are always available to the powerful. With the right *guanxi*, you might even be able to get a car assigned to you, or get your children into a school they could never enter just on their own test scores. In this politics-over-economics environment, the party secretary of the typical state-run factory has a position a Prendergast or a Daley could never have imagined. Every new apartment assignment, every new water line, every school admission, every bicycle ration card assigned by the work unit is potentially or actually subject to review by the party secretary.

Typically, the factory's Communist party secretary is a man in late middle age who has bobbed and weaved through decades of the never-ending vagaries of Maoist campaigns and changes of the party line, humiliated himself in numberless rounds of that special kind of confession the Chinese Communist party calls "self-criticism," and spent months or years in Cultural Revolution labor "schools." He has mastered this milieu sufficiently to rise up through the party into a place where he at last has his hands on real strands of local *guanxi*. Those decades may or may not have taught him anything about what kind of tires people need or want, for that has not been his responsibility—an often faceless central planner tells him what his factory is supposed to make. But his decades in the party have inevitably taught him much about the flow of power and *guanxi* in his corner of the country. His experience, his training—and, not to be ignored, his ultimate responsibility—are all far more political than economic. He has spent virtually his entire adult life in an environment where the word "businessman" has been a form of invective.

When a factory's Communist party secretary contemplates a decision, he inescapably approaches it with a mental set that is far more political than economic. He may or may not be influenced by arguments about whether anyone wants to buy the tires his factory makes, or about how the issue being weighed will affect quality, efficiency or profits. But he will surely consider how it will affect his *guanxi,* not only with his superiors but also with, for example, the local water company, where he will surely sooner or later need connections to get hookups for apartments he wants to distribute. He knows that even if his factory fails to meet its assigned quota for rubber boots, the system is rich in excuses that will diffuse the blame across a broad range of late supply deliveries, electrical power failures, worn-out equipment and endless other factors beyond his control. If the excuses seem pale, he still can probably call in a favor on the *guanxi* network. But he knows equally well that he can be held personally and directly accountable if he fails in some political sense—if, for example, he rewards superior workers in an innovative way that produces rebellion among the ordinary and the laggard. It has been his experience for decades that this kind of incident, far more than a deficit or a failure to meet a quota, is likely to produce a demand from higher-ups in the party for a new round of self-criticism. Little if anything in his experience, his training or his responsibility would suggest, to him or to any impartial observer, that he has anything to gain by applying economic, rather than political, principles to his stewardship of the factory.

By the late 1970s, the new central leadership under Deng Xiaoping was deciding, with much difficulty and reluctance—and with substantial dissent that remains visible to this day—that China could never become economically modern under the existing state factory system. By the early 1980s, with much accomplished in agriculture, the time seemed ripe to start work on the factories. But the painful realization that the country's industries were wholly unsuited to cope with the modern world was closely followed by realization of how vastly difficult factory reforms will be. Not only is each factory much more complex than each farm, but each factory is part of an interrelated system of commercial, production, transportation and institutional sectors. A factory depends on universities for engineers and chemists, on vocational schools for technicians and trained workers. Complexity begins at the mine and extends through smelters, rail lines, and stamping plants before the earth's ore becomes the threaded metal tube that is delivered to be shaped into a valve stem at the South Seas Rubber Products plant.

The very complexity of the factory and the system of which it is part poses daunting hazards for anyone proposing major changes, no matter how sluggish or even self-defeating the existing way may be. Assuming that the Chinese Communist party could find the political will to take major economic decisions away from party secretaries and give them to factory directors, where was it to seek these directors in a country that had opened its first management schools in 1981? Assuming that the party was willing to jeopardize the national treasury and give up the existing system of collecting all profits and making all investment decisions centrally, how was it to hold factories accountable for their profits and their investments if their working budgets— what they paid for their labor and their supplies, and what they charged for their products—all were determined more by government fiat than by market forces?

When they had set out on economic reform of the countryside, the new leaders could adopt the pattern Zhao Ziyang had set in Sichuan Province, and could basically return to something resembling the family farming system China had practiced before Mao's communes. But, having demonstrated how much more the family farm could produce than could the commune, when it came time to extend reform to the factories, they had no such thing as a pre-Maoist system to return to. When the Communist party won power in 1949, the industrial base was so scant, and so damaged and depleted by decades of war, that it stands today essentially as a creation of the three decades of Communist rule. If it is replete with comic inefficiency and Dickensian working conditions, and if it is redolent of politics where most of the world would put economics, it at least does exist today in some form and does produce some goods, neither of which was true to any comparable extent in 1949. But the fact that most of the system has been built since 1949 also means that China is essentially without factory managers who know anything but the Soviet-style system and its Maoist adaptations.

When China set out in 1985 to put factory directors, rather than party secretaries, in charge of economic decisions, the pool of people available had taken training either under Soviet advisers who had helped with the initial construction in the 1950s, or at Soviet universities, or in the Soviet-style educational system installed under Russian tutelage, or on the floor of the factories created under the Soviet system. As a consequence, the most elementary management concepts, the daily working tools of production supervisors and factory administrators, simply are not part of the vocabulary of the Chinese factory director. Over lunch in Beijing, an American economist who had just spent two weeks visiting factories in Shanghai and neighboring parts of Jiangsu Province, China's most productive industrial area, spoke of this phenomenon in tones approaching disbelief. "The reality," he said, "is that the typical Chinese factory director doesn't have a clue how much it costs his factory to make its widgets." My own experience in interviewing Chinese factory officials was that, while most could readily read off figures on worker productivity or production cost from a well-worn factory briefing book, questions aimed at analyzing the figures soon produced confusion and vagueness about how they had been derived.

Concepts that have only more recently become widespread among modern industries, like market surveys, seem better known in China, perhaps because they still have a freshness that keeps them in print in foreign newspapers and journals that are now sometimes translated into Chinese. But while some factory officials show some awareness of these concepts, they seldom know much beyond the jargon. I asked a new director how his piano factory in Guangzhou could confidently increase production as fast as it had, given the scarcity of market information. "We have surveyed the market very seriously," he replied, and for a passing instant I found myself reflexively bracing for the flood of data that would have followed from any comparable official of an American or Japanese firm. I soon found I could safely turn off my mental calculator. "We think many Chinese families have more money now, and with the one-child policy we believe many people will want to do special things like providing pianos for the one child. Besides, we keep falling farther and farther behind on our orders even after we increase production, so we know there is a strong market." In one sense, he may have said all that needed saying about selling pianos in the shortage-dominated economy his factory serves. But his assumption that his comments could pass as the product of any serious market study also struck me as a measure of how close Chinese factory managements are to functional illiteracy in the most basic business concepts of the modern world China now seeks to enter.

———————

Like many of the obstacles faced by the industrial reforms, this human dimension had its clear manifestations at the South Seas Rubber Products factory and many other plants I visited as the reforms proceeded. Liu Maoxing, the deputy director I had met, was a graduate of a high school–level technical school. In a land where education is scarce and schools were closed for much of the decade of the Cultural Revolution, Liu's technical school diploma qualified him for the rarefied status of what Chinese call an "intellectual." The plant's new director, Liu Guyin, a woman then fifty-three years old and no relation to the deputy, was a graduate of a junior high school. Given the character of China's schools, such backgrounds are not likely to produce the dynamic reformer who can lead a factory into the modern world.

But the leadership factor was only one of the constraints on reform in the factories I visited. Another important factor by late 1985 was a major dissonance between the ambition of bringing real management to the factory and the very cautious nature of the reforms actually being attempted. Liu Maoxing and officials of other factories outlined limitations that seemed at least as impressive as the extent of the reforms. The South Seas Rubber Products factory director now had autonomy and responsibility never seen before, but still nothing resembling counterparts in modern economies. For example, her deputy explained, a factory affairs committee oversaw her decisions, thereby both inhibiting them and delaying them. A state agency still told the director how many workers to keep on the payroll, thereby blocking action on an issue most factory directors say needs attention. The factory could distribute some of its profits as bonuses to top workers, but only within limits that were enforced by taxes, amounting in effect to penalties for any factory that paid out more in bonuses than the state wanted. The director's power to fire a laggard worker turned out to be subject to approval by a state agency. The factory was free to sell a portion of its products at market prices, but there was no real market for tires or hoses except through the same old state purchasing agencies, which bought only at fixed prices.

If the reforms themselves were limited, the persisting subculture created by the Stalinist-Maoist factory system added limits that hemmed them in still further. The South Seas Rubber Products plant, like all but a few of the factories I had visited, found only a handful of workers worthy of much more than the average bonus paid out in any one of its shops. It found an even smaller handful worthy of significantly less than the average. Consistent with the "groupism" orientation of both traditional and Maoist culture, the factory preferred to make its distinctions from shop to shop, far more than from worker to worker. This practice added a dimension to the already complicated job of measuring human performance and diluted the Beijing reformists' idea of putting more focus on individual workers. The right to dismiss laggard workers proved to be, effectively, a dead letter a year and a half after the factory had set out on its reforms. Workers might be dismissed, Liu Maoxing reported, only for the grossest nonfeasance, such as forty or more days of unauthorized absence in a year. Despite continuing absenteeism much like that experienced in most Chinese factories, Liu noted that, in fact, no one had been dismissed on that basis, either. One worker had been fired so far, not in the name of labor discipline but because he had been convicted and sentenced to five years in jail for a street assault.

On the critical question of how far the reforms had succeeded in putting power into the hands of people who would make economic decisions on economic rather than political grounds, the record at the South Seas Rubber Products plant, as at every factory I would visit, was at best ambiguous and at worst suggestive of something somewhere between fraud and sabotage. Liu Guyin, the new director, was somewhat younger than her predecessor, and her junior high education was somewhat better than his. But she had been promoted into the directorship straight from a tour as deputy Communist party secretary for the plant. "She joined the Chinese Revolution at a young age, and that was taken into consideration," Liu Maoxing answered when asked what had been decisive in the appointment of the director. So the new autonomy of the factory director, which had been intended by Beijing's reformers to get the factory's economic decisions out of the party's hands and into a professional manager's, had itself been simply put into the hands of a leader of the factory's Communist party committee.

If this were not sufficient, the new factory affairs committee, like its counterparts at most of the factories I visited, was heavily laden with Communist party officials and workers. In most of the factories I visited, party cadres and members held between 25 and 40 percent of the seats on these committees, not counting representatives of labor unions, the women's federation and other organizations that are required by law to accept "the leadership of the Chinese Communist party." This was far more than the leadership ratios the party had found fully adequate even in its clandestine years, before it had won power, to seize effective control of organizations that were not under any legal obligation to accept its "leadership." I did find a few factories where the new directors themselves were something other than party careerists, but I left their factories impressed by the narrowness, not the breadth, of any autonomy they were likely to have without strong backing from their local party cadres.

As I left China in the summer of 1987, the early stirrings of real industrial growth were visible on the streets of almost any city. Manufactured goods were spreading beyond the cities and even beyond the county seats into rural marketplaces that had never offered them before. The big state-owned factories that had consumed so much of the country's investment in the Maoist decades clearly were beginning to participate in change, and their products—bicycles, refrigerators, and television sets—were far less scarce than they had been a few years earlier. But the central leadership seemed less satisfied with what it was accomplishing in these state-owned factories than with most aspects of reform. The factory reform could proceed only so far, in any case, without major progress on other fronts, particularly in stubborn areas like getting the country off its system of arbitrary, bureaucrat-ordered prices, related neither to supply and demand nor to production costs, and onto a market-price system. Real progress in getting factories to make economic decisions mainly on economic rather than political grounds would also depend, in many cases, less on isolated attempts to reform factories than on the Communist party's internal attempts to reform itself.

My impression was that the reformers themselves were not yet sure how to go about restructuring the factory system, even had there been no resistance from conservatives at the top of the party. So their dissatisfaction with progress to date translated itself, not into a coherent reform program, but into further groping, in the form of a seemingly eclectic collection of ideas all being tried at once. Some factories were to be put on a "director responsibility system," not unlike those tried at the South Seas Rubber Products plant and other early sites of experimentation. The word "responsibility" was taken directly from, and was clearly intended to borrow some of the cachet of, the terminology used when Zhao Ziyang gave rural families "responsibility" for the land they farmed. But in the factories, the "director responsibility system" was taking far more forms, with some directors signing contracts for terms as short as two years and being subject to dismissal if they had failed to show profits and satisfy their Communist party–laden factory affairs committees by the ends of their contracts. Some smaller factories were being turned over to "cooperatives," often in effect headed by one strong individual, that were expected to run them for the state.

Since 1986 the trend in reforming state factories has been to permit "separation of ownership from management," a concept borrowed from capitalistic, publicly traded corporations, owned by shareholders but run by hired managers. The concept offers the philosophical convenience of keeping major industries "socialist"—at least in the sense of being "owned" by the state—while permitting the state to farm out the management to workers' congresses, to cooperatives and even to individual operators. That concept contains the potential of what would amount to a privatization that could rival the transfer of state-developed industries in Meiji Japan, the gestation era of what has become 100 years later the world's most dynamic industrial economy. That, in turn, would contain the seeds of reforms that could give factories much more of the remaking they need than any other plan visible today. But political power in Deng Xiaoping's China remains more diffused, and less in agreement, than it was in Meiji Japan. To turn the "separation" concept, still struggling for acceptance as I left Beijing, into a source of dynamism on the scale the factories need, would require political unity, and accompanying political will, on a scale not yet in evidence. I left the country convinced that, of all areas of China's economy, reform in the state-run factories, one of the sectors most vital to any real modernization, has been the least effective and is meeting the most effective resistance.

4

Pop Stars, Preachers, Party Lines

"In the division of labor within our society," Zang Yihua told me when I visited her work unit in the late summer of 1984, "it also serves the people if you work as a nude model." Zang Yihua, a lanky nineteen-year-old with a saccharine smile, had graduated from a Beijing high school the previous spring. Lapsing into the Orwellian Newspeak of post-Mao Marxism, she explained how she had reconciled her new job at the Central Academy of Fine Arts with the demands of Chinese traditional and socialist modesty. As we talked, the contrast between her work and her phrasing echoed the contrast between her clothing and the schoolhouse dustiness of the academy reception room's gray walls, gray slipcovers, gray desks, gray fans and gray floors. She wore all the trendiest stuff of 1984 Beijing—black leather shoes with thick high heels, nylons under a tight-fitting pair of Shanghai blue jeans, and a long, pink-and-black striped sweater. Stenciled across the front of the sweater, in ten-inch-tall yellowish metallic script, was the word "Physical!"

Zhang Yihua was one of 171 young Beijing men and women who had responded to a single, discreet advertisement in the Beijing *Evening News* earlier in 1984. Qian Xiaowu, the academy's dean, sat in on the interview and explained that the advertisement marked the first time since schools were closed in 1966, at the onset of the Cultural Revolution, that Chinese art institutes had been permitted to hire nude models for life-study classes. Instruction in figure sketching itself had resumed only a few years earlier, in 1981, after an interruption of fifteen years. When the classes were at last permitted to meet, the professors discovered that while Beijing's small corps of professional nude models had waited out a decade and a half of political tumult, they had developed wrinkles, pot bellies and saddlebags. Some had acquired ill-placed and unaesthetic marks of Cultural Revolution beatings. It had taken three more years, working patiently through China's bureaucracy, to get permission from the Ministry of Education and the Ministry of Culture to advertise for some new models who more closely matched the ideals of the art form. Zhang Yihua was one of thirty female and male models hired from the group who had answered the ad. With the addition of the new thirty, the academy was able for the first time in eighteen years to supply all the life studio needs of ten Beijing-area institutions, ranging from universities to the Art College of the People's Liberation Army.

But in today's Chinese society, the ancient Confucian modesty of the young woman is overlain with the prudery of Cultural Revolution Maoism, and with the just plain clucking of housewives and guffaws of balding men along the labyrinthine lanes where many Beijing people live. So the same hiring that had solved a set of old problems had also created a set of new ones. After more than a month on the job, Dean Qian explained, for Zhang Yihua and several of her colleagues the problem still was how much to tell the family. By the time of the interview, she had not let her parents know much more than that she had found unusually well-paid work at the art academy. The faculty was arranging to help her talk to her parents, the dean said, but "she has a big job to do to help her family understand that nude modeling is a respectable and necessary occupation in modern China." So Dean Qian wondered whether "Mr. American *Baltimore Sun* Correspondent," as he and many other officials called me in formal interviews, might be willing to use a name that was not actually hers. Accordingly, "Zhang Yihua" is not her real name but one invented for use when I wrote about her for the paper.

———————

Zhang Yihua's new job at the Central Academy of Fine Arts is a minuscule part of a vast but still highly selective relaxation that has taken place since 1976 in the cultural, recreational, religious, and entertainment lives of hundreds of millions of people. Sensitivity about her new line of work is one facet of a persisting and pervasive ambivalence toward that relaxation, an ambivalence that has contributed to divisions among the men at the apex of the Communist party, that deeply permeates society, and that ocasionally boils into public controversy or confrontation despite the enduring Chinese and Communist preferences to keep disagreement out of sight.

The sources of ambiguity lie deep in history and create not only fault lines between individuals, social groups and political factions but also a fundamental schism within each individual. Each educated Chinese is conscious that his country invented gunpowder and moveable type, but that it now lags desperately behind after a century of trying to catch up with Western technology; that his country once so outshone its neighbors that its ancient styles of architecture, art and literature still dominate much of East Asia, but that it more recently needed a violent revolution to drive foreign overlords from its cities. Beginning in the late nineteenth century, this admixture of pride and humiliation has often seemed to keep both individuals and the nation in an enduring state of personal confusion and public controversy, especially whenever a national leadership has tried to open the country to outside influences.

This schism is a question of how much of their sense of their nation's uniqueness and glory the Chinese, as individuals and as a people, are prepared to give up in order to join the advanced world. In its simplest and most directly political expressions, this schism is visible in whatever is the latest shape of the country's timeless antiforeignism. In the fall of 1985, students in several cities demonstrated against waves of imported goods from Japan, carrying placards denouncing "THE SECOND JAPANESE INVASION." In talking with foreign newsmen who covered these demonstrations, many of these same students acknowledged that their own homes and dormitory rooms contained Japanese televisions, tape recorders or refrigerators, and that they would buy Japanese appliances in preference to local any time they could. Most of the students saw no irony in demonstrating against a "second Japanese invasion" and then going home to watch a

Socialism with a Chinese face. Photographed in her double mirror, a dancer works on her eye makeup before going onstage in a 1986 pop concert. Western-style makeup like this was banned from the stage for more than a decade as too "bourgeois."

Zhang Qiang, left, a pop singer who was eighteen years old and already two years into a lucrative career when I took this picture in 1986. At right is her mother, Zhang Bo, who launched her daughter on a recording career at age sixteen as pop music began to take off in China under Deng Xiaoping's reforms. Behind them are posters for some of Zhang Qiang's more than a dozen earlier tapes.

Old and young priests at a Daoist temple in Shanghai pose for a visiting American journalist. Daoism is China's only major indigenous organized religion. It is being revived under official Communist party sponsorship, along with major imported religions like Buddhism, Islam and Christianity.

Visiting faithful from Hong Kong join in worship at a major Buddhist temple in Guangzhou. Buddhism has again become a growing religion, and the Japanese and Overseas Chinese followers it draws to China make it a promising source of foreign hard currency needed for modernization.

Worshippers at a Daoist temple in Shanghai light votive candles. At most shrines and temples, tourists outnumber worshippers by wide margins, but this 1986 photo was taken on a major festival day.

In Nanjing, at the country's main Protestant seminary, students practice singing hymns while their teacher plays the piano. All Protestant faiths—Episcopal, Methodist, Baptist, Salvation Army and Adventist among them—have been lumped together in a feat of ecumenism that the Communist party officially describes as "postdenominational" Protestantism.

With painted face and elaborately embroidered costume, a Beijing Opera star performs on one of the capital's most famous stages. Beijing Opera was allowed to resume traditional stories and legends in the early 1980s, thereby restoring to older Chinese a familiar entertainment that had been banned during the Cultural Revolution. In those years, Jiang Qing, wife of the late Chairman Mao, quashed these and other traditional forms of culture in favor of her own brand of "revolutionary" stage productions.

Right: A girl "Big Head" dancer peeks out from under her papier-mache mask during a break in the 1986 Chinese New Year's Day celebration at Feng Tai. This Beijing suburb is now famous for its elaborate revivals of the annual street dances.

The dragon dance begins at Feng Tai, a new suburb of Beijing. Chinese New Year's festivals have been permitted since 1981, after being banned for years during the Cultural Revolution.

Brass stars stand out on the red collar flashes of two People's Liberation Army soldiers, dressed up to perform as monkey dancers in the 1985 New Year's celebration at Feng Tai.

Japanese-made TV. In fact, the issue need not directly involve foreigners or even foreign goods. The schism is palpable today wherever reform reaches, and it interacts everywhere with the reformers' own ever-changing definitions of how much control the Communist party still wants to exert over the commonplaces of daily life.

As seemingly simple a matter as whether to permit public balls and dances can thus become a matter of high politics, commanding the attention of the highest councils of political leadership and occupying literally acres of scarce newsprint and magazine paper. Ballroom dancing was not a Chinese invention. It was introduced mainly in this century, by foreigners who had torn whole cities from Chinese sovereignty. But novels, songs and movies of the 1930s have indelibly associated ballroom dancing with places where foreign men went to pick up local girls for a night's pleasure. Many older couples, who may even treasure memories of the ballroom dances they attended in their own younger years, can work up a high dudgeon over reports of today's youth dancing cheek-to-cheek or chest-to-chest, not to mention the occasional foreigner taking home a local woman after a dance. When the new leadership tentatively permitted a few public dances in the late 1970s, young people and some middle-aged couples flocked to them. But these events were unceremoniously choked off in 1980 after being accused of harboring every sin from smooching to prostitution, from "bourgeois individualism" to talking with foreigners. Dances resumed in January and February of 1984, but only after several months of articles in which *China Youth News* and other publications set forth a code of behavior for what were being publicized as a new kind of "healthy collective dancing parties." The new code laid out diagrams of the acceptable dance steps, prescribed how far apart cheeks should remain and instructed dancers to change partners every few minutes rather than try to spend the whole event with one person.

I was one of several foreign correspondents who went to one of the first of these healthy collective dancing parties as Chinese New Year approached in the winter of 1984. As if to stress the contrast with the "low lights" dances of the indecent past, the party started promptly at

2 P.M. in the Beijing Exhibition Hall, a cavernous and amply sky-lighted structure in the Sino-Stalin Gothic style. A red banner above the bandstand identified the event as the "Chemical Industry Bureau Spring Festival Youth Gathering." A dozen musicians on the band-stand, bundled against the cold in heavy padded coats, worked their stiff fingers to make "Jingle Bells" and "Beer Barrel Polka" come out of their clarinets, flute, trumpets and castanets. Gold-foil Chinese characters taped to the bass drum, a 1930s model with transparent heads and a naked light bulb glowing inside, said the band came from the First Ministry of Machine Building. The band played foreign tunes for intermissions, but all the dancing was done to taped versions of acceptably socialist pieces with names like "Youth Friendship Waltz" and "A Silver Feather Bestowing Deep Sentiments."

Two floorwalkers with battery-powered bullhorns paced the red-painted cement floor of the exhibition hall, seeing to it that the dancers stuck to the course—a huge oval around the edge of the room, females on the outside and males on the inside, decorously keeping their cheeks and chests apart and switching partners on cue every few min-utes. With a Canadian television crew, I climbed the stairs to the second balcony to get an overview. There we discovered that even the months of propaganda and the elaborate precautions on the floor below had not kept a few couples from finding ways to get in a bit of smooching, one of the reasons young people like to go to dances in China just as in other countries. But the "healthy collective dancing parties" of February 1984 did successfully re-break the ice. By the next fall, hotel managers in some cities were closing dining rooms to make room for more profitable dance parties, at ticket prices roughly equal to a day's pay. At most dances I saw that fall, the lights were distinctly low, there was no bullhorn and couples danced cheek-to-cheek if they chose. A few dances were held on weekend afternoons, but only be-cause the tickets were sold out for the evening sessions. In some cities, foreigners and locals were beginning to be permitted to dance with each other. Sometimes, people were beginning to get away with danc-ing disco-style, though another year would pass before I would regu-larly notice disco music and contemporary pop songs in dance halls.

How far and how fast this relaxation has been allowed to progress varies widely from city to city, and from one form of art or entertainment to another, but no facet of either high or pop culture has failed to have at least some degree of reawakening. Beijing has a brand-new symphony hall, and orchestras based in Shanghai and Beijing put on respectable performances of the classics, often heavy with traditional favorites like Mozart, and of contemporary avant-garde works by both local and foreign composers. Art and music students go abroad to study and sometimes to win significant foreign competitions. In 1986 I took a walk with a Chinese artist friend through the Beijing Museum of Art to see the capital's first public showing of nude figure sketches in twenty years. A few months earlier, Robert Rauschenberg, the American modernist, had put on a one-man exhibition in the same museum, also a first. Every year, a handful of foreign films—French farces and American superhero flicks like "Superman" and "Rambo"—are selected to tour movie houses, appearing in most major cities.

These are stunning changes when looked at from the perspective of the times, not much more than a decade earlier, when Jiang Qing, Mao's wife, still exercised a stranglehold over cultural and entertainment life. She reduced the principal sources of many art forms to seven legends from the guerrilla decades. With names like "The Red Detachment of Women" and "Taking Tiger Mountain by Strategy," these were the only stories "revolutionary" enough to form the basis of operas, ballets or major films. By the time I visited Guangzhou in 1972, a few of these shows had been developed into a full expression of the Jiang Qing version of the new Socialist culture. Those I saw were staged in a loud, macho style, full of flexed biceps, inflated chests and jutting jaws. They were populated by stereotypically heroic workers, peasants and soldiers who lived only to "serve the people," and by hateful landlords and reactionaries who lived only to get rich, suck blood and abuse women and children. In this Maoist vision of life, an entire nation of some 900 million, heir to a 4,000-year history that had produced one of the world's major cultures, was to draw all its cultural sustenance from the war stories of a single generation of guerrilla fighters. A love story, a traditional novel, or anything else that didn't concern itself with the edifying force of Mao's peculiar notions of socialism, was banned as decadent bourgeois trash or as a remnant of feudalism.

Those years of cultural suffocation were an exaggerated expression of Mao's own dictum of the 1940s, that there could be no such thing as art for art's sake, that all public expression must "serve the people"—that is to say, serve the Communist party's political ends of the moment. To enforce this rule, Mao made all high and popular culture and all news media answerable, either directly or through a government ministry, to the propaganda department of the party. That remains the organizational setup today, but after the arrest of Jiang Qing, this apparatus came under orders to relax its grip in stages over the years. By the mid-1980s, the party increasingly gave explicit sanction to entertainment for entertainment's sake. Movies, plays and musical performances began to explore their increased leeway. Popular entertainment, in particular, mushroomed in these years of relaxation. With love stories and love songs no longer classified as "bourgeois," popular music from Hong Kong, Taiwan, Japan, England, and the United States leaped from the underground network of bootleg tape copies directly onto the stage.

"Get off the stage!" an audience in Chongqing shouted at a singer named Li Yumei during a performance I watched in December 1985. "We don't want to hear it. Bring back the other singers." Li Yumei's problem was that, in the middle of a night of sequins, vinyl pants, strobe lights, loud guitars and New Wave songs from England and Hong Kong, she was the one who had to stand in a demure pink gown and sing the handful of socialist pieces still required at that time to make the rest of the program politically tolerable. She had hardly begun to sing her first number, "Heroic Sons and Daughters," when the jeering began. But the golden days of songs like "Heroic Sons and Daughters" were numbered, for the new economics of the Deng Xiaoping years was already advancing upon the pop music scene. For decades, anything put on a public stage had been required to be mounted by some official "work unit." Through the late 1970s and early 1980s, a few recording companies and many provinces and cities had organized song-and-dance troupes that they sent on tour, usually to put on primly socialist events using performers who were typically paid $25 to $30 a month, about what a factory worker was paid. By the early 1980s, as these work units were increasingly expected to make profits rather than collect subsidies, they began to encourage their most popular performers to work more often, offering them an extra $10 or $15 for each performance and often much more for making a tape. Several pop singers I knew were even beginning to get contracts that called for what amounted to royalties on tapes that sold well.

By the mid-1980s, the pop music scene was changing so fast it was already producing ambition-driven stage mothers and glitzy teen-aged stars. One stage mother, Zhang Bo, had propelled her sixteen-year-old daughter into a career in which she had made more than a dozen tapes by the time I met them two years later. Zhang Qiang, the daughter, sang Michael Jackson numbers, Taiwan and Hong Kong rip-off songs and a variety of other trendy pieces in a squeaky falsetto. She was eighteen and stagewise when I met her in 1985. Zhang Bo once asked me to take some photographs for one of her daughter's tape jackets. Soon after I arrived, the singer quickly demonstrated her expertise at doing her face in mahogany makeup tones and gyrating through a series of coy poses that evoked the squeals and squeaks of her tapes. Her posters and tapes were in record and department stores everywhere, and all of them showed her in similarly contrived poses. She regularly had her hair permed into a huge puff resembling an overgrown Afro, and when she went out in cold weather, she set off her curly black locks with a lambskin wrap of cascading white curls. Her face and figure were essentially ordinary, but she had become so entranced with the glamor she had studied for her career that she literally could not go five minutes without a glance in a mirror. Over tea and Cokes at Beijing's Great Wall Hotel, where most of the walls are mirrors, she left her seat every few minutes, walked over to get a glance at her face, then came back and sat down, often pulling out a pocket mirror several times before getting up again to check out her reflection on the walls. Zhang Bo complained now and then that she felt sure her daughter's record company was not paying all the royalties due her, but by the time I left Beijing, the singer had saved up enough to go to Australia to study English for a year, an extraordinary feat for a Chinese teen-ager.

Riches like Zhang Qiang's had not yet stopped seeming fabulous to most Chinese when the economics of reform began to open doors to still bigger treasures for some pop singers. By 1986 the private impresario was finding his way to the fringes of big-name entertainment. I met one of these, whom I shall call "Mr. Zhao," which is not his name, when I went to photograph dancers making up for a pop concert. Mr. Zhao had signed only one genuinely big name for his show and had filled out the first five-sixths of the evening with splashy but little-known and semicompetent performers he could hire cheaply. But entertainment was still so scarce in most cities that with just the one real name, a single advertisement in the local paper had sold out eighteen performances in a 1,200-seat movie hall within twenty hours. Mr. Zhao's own investment had consisted mainly of some underpowered and scratchy-voiced sound equipment that kept all the performers complaining. At the performance I watched, a singer took a yellow Walkman out of her purse and loaned it to a sound technician, who plugged it into the system to boost the amplifying power.

But with some 20,000 tickets already sold out at 3 yuan each, or about a day's pay for most young factory workers, Mr. Zhao seemed likely to do well with his shoestring promotion. I talked with him and several performers over dumplings and noodles at a nearby restaurant after the show. He wore the same camper's shorts and rumpled gray short-sleeved shirt he had worn backstage when he brought in sandwiches and soft drinks for the performers and technicians, but there was also an intensity in his manner that never seemed to leave him. In confidential tones, he explained the secret of his success: "I always keep good relations with the star singers." The key to good relations, it turned out, was good pay—anywhere from 250 to 1,000 yuan an evening, depending on the size of the house, plus the usual free meals and lodging during rehearsal and performance weeks. A big house, he said, would be a gym or a stadium. This show's star would get 400 yuan—eight 50-yuan notes, the biggest bill of People's Money in circulation—for each performance at the movie theater. That meant that for a demanding schedule of eighteen performances in two weeks, the singer would get 7,200 yuan, or nearly $2,000 at the legal exchange rates of the times. That is a sum beyond the imagination of most Chinese. For several years in the 1980s, the press had made front-page news of farmers who managed to make 10,000 yuan in a year. Working with Mr. Zhao, a moderately energetic pop star could now make that in a month or two and still have plenty of time to meet any obligations to the provincial troupe or recording company that was the singer's legal work unit.

The fistfuls of 50-yuan People's Money notes that lubricated Mr. Zhao's "good relations with the star singers" were not, in fact, the only secret of his success. At least equally important was the swift pace of change in the economics of the entertainment business itself. One vital key was the changes the reforms had brought to the work units that owned theaters, gymnasiums and other halls. They were coming under intense pressure to get off the state subsidy system. Some were already required to be self-supporting. At the same time, their workers were pressuring for bigger bonuses, like the ones they saw being given out in some factories. For decades, many of these organizations had usually found it safest to keep their halls empty except for events with clear and explicit political sanction. Now, sometimes in the space of a few months, their position was reversing and it became economically necessary to fill their halls and make money. But their directors were more experienced at politics than at entertainment, and they often ended up losing money and looking foolish when they tried to put shows together to meet their new circumstances. One ready solution was to bring in people like Mr. Zhao, who knew what these work units usually didn't—how to put together a show that would pay the rent. Short-sleeved impresarios like Mr. Zhao have begun to spring up everywhere. "Now there are lots of people who hire singers the way he does," his star singer told me. Besides Mr. Zhao, I met them in Shanghai, Xian, Beijing and Guangzhou.

Like tens or perhaps hundreds of thousands of other entrepreneurs in all kinds of businesses all across the country, these short-sleeved impresarios tend to find opportunity in shadowy and uncharted spaces between the old system and the new. They already seem to exist on a scale, and to operate with a leeway, unlike any ever before reported anywhere in the Marxist-Leninist world. But it is too soon to guess how many of them will prove to be the vanguard of enduring new enterprises and how many will prove to be passing phenomena, spawned by Deng Xiaoping's experiment and then left behind by its next twist or turn. Not all of them worry as Mr. Zhao does about "good relations with the star singers." Several singers I met have learned the hard way that they must demand payment at the end of each night's performance. If they wait until the end of the series, they might not be paid. In several cities, Shanghai and Xian in particular, singers told me that some impresarios have devised schemes in which they make generous offers and then find ways out of paying what they promise.

The new economics of reform thus is rapidly drawing commerce into the foreground of the pop scene and is pushing politics into the background. But even in pop music, politics had not yet altogether faded from the scene by the time I left China. The night I met Mr. Zhao, his star singer had done perhaps half a dozen songs, one American, one Japanese, two from Hong Kong and the rest local. American love songs tend to dominate pop music in most of the world, and Taiwan love songs tend to dominate in the Chinese parts of Asia. At the restaurant, I asked the star singer why there had been only one American tune and none of the Taiwan songs that can be heard on boom boxes on every street in most cities. "Chinese audiences only want to hear so much in English," the answer came, "and you can have problems if you do Taiwan songs on the stage very often." Yes, audiences love it when a singer does Taiwan songs, especially those made famous by Teresa Teng, the Taiwan superstar whose voice has been the most famous in East and Southeast Asia for more than a decade, the singer acknowledged. "But in China, it is still safer to wait and only do Teresa Teng's music on the stage when someone asks you to."

Guo Jincheng was in her early twenties in August 1966 when the late Great Helmsman's teen-aged Red Guards arrived at her parents' home and dragged her sixty-year-old mother and father into the court-yard for "struggle." By the standards of Mao's Cultural Revolution-aries, her father, Guo Lizhong, had a bad class background. He had once been the owner of a shop that sold traditional herbal medicines. By the standards applied in the summer of 1966, that qualified him as a "bourgeois element," even though his shop had been confiscated in the 1950s and he had long since been put to work in a factory. One band of the Red Guards shouted slogans at Guo Jincheng and her older sister. A second gang of teen-agers put dunce caps on the elderly husband and wife, pushed them around the courtyard and ordered them never to go back into their home. A third gang ransacked the house, carting off books, paintings, furniture, antiques and other valu-ables.

I met Guo Jincheng more than eighteen years later, in February 1985, when the Beijing city government finally granted me and a few other resident correspondents a long-sought chance to visit one of the last in a series of "Cultural Revolution Returned Goods Exhibitions" conducted in various parts of the capital over a period of some three years. Residents or former residents of the capital's Chongwen Gate district were invited to come to the Enlightenment Primary School during a ten-day recess and to search through some eighteen class-rooms chock full of paintings, books, porcelains and other heirlooms. If they could identify items that Mao's teen-aged iconoclasts had hauled away from their homes, they could fill out a small claim card and paper-clip it to each item they thought was theirs. A walk among the more than 30,000 objects on display in the classrooms was a reminder of how many lives still have not been put all the way back together, more than two decades after Mao called teen-agers into the streets to "make revolution." The exhibition had only a day to go when I arrived, but no more than a few thousand of the items bore claim cards. The rest would never find their way back to their owners. Similar exhibitions had been going on for two or more years in most cities. Literally millions of additional objects confiscated by Mao's teen-aged zealots were not saved at all but went into gigantic pyres, or to the bottoms of rivers and lakes, or into smelters to become state property in the form of brass artillery cartridges or gold bars. Guo Jincheng and her older sister, Guo Xunlong, told me they had found their *gu qin,* an ancient musical instrument resembling a lute. Their mother had been the only person in the family who knew how to play it and had died without ever seeing it again. They had also found their nineteenth century scroll painting of plum blossoms, pines, and bamboo. "Chinese people call the plum, the pine and the bamboo the three winter friends," Guo Xunlong said, "because they can survive the storms."

The Guo family's painting of the three winter friends had survived the long winter of the Cultural Revolution and the convoluted political storms that had followed. It was on display that week as part of a new twist in the Communist party line. What was going on was a massive rewriting of history that the party officially terms "thoroughly negating the so-called Cultural Revolution." The undertaking extends into virtually every walk of life, even to the once-sacrosanct People's Liberation Army (PLA). Not long after the 1985 exhibition in Beijing at which the Guo sisters recovered their family's *gu qin* and painting of the three winter friends, some top officers of the local PLA units in South China stopped in for what was officially described as a "tea party" with members of the Communist party committee in Fuzhou, the capital of Fujian, the province on the mainland side of the Taiwan Strait. The local papers reported that the soldiers and the party officials ate sweets, smoked cigarettes, exchanged wishes for Chinese New Year and talked about old times.[1]

The point of the exercise was the talk about old times. The old times in question were the weeks some eighteen years earlier when the PLA had been sent in to "support The Left," which meant saving the day for the Red Guards and other radical followers of Lin Biao, the defense minister and Chairman Mao's officially designated heir-apparent, who were then in danger of losing out in Fuzhou and many other cities. Only with army support had The Left managed to win control in many places. In Fuzhou, even the army had its problems winning power for The Left. When public realization sunk in that the army was being used to support a faction the masses had already once successfully fought off, thousands of people assaulted the local military headquarters in one of the most famous antiradical outbursts of the Cultural Revolution. Before the army could manage to carry the day for The Left, hundreds were dead and hundreds more were sent "down to the countryside" to "learn from the peasants."

Now, eight years after Mao's death, it fell to Fu Kuiqing, the political commissar of the Fuzhou Military Region and a member of the Central Committee of the Chinese Communist party, to lead an army delegation to the Fuzhou Communist party committee's offices to apologize for events already eighteen years in the past. "On behalf of the party committee and the leading organ of the military region," he said, "I take this opportunity to make a sincere self-criticism of the shortcomings and mistakes of the military region . . . and offer my apology and give my cordial regards to the comrades who were hurt and to their families." Provincial newspapers and radio and television broadcasts in many provinces reported army delegations attending similar tea parties that year, one of the biggest helpings of humble pie any Communist party anywhere has ever forced down the throat of its own army.

But "thoroughly negating the so-called Cultural Revolution" is a job for the Communist party itself. Not just anyone can casually take part. Allowed to get out of the party's own control, such a massive rewriting of history would be too fraught with potential for raising obvious questions about the party itself. Playwrights, movie directors and authors, in particular, have had a wealth of reminders that anything they do along this line must be done "under the leadership of the Chinese Communist party." In stage drama, an art form that is known in Chinese as "Western theater" and that has shallow roots in China in the best circumstances, one of these reminders is the history of a modernist play called "Bus Stop." In the play, in an atmosphere reminiscent of "Waiting for Godot," a group of would-be passengers stand waiting for a bus, talking and complaining about how bus service and everything else isn't what it used to be. Finally, one of them looks at his watch and says with some shock that ten years have passed and their bus still hasn't come—an obvious allegory of the feeling millions of people have that their lives were wasted by the ten years of the Cultural Revolution.

The screening committee of the People's Art Theater, which is the experimental company at Capital Theater, Beijing's main resident acting house, initially turned "Bus Stop" down in 1982 on grounds that its technique was too avant-garde for Beijing's audiences to understand. So Gao Hangjian, the playwright who wrote it, and Lin Zhaohua, a director who wanted to stage it, devised a plan to introduce contemporary Western-style drama to Beijing audiences. They started by staging, in 1983, a politically inoffensive modernist piece called "Warning Signal," written by Gao specifically for the purpose. Despite its extensive use of contemporary dramatic effects, including sudden appearances of characters in the aisles amid the audience and use of ghastly colored spotlights to demarcate sequences when characters were dreaming, the play did well enough in the backroom little theater to get a chance at the main stage, where it filled the house for most of a brief run.

About the time "Warning Signal" was to move to the main stage, I interviewed Lin Zhaohua, the director. He told me that the next step in introducing modernist drama would be to bring Arthur Miller, whom he identified as "America's greatest living playwright now that Eugene O'Neill has died," to Beijing to direct a production of "Death of a Salesman." Mr. Miller's play filled the main house of Capital Theater for several weeks, to enthusiastic reviews from newspapers and broadcasters. Then, Mr. Lin and Mr. Gao tried again with "Bus Stop." But even after all the preparations, the play closed without explanation after a few little theater performances and never did have its scheduled main stage run. After months of silence, the Communist party's leading cultural magazine, Wen Yi Bao, suddenly attacked "Bus Stop" in February 1984, in terms that made clear that the problems were at least as much political as technical. "After the play, one could feel that our life is a complete mess and there is no prospect and hope," the magazine complained. "Ideologically, the play spreads depressionism and decadent emotions. Technically, it is a product of blindly worshipping and mechanically imitating the Western plays of modern schools."[2]

Beijing audiences now and then make it clear that modernism is not beyond them and that they are only too eager to see plays that challenge the party. In 1985 a play called "We" was winning enthusiastic audiences with its portrayal of Cultural Revolution victims. Then it was summarily cancelled. In 1986 a Chinese friend took me to a play called "Uncle Dog," a modernist show in which the protagonist goes mad early in the first act and stays that way through a series of witty dialogues and soliloquies until near the end of the final scene. My friend nudged me to make sure I would be listening when, still mad, the character pronounced the line that was drawing the audiences. Before 1949, the madman recalled, the people could go to the Communist party's legendary Eighth Route Army with their grievances. Now, he said, the Communist party itself is long accustomed to being in power. "Now, whom can we turn to?" the madman asked. The line drew a long laugh from the audience, who then applauded, briefly interrupting the dialogue on stage. A few days later, Chinese-speaking foreign friends who went to see the show waited for the line, but it had been removed. My Chinese friend soon reported that the show had lost its audience and had closed.

A walk under a triple-canopy jungle of laundry, down a street named Big Horse Station in the heart of the South China city of Guangzhou, leads to a tiny, plaster-faced row house. A stairwell, so narrow that both elbows brush its walls, leads to a fire-safety inspector's vision of purgatory—second-floor rooms crammed with hundreds of Cantonese people of all ages, sitting shoulder-to-shoulder on stools, on chairs, on benches and on stairsteps until there is no aisle to the door and almost no space on the stairs. Another narrow stairwell leads to the third floor, where more tiny rooms are packed shoulder-to-shoulder. There, a Cantonese man in his seventies, scarcely five feet tall and surely no more than 110 pounds, stands at an altar, pointing his finger toward Heaven and preaching Baptist fire and brimstone— the old-fashioned way but in the local Chinese dialect.

Steven Lamb, as the preacher calls himself in English, showed no sign of compromising with the Communist party on the day in 1986 when a Chinese friend led me to Big Horse Station to watch him preach. "Policemen and officials came here to watch a few years ago," Mr. Lamb had told me when my friend and I had stopped to see him a few days earlier. "After they watched a few times, they told me everything I was doing was illegal. I told them I was ready to go to jail for the third time, if that was the Lord's will. After they went away, I never heard anything again." Mr. Lamb said he had spent his first year in jail in the early 1950s, soon after Mao Zedong's armies had won power in 1949. He had refused to bring his flock into the fold of the Three Self Movement, the officially sanctioned "mass organization" through which Protestants are permitted to worship "under the leadership of the Chinese Communist party," provided they keep free of foreign influence and remain self-sustaining, self proselytizing and self-governing. When he got out of jail, Mr. Lamb went directly back to preaching at Big Horse Station, and by 1959 he was back in jail again. This time, it was a twenty-year sentence, and he served every day of his term, much of it pushing underground train cars in a coal mine beneath the barren hills of Shaanxi Province. It was an unhappy time, he said, not because of the work or the confinement but because, "I could only manage to talk about Jesus Christ very secretly to a few other prisoners." He went back to Big Horse Station in 1979, as soon as he recovered from his twenty-year sentence, and he has been preaching there, illegally but without interference, several days a week ever since. By the time I went to see him, he had helped to open similar Baptist centers in several other parts of the city. He said those services resemble his—jam-packed rooms, fire, brimstone, hymns and tape-recorded organ and piano music on a loud boom box.

No one knows how many of these "house churches" there are today, but the visible number has grown substantially since social controls began to relax as part of Deng Xiaoping's reforms. Protestant house churches are especially active across South China's Guangdong and Fujian Provinces. Catholic house churches are most active in Shanghai and the adjacent areas of Jiangsu Province, but the party sometimes seems harder on Catholics. Now and then a priest will still go to jail as the Communist party enforces its insistence that Chinese Catholics sever their allegiance to the Pope. In many places, some American and Australian Protestant sects are taking the burgeoning need for English teachers as their chance to send in missionaries, who get jobs on campuses and then bring in suitcases full of Bibles and discreetly set out to make converts. Overall, Mr. Lamb opined, religious life even outside the Communist party's sanctioned churches, "is better now, safer."

For tens of millions of religious Chinese who do accept the leadership of the Communist party, life is better and safer yet. Preachers who have joined the Three Self Movement, priests who have joined the Chinese Patriotic Catholic Association, imams, monks and scholars who have joined the Communist party's officially sanctioned organizations for Islam, Buddhism and Dao, are back in control of many of their halls. Thousands of places of worship remain in the hands of warehouses and factories that still refuse to give back buildings they got when Red Guards closed down all religion during the Cultural Revolution. But most of the reopened places of worship have received modest sums of state money, explained usually as "back rent" for the years between the confiscation by Red Guards and the return to religious use. These grants will never restore nineteenth century stained glass windows the Red Guards smashed in many churches, or centuries-old Buddhist and Daoist icons the rampaging teen-agers burned, defaced or melted down, but they help to get buildings back into shape to receive worshippers. A few Catholic and Protestant seminaries, and training centers for Buddhist, Daoist and Muslim holy men, have reopened in some places. In the Three Self churches, Episcopal, Methodist, Seventh Day Adventist and Salvation Army preachers often are obliged to share the same building and the same congregation—a government-approved miracle of ecumenism no other country has yet achieved. But their congregations are growing, attracting new young converts as well as old followers who had not dared practice the faith during the Red Guard years.

At this officially sponsored level, relaxing the party's control over religion is part of the broader reopening of society, within the country and in its relations with the outside world. Wherever I went to report on religious life, local officials would speak of the "restoration of the party's correct line on religious freedom" after Deng gained power. The way they pronounced the words often sounded as if neither the Cultural Revolution nor the Red Guards that Mao sent to burn hymnals and smash altars had anything to do with the Communist party. In fact, the current line on religion often shows signs of being closely integrated with the economic reforms, much as past mass repressions of the religious were themselves parts of twists in the party line in other times. At a Daoist school in Shanghai, I attended a class where novice monks were studying English, a language not previously associated with China's only major native organized religion. One use they will have for their new language skills is suggested by a regular fixture that today adorns the entry to every Daoist shrine and Buddhist temple I visited. That is the ticket office, where visitors must stop to buy a small slip of flimsy paper before going in. At many of these places of worship, admission-paying local and foreign tourists overwhelm the handful of neighborhood people who have come to light joss sticks and ask the ancient deities for a happy marriage, relief from an illness or good scores on an examination. Especially among Buddist sites, which attract large numbers of Japanese pilgrims, and among Muslim mosques, which often attract support from oil-rich Middle Eastern fellow-Muslims, religion shows signs of becoming a promising source of hard currency as well as domestic ticket sales.

In the winter of 1984–85, many writers believed they were making a major breakthrough against the party overlords who had stifled them for decades. Top Communists appeared before a national conference of writers in late December and early January, stressing the freedom of expression technically guaranteed by the national constitution rather than the limits traditionally demanded by the Communist party and Mao's requirement that all public expression "serve the people" by serving the party. Writers who attended that conference spoke afterward of having had a sense of purgation, of feeling the exhilaration of a major victory.

It was not to last. Within weeks Hu Yaobang, who, as secretary-general of the party, was formally the leading Communist, would go before a meeting of journalists to offer a very different emphasis. Whatever may be true for writers, he said, journalists must never forget that their job is to serve as "the mouthpiece of the Communist party."[3] By summer, writers I talked with had lost their exhilarating sense of new times and were back to the humdrum of trying to figure out how far they would have to compromise to get their work published. By fall, Wang Meng, the head of the Chinese Writers Association, was on board with the party, speaking of limits. *Red Flag*, the Communist party Central Committee's chief theoretical journal, published a November commentary to make clear that limits, and not freedom, were still the order of the day.

"It is imperative to stress socialist orientation and writers' responsibility," declared Wang Meng, who was soon to become the Minister of Culture. "Our freedom of creation is the freedom of socialist creation."[4] Wang proposed a test that could be applied to literature: "The literary work's inclination toward promoting the socialist cause is demonstrated primarily by its inclination towards patriotism, collectivism, socialism and communism and by its intention to turn us into people with ideals, morality, culture and discipline." *Red Flag,* for its part, declared that writers must use their freedom first and foremost to uphold the fundamentals of Chinese Marxism. "Without this fundamental requirement, the creative freedoms would lose their proletarian character and would degenerate into bourgeois liberalization."

Only slightly more than a year later, after students in the streets had given orthodox Leninists at the top of the party a crisis to use against the reformers, would it become clear how fundamental an inner-party struggle was reflected by these unexplained changes of tone. Hu Yaobang, the man who had told the journalists in March 1985 that they still existed first and foremost to serve as the party's "mouthpiece," would resign as head of the party in January 1987, confessing "major errors on important matters of political principle." The word would be passed that chief among his errors was a long track record of being too soft on "bourgeois liberalization," Deng Xiaoping's epithet for all seasons, especially for the seasons when freedom of expression begins to embrace any serious questioning of the party's exclusive right to rule.

When I arrived in Beijing in October 1982, a favorite topic among some younger Chinese was the movie "Unrequited Love." Based on a story by Bai Hua, it had been withdrawn after a few showings in 1980. Its crime lay in the lines on which the title was based, which suggested that even if you love your country, you have a right to ask whether your country loves you. Too pessimistic, declared the party's watchdogs. Analyses of the movie's political transgressions were still being printed more than a year after I had arrived in China.

A movie takes a long time and a lot of work and money to produce, and Chinese moviemakers, like their counterparts in many other countries, have often been slow to take unnecessary political chances. The "Unrequited Love" experience seemed to have had a chilling effect. For the next few years, Chinese moviemakers satisfied themselves with exploring new themes permitted by the party's increasing willingness to countenance entertainment for its own sake and discussion of personal problems without reference to politics. For many audiences, accustomed for more than a decade to the aridity of a screen that was used mainly to give larger-than-life proportions to revolutionary heroes, the new topics movies could explore were like a breath of air. One movie, "Under the Bridge," seemed daring in 1983. It took up bastardy as a topic and even let young boys shout the forbidden word while taunting the film's child star in a scene on a Shanghai side street. Another film of about the same time, "Our Niu Bai Sui," portrayed a group of village-level Communist party officials as clowns, whose antics left audiences rocking with laughter.

These films broke taboos, but the taboos they broke were the dead Mao Tsetung's taboos, not the living Deng Xiaoping's. The Cultural Revolution thus could be cast in a negative light as the setting in which the young mother in "Under the Bridge" had made the mistakes that left her with a bastard son, or as the source of wrong thinking that had run the village Communists in "Our Niu Bai Sui" afoul of reality. To that extent, film writers and directors could participate in the movement to "thoroughly negate the so-called Cultural Revolution." But the Cultural Revolution as millions lived it, the formative trauma that indelibly marked several generations, remained forbidden territory and was still far better explored by writers outside the country than within. That political minefield, deeply imbedded with potential to call into question the legitimacy of the Communist party itself, was still too laden with explosives to be explorable.

A few weeks after Hu Yaobang resigned in January 1987, a Chinese friend with decades of association with the film industry took me to see a new movie, "A Small Town Called Hibiscus." Based on a widely read 1980s novel of the same name, the movie was creating a sensation for the sophistication with which it portrayed its characters as real, three-dimensional people rather than the usual caricatures of good and evil. It was drawing big audiences and was the talk of Beijing for weeks. But my friend felt that it still fell short of exploring the traumas millions had experienced in Mao's failing years. "The movie was about to come out when the student demonstrations started and Hu Yaobang resigned," my friend said after we watched the show. "At the last minute, they called it back and cut out sixteen minutes before they released it. The party people in the ministry actually proposed twenty-eight minutes of cuts, but Xie Jin, the director, said if they cut that much it would no longer be his film. He's very famous, and the movie had already been advertised all over China, so they compromised some with him. Some of what they cut included bedroom scenes that didn't matter, but more than half was political. Most of it was footage that told the real truth about what happened in the Cultural Revolution."

5

Women:
Big Strides,
Forward, Backward,
and Sideways

For Dong Liya, a thirty-one-year-old computer technician at a printing house in Beijing, a wish came true in the late spring of 1984. That was when Jia Xiuhua came to live and work in Dong's Liya's home. For about $12.50 per month, Miss Jia would clean the minuscule flat—about thirty square yards of bare cement floor space divided into about a room and a half in one of the five-story, cold-water walkups that house tens of thousands of Beijing families—and take care of Chen Yuan, Dong Liya's four-month-old infant, in the daytime. Miss Jia, the daughter of a coal miner and a farmer, thus joined thousands of other teen-aged girls from the hardscrabble mines and farmlands of Anhui, one of China's poorest provinces, who have been coming to Beijing to do household work ever since the end of the Cultural Revolution.

In June 1984, a few weeks after Jia Xiuhua had arrived in Beijing, two other foreign correspondents and I met with her and Dong Liya in a formal interview arranged by the Beijing branch of the All-China Women's Federation, the official government-sponsored "mass organization" for China's women. We had separately asked the women's federation to help us set up the meeting, after becoming intrigued by articles in Beijing newspapers. The articles reported that the local women's federation had struck a new blow for the liberation of womanhood by organizing a company that scoured Anhui and other poor provinces, recruiting girls in their late teens to come to the capital to work as live-in servants. As if they felt a need to stress the revolutionary legitimacy of the new company, the women's federation leaders had named it for the Socialist International Women's Day—the May Eighth Household Service Company.

The new company was palpably a product of the quickening pace of political and economic reform as Zhao Ziyang, Hu Yaobang and other allies of Deng Xiaoping sought to provide social breathing space for modernization. Maoist orthodoxy had required that household servants be banned, especially for people categorized as "intellectuals," as anyone with a high school education is likely to be in China. Not that there was ever a time when no one had servants. One well-connected friend once took me on a tour to see some of the places in Beijing where Jiang Qing, Mao's wife and a high-handed leader of that Cultural Revolution radicalism that demanded spartan simplicity of ordinary people, had lived a life of imperial splendor. Madame Mao had taken over a series of private chambers at places in Beijing as diverse as the old summer palace, which had been the empress dowager's favorite home in the late nineteenth century, and the post-1949 Mandarin Garden, where she maintained a bridle path, a stable and a pedal-powered monorail to entertain herself and her visitors. Each place had quarters not only for Jiang Qing but also for her household, secretarial and personal staffs. Elsewhere in the hierarchy, even at the peak of alleged egalitarianism, fast-rising Maoist loyalists, old revolutionary generals who had avoided the lash of the Cultural Revolutionaries, and many of Madame Mao's top political confederates—not to mention the Great Helmsman himself—had staffs of drivers, housekeepers, cooks, orderlies and assorted others, often provided by the People's Liberation Army even if the person had no military role.

It was only after 1976, when Mao died and Jiang Qing was locked up in the Qin City prison outside Beijing, that having household help, like wearing pretty clothing, ceased to be publicly and officially denounced as a form of "chasing after the bourgeois lifestyle." A few daring Beijing residents, sensing personal opportunity in the changing political winds, soon resumed the timeless tradition of taking in girls from Anhui Province as household servants, though it remained technically illegal to hire such help directly. By the time we met Dong Liya, Miss Jia and several officials of the Beijing branch of the women's federation, the practice had become so commonplace that one corner in a park near the Beijing Ring Road had become the known place for wives to meet Anhui girls. There, in the lifting morning mist, the girls would stand in knots of a dozen or two, waiting for housekeeping jobs. By the time of our interview, most estimates were that thousands of girls had illegally found jobs in the city in the several years since the practice had been resumed. By the time I left China, most of my Chinese friends believed the number must be well past the 20,000 mark. It was in an attempt to bring order to this persistent and flourishing, but patently illegal, job market that the women's federation had organized the May Eighth Household Service Company.

To the three foreign reporters in June 1984, the new company seemed to pinpoint a dilemma that was becoming increasingly apparent in the reforms. To a very considerable extent, the reforms were proving to be a mixed blessing for women. [On the one hand, many women, along with men, were eating, dressing and generally living better in the freer economic and cultural climate of the Deng Xiaoping years. On the other hand, many of the reforms were being accomplished by abandoning favorite doctrines of the Maoist years and reverting, in greater or lesser degree, to traditional social patterns. This often has meant a return to patterns that have for centuries been deeply sexist in both philosophy and practice] In nearly five years in China, no facet of daily life under the reforms struck me as more complex, more swept by crosscurrents of gains, losses and contradictions, than the effect the new ways were having on the lives and prospects of women.

As we talked with Dong Liya and Jia Xiuhua it became clear that a major question on our minds was how much of the new May Eighth Household Service Company's work represented steps forward for women and how much might represent steps backward. For Dong Liya, the step forward—a degree of liberation from China's numbing housework—was clear enough. But when we focused on Miss Jia, we seemed to be wondering how doing laundry and tending a baby in another woman's house could be anything but a step backward, even for a country girl. Miss Jia assured us that all she could see at the moment was the chance to live in the city. The Women's Federation assured us that their company had been organized not only to help Beijing women find household help but also to help the Anhui girls by regularizing a practice that had grown up spontaneously and needed supervision. Many of the girls who had found work in the unregulated market had begun to complain that their employers had cheated them, or wrongly accused them of theft, or, to the horror of a still avowedly Marxist leadership, in some way exploited them. Some of the housewives had written letters to the editor complaining that some of the girls had even formed illegal organizations to deal with their employers. Such a step is always taken seriously in any Leninist system, which tolerates organized activity only if it is "under the leadership of the Communist party."

In practical terms, the May Eighth Household Service Company seemed to provide an alternative to the old-style freemarket, in which the teen-aged housekeepers and nannies had offered themselves for hire in the park, but not to put an end to it. By the time I left Beijing, the city had tried a couple of times to crack down on the unauthorized labor exchange but was having only sporadic success. From time to time, police were posted to keep the girls and the housewives apart, but the market would soon spring up at some other discreet point on public property until someone discovered that the corner of the park was again free of police. One well-fixed housewife I know hired a series of four Anhui girls through this unauthorized free market during my time in Beijing, the last one several months before I left and a few months after one of the police interventions. Her son later explained why his mother changed housekeepers so often. "She's always accusing them of stealing things. I can't tell who's really right. These girls seem so scared when they come from the country and so happy to be in the city; I don't believe all three of the ones she's yelled at were stealing. But people have been poor for a long time. I think now that there's some money, and we're able to have a few nice things in the house, it's hard for my mother to trust anyone." He told me his mother never had trouble finding the market when she wanted a new Anhui girl.

Traditionally, Anhui girls who have come to Beijing and other cities to do housework have stayed long enough to save up for marriage and to send some money back to their parents. Miss Jia said she had no specific plans but acknowledged that she expected marriage to be part of her future. Rural parents often see the effort and expense of raising a girl as something for which they deserve compensation, for at marriage the enduring practice is that the daughter will enter her husband's family and be basically lost to her parents. The practice of paying bride prices—in cash, or in gifts to the bride's family that can often run to more than $1,000 or $2,000 worth of televisions, fans, refrigerators and other big-ticket appliances—has come back with a vengeance, especially in much of the countryside, since the elimination of Mao's communes and the consequent relaxation of social control. A few years of housework in the city, aside from holding some prospect of finding a relatively well-fixed city husband, is a chance for an Anhui girl to repay some of the cost of her upbringing and to save a bit toward her own marriage. This kind of return to old social patterns, many of them deeply rooted in traditional sexist practices and attitudes, was part of what the correspondents wanted to discuss. But the women's federation representatives declined to be drawn into any discussion of whether the May Eighth Household Service Company might be in any way participating in this revival of ancient ways that peasants had paid dearly to suppress, at least partially, in the Maoist years. Instead, they assured us that the May Eighth Household Service Company would be a way of seeing to it that peasants would never again have to sell their daughters at city teahouses, a scene searingly drawn in some novels and plays of the 1930s and 1940s—but one nobody has reported seeing since the early 1950s.

Jia Xiuhua, a robust but shy eighteen-year-old who frequently found ways to avert her eyes as she answered our questions, came to the interview wearing a new maroon jacket that matched one worn by Dong Liya. The jackets had been bought at one of Beijing's rapidly reviving streetside freemarkets by Dong Liya's husband, Chen Ying, a thirty-five-year-old Japanese-language tourist guide for the China International Travel Service. Dong Liya explained that she and her husband were providing Miss Jia's board, clothing and monthly $12.50

out of a total household income of about $75 a month. Their willingness to use that big a chunk of their monthly income, and to provide sleeping space in an entryway of their crowded flat, was tangible evidence of the need the women's federation was setting out to meet when it organized its new company. Millions of urban Chinese live lives of unrelenting tedium, consisting largely of a series of chores that provide their own irrefutable answers to the question of what city people do with their leisure time. A typical commute within Beijing may entail more than an hour each way by bicycle, or about the same by bus, with sometimes two or three intervals of standing in bitter wind or hot sun waiting for the next transfer. Along the way, each partner in the couple may have a daily shopping assignment, often two or three stops a day, to stand in line for vegetables or other necessities. Commuting, chores and the regular six-day, forty-eight-hour work week combine to make a good night's sleep scarce. One of the first comments many new foreign residents make is that Chinese seem able to sleep anywhere—on buses, at rail stations, in political meetings, at tourist attractions, at their desks.

The typical Beijing cold-water flat has plumbing, especially drains, that cannot handle an automatic washing machine. Factories in some cities have begun to make rudimentary washing machines in recent years, but they are tiny and largely powerless and often look like toys to Japanese or Americans who see them for the first time. The spin cycle is unheard of, and only a few have even a wringer, so the user is left to squeeze out the excess rinse water by hand before hanging the clothing to dry. Many of the washers have to be tipped on their sides and dumped each time they complete the wash or rinse cycles. Most city people don't think the tiny washing machines made in China are worth either the cost or the trouble, so laundry tends to be a matter of heating water on the stove and then bending over a scrubboard.

Socialism has produced a sameness in Beijing apartment designs. The most consistent feature is the kitchen, roughly the size and shape of perhaps three ordinary American dining room tables side by side. It most commonly comes equipped with one or two six-inch-wide planks of shelving, a patch of stone or composition countertop two or three feet wide by three or four feet long, and a one-faucet, cold-water sink that resembles the small set-tubs found next to the laundry area in an American basement. Cooking is typically on a two-burner, cast-iron, table-top contraption, attached by rubber hose to a gas tank that has to be hauled down the stairs, strapped onto a bicycle and carried off for refilling every time it is empty. Beijing kitchens are far too tiny to hold even a motel-sized refrigerator, but the convenience of shopping less frequently holds more and more appeal. In my last two years in Beijing, the refrigerator was becoming a standard item of living room furniture alongside the television set.

Most of my Chinese friends had jobs that would have ranked them in the middle classes of Western countries—professors, electricians, entertainers, journalists—but I found little from my middle-class American background that could help me relate to some of the most ordinary facets of Beijing daily life. There is not much work left in the typical American middle-class home to compare with chores like housekeeping without a vacuum cleaner, keeping bare cement living room and kitchen floors clean, keeping the fire chamber of the living room stove full of the compressed soft-coal-dust bricquets that keep the winter cold away, or keeping the capital's relentlessly grimy dust and air pollution from taking complete control of apartments in which windows leak copiously around the edges even when closed.

In most cities, men participate in many of these household chores, possibly more than Western men join in keeping house, even after allowing for the fact that Western men often have a lawn to mow, or the exterior of a house to maintain. But men do not participate equally with women, and that is why the Beijing branch of the women's federation felt it was striking a blow for womanhood, rather than for couples, by organizing a company to recruit girls from Anhui to work in Beijing households. Studies of housework in urban families were among the first surveys undertaken in the early 1980s, after Deng Xiaoping had personally intervened to reestablish social sciences as a legitimate field of inquiry, ordering the establishment of the Chinese Academy of Social Sciences. The academy's journal, *Social Sciences in China*, was soon being published quarterly in English as well as in Chinese, and in 1982 and 1983 it published results of several surveys that dealt either directly or indirectly with the burden of housework, and with the socially and politically sensitive question of who does how much of it.[1] These surveys consistently found that while men complain about household chores as often as women, a working wife is likely to put twice as many hours, or more, into the tedium of tending the apartment and the family every week, especially if there is a child.

———————

As I read the results of these studies, I was reminded of Hu Yieh-yu, who had left the Mainland after the revolution and was my family's cook when I was based in Hong Kong from 1970 to 1973. "China had a revolution in 1949 and liberated women," A-Hu was fond of remarking. "Marx said women can't be free unless they work, so New China makes every woman go out to work. Now, every Chinese woman has two jobs, one at work and one at home." The housework studies I read in the early 1980s persuaded me that A-Hu had understood something important about the limitations of women's liberation in the new system. But his comment focused on only part of what had happened after the Communist party won power in 1949. There are important respects in which the lives and prospects of women, especially in cities, did change dramatically in the early years of Communist party governance. The party all but eliminated prostitution and venereal disease, sent prostitutes off for "reeducation" at labor camps and made the customer, as well as the woman, subject to arrest. The new Communist government made it national policy to send girls to school, without reference to class background or ability to pay, for the first time in China's history. Universal education of girls is yet to be realized in large parts of the countryside, but, since 1949, girls have gone to school, and so have boys, in numbers no Chinese government ever before contemplated. The new requirement that women work was accompanied by a network of child-care centers patterned after the Soviet system, though it had numerous and big gaps that created cruel dilemmas for millions of parents.

The early Communist administrations also gave women political rights equal with men and promulgated a series of new marriage laws that gave women legal rights unprecedented in Chinese society, like equality in divorce and choice of a mate without parental bartering. Men had traditionally held a virtual monopoly on both education and work outside the home. For centuries, men had the power in effect to annul a marriage unilaterally if the wife bore only daughters, and to divorce a wife by announcing the end of the marriage to friends over dinner. While it had not been unknown for a man to have several wives, whether in sequence or at the same time, a woman ran some considerable risk of ostracism if she did not remain faithful to her first husband until she died, even if she lived a long widowhood. In such a society, the new laws and schools of the 1950s were genuinely revolutionary.

The revolutionary changes of the 1950s proved, however, to be the easy part of the job. Passing laws, building schools and opening urban day-care centers, however big these undertakings were and however unevenly and incompletely they were carried out in a vast and varied country, was much more manageable than changing deeply ingrained attitudes about the sexes, or the social practices that grew out of those attitudes. "Why aren't there more women in this classroom?" my daughter Nancy asked one morning at Qinghua University, Beijing's premier engineering college, where she taught English for a year to overwhelmingly male classes of graduate students. "Because women are not as smart as men," her students replied. "At first, I thought they were joking, teasing the foreign woman teacher," she said afterward. "But they really believed it. The girls believed it, too." These were not the casual attitudes of one classroom of students but a fundamental and explicit strain of traditional thought, carried over from the Confucian past and palpable throughout society today, nearly four decades after the Communist party won power. I asked many of my Chinese friends and acquaintances about this, and all but a few, women and men alike, assured me that they themselves believe lore that millions of children hear from a young age—that girls are smarter in primary school but become unstable after puberty, that women cannot be counted on under pressure, that women have neither the creativity nor the initiative that equip men to be scientists and managers.

The laws passed in the 1950s, and succeeding laws passed as recently as the 1980s, contain in their wording, their provisions and their implementation certain undertones of chivalry that make women not equal but special. The law provides, for example, that women retire five years younger than men. In my talks with leaders of the

All-China Women's Federation, I was impressed with how often I was told, "In China, women and children enjoy special protection under the law." These officially assigned custodians of feminism never once betrayed any consciousness of such questions as whether laws singling women out for special protection added up to an unstated assumption that women were by nature inferior and in need of special attention from men, or whether these laws might raise women onto the kind of pedestal many Western feminists resent. In some cases, the same laws that protect women also protect children. These assumptions that interlace the protection of women with the protection of children are further reinforced by institutional arrangements. The All-China Women's Federation, for example, is the government's and the Communist party's main communication channel on a broad range of children's issues, an implicit acceptance of the proposition that child care and protection is inherently women's work more than it is men's.

The very pervasiveness of these attitudes may well do much to make some of them self-fulfilling. In a 1983 visit to two Shanghai schools where high-school-aged offenders were confined for "reeducation through study and labor," the most striking single fact was the sex-role assumptions in the labor the inmates were given. At the boys' school, the main form of labor was assembling one of the city's most prestigious brands of bicycle, the main national commuting vehicle. At the girls' school, reeducation began with scraps of coat linings, which the inmates stitched into dolls that would be donated to kindergartens. Most of the boys had committed crimes like theft or assault, and the emphasis was clearly on making these young male offenders fit for full and productive roles in the economy. Most of the girls had done no more than get pregnant by a schoolmate or neighbor. The emphasis in their school was on restoring their marriageability after the mandatory abortion, and on making them fit for a role in the household. Much of their training was in housekeeping skills, and they were expected to stay at the school for a year or two before returning to society. The boys with whom they got pregnant, the school officials assured me, also were brought in for reeducation. I learned as we talked more that those boys seldom stayed more than a month or two.

Such separate standards for men and women are seldom subtle, and they are frequently an acknowledged part of institutional policy. Housing assignments are one of the areas where this is most noticeable and systematic—and burdensome to women. In an economy where housing shortages remain severe in most cities despite ten years of breakneck construction under Deng's reforms, a housing assignment is still one of the most critical ways a work unit affects a worker's life. For a young married couple in many cities, the apartment assignment can often be a major factor in marital harmony. Wang Zhiming, a Beijing friend in his late twenties, told me his wife had felt desperate by the time they got their apartment, after nearly three years of marriage: "My mother was always very polite to my wife, and they never fought the way some mothers fight with their daughters-in-law. But for all the time we lived with my parents, everyone assumed that my wife would be my mother's personal servant, because that has always been the Chinese way. My wife went to my parents' bedroom before work every morning and carried the overnight bedpan down the alley to the public toilet and emptied it, cleaned it, and put it back in the bedroom for the next night. That was how her day started, and doing chores for my mother and father was how her day went until she left for work and again as soon as she came home. When we got an apartment and moved out, my parents seemed to have hurt feelings that we would leave them."

In families that still live by these ancient assumptions, as many do in one degree or another even in major cities, it is often the young wife who most needs to have the couple get an apartment. But in most work units, when apartments become available, it is the woman worker who stands at the end of the queue. Most work units, either by rule or in practice, give overwhelming preference to married men in assigning apartments. In most cases, a married woman stands a chance of getting an apartment from her unit only if she can show that there is some extraordinary reason her husband's unit cannot provide one. Since most work units try to provide housing fairly close to the office or factory, this means that the wife usually lives much nearer to her husband's work unit than to her own. So the wife, already burdened at home with most of the household chores, also stands a good chance of spending longer hours pedaling a bicycle into the North China wind every week, or standing at bus stops in the South China sun. The single woman most often gets even worse treatment in housing assignments. At one company, a divorced woman I know had five years' seniority and complained to her boss, a woman, when an unmarried man with three years on the job got an apartment that became available. boss said if I want an apartment I should get married to a man who can get an apartment," she said angrily afterward. "It's disgusting—I have to live in a dormitory room with three other girls and no kitchen, and I have to go down to the next floor to the women's toilet and shower." Most of the unmarried young people I knew lived in similar dorm arrangements if their work was too far away to live with their parents. Except for two young women who managed it with sheer political pull, every unmarried acquaintance under thirty who had an apartment was male.

By the time I met Ming Yueliang and his wife, she had had her fourth abortion. I learned this much later, after I knew them well enough to ask about their experiences with birth control, the face of Deng Xiaoping's modernization drive that has been most controversial outside China and one that arouses much feeling within the country as well. "My first abortion was when I was seventeen years old," she said over orange drinks in their half of a small apartment that they shared with another couple. "I had a boyfriend who was about twenty, and we had been making love a few times a week for about a year when I discovered I was pregnant. When I told my parents, they ordered me never to see him again and made me move in with an aunt on the other side of town so he couldn't find me. They invited a teacher in to lecture me, because the Communist party always teaches that this kind of case is too serious for a family to deal with by itself. They made me feel so ashamed that I never questioned whether I had to have the abortion. A few days after the abortion, my boyfriend found out where I was and climbed a tree outside my window to talk with me. I felt really happy, like someone really cared about me, and just not about their own face, but he got caught and never dared to come back. The next time I dared to have a boyfriend was four years later, when I met Yueliang. Chairman Mao was still alive that first time I got pregnant, and everyone acted like this was such a huge problem. Only after Yueliang reassured me that he could still love me and wanted to marry me did I begin to feel that I was a normal human being after all."

By the time of that conversation, in 1986, she had been married for four years and had undergone three more abortions during her marriage. "I don't like to use condoms," Ming Yueliang said. He showed no trace of embarrassment in discussing this intimate topic, perhaps because by that time we knew each other well. "The Chinese ones are so old-fashioned you can't feel anything, and foreign ones are expensive and much harder to find here in Beijing than in Guangzhou or Shanghai." His wife had her own objections to female methods of birth control: "I really don't feel right with anything inside me that is not natural, and I hate to take any kind of medicine. Anyway, the way the government wants you to use, the intrauterine device, is too dangerous in China. I've heard too many stories about it." So Ming Yueliang and his wife, like many Chinese couples, try to confine their lovemaking to safe times of the month, which is not very reliable as birth control. "That is why she had three more abortions even after we got married," Ming Yueliang explained.

Ming Yueliang and his wife are fairly typical of young urban couples. They have signed the one-child pledge that is at the core of the birth-control program. They plan to have a child, but they are content to wait until they have a whole apartment of their own, some savings and more furniture. And they will be happy with a single child, regardless of its gender. "Of course we want a child, like everyone else, but a daughter would be just fine," he said. "And one child is enough—any more would cost too much." Among city folk, it is common, though far from universal, to feel that more than one child would be too expensive, even without the system of financial rewards and penalties that is part of the population-control plan. So in China as in much of the world, population programs are easier to enforce in the city. With the help of a program that offers subsidies and educational benefits to families that make and keep the one-child pledge, and an ascending scale of financial penalties for families that break the pledge or go beyond two children, many cities easily make their birth-control targets, and many more stay well within reach of making them.

———————

In the countryside, the picture is very different. The combined weight of traditional attitudes and the economics of the return to

Housewives do their daily laundry in the dark-colored, smelly, polluted waters of one of Suzhou's canals. Earlier in the day, many of them had dumped their family's bedpans and nightsoil buckets into the same waters. For millions of city people, the tiny and hard-to-use washing machines available in China are not worth the trouble. For millions of others, indoor plumbing is not available to hook up machines. So washing by hand is still the norm.

Drudgery consumes much spare time and often shortens the normal night's sleep, so people catch naps wherever they can. The first comment of many newly arrived foreigners is that Chinese seem able to sleep anywhere.

Right: Split pants like these are standard wear for a North China toddler. Their convenience saves hours of diaper washing but sometimes makes a walk down a back lane a bit treacherous for the uninitiated.

A boy's trousers are often as convenient in front as in back, a fact of life generally taken for granted by parents and children alike until school age.

Three sisters, still not recovered from the surprise of finding a foreigner in their lane in central Beijing, pose for his camera in the doorway of their family's courtyard-style house.

Facing page, top: Deng Xiaoping poses between, left, former Defense Secretary Caspar Weinberger and, right, U.S. Ambassador Winston Lord. The political mastermind of the coalition that made possible the reforms of the 1980s, Deng regularly posed for group photographs before meetings with foreign leaders. Journalists of the country involved attended these "photo opportunities" for the chance to see Deng close up. Most were impressed by the vigor and mental alertness of the octogenarian Chinese leader, who liked to remark that he started each day with a cold bath.

Facing page, bottom: Zhao Ziyang, then the Premier, just before newsmen were dismissed from his meeting with an American delegation at the Great Hall of the People. Zhao often wears western-style suits and neckties. For this meeting his suit is double-breasted. He is now secretary-general of the Chinese Communist party, second in power only to Deng Xiaoping.

A Beijing mother stops at a staging area outside the Chinese history museum in central Beijing for an advance peek at a new version of history. These floats were for the October 1, 1984, National Day parade, the first in which Mao Zedong, here in the foreground, had to share top revolutionary honors with General Zhu De, still under a plastic shroud in this picture, Premier Zhou Enlai and President Liu Xiaoqi. The floats are part of a vast rewriting of history, still under way, to provide a context for the new Communist party line under which the reforms are taking place. The new version makes Mao a mere mortal superhero among heroes, but the party still needs to keep his memory alive to preserve its own legitimacy.

In the foothills of Sichuan Province's mountains stands the launch pad China offered the world to get satellites into orbit after the American space program was delayed by the Challenger disaster. American journalists got a look at the pad during Defense Secretary Caspar Weinberger's visit in 1986. Perhaps fifty feet behind the camera, the concrete pad gave way to a corn field where children played with chickens and ducks. China did sign some launch contracts with foreign countries in 1986 and 1987.

In Shanghai's harbor on the Huangpu River, a timeless junk, home and source of income to the family that inherited it from generations of waterborne forebears, passes a modern freighter, forming a contrast that summarizes the gap between where China's economy long has been and where Beijing's reformers want it to go.

family farming create intense pressures to have at least one son. A son is regarded as a stronger back to help in the fields. He is the only way to perpetuate the family name, an imperative of filial piety that Mao-ism never stamped out and that now is in full vigor in many places. He is counted as a more reliable source of support in his parents' old age, despite Communist-era laws that make married daughters and their husbands equally responsible. These ancient social and economic pressures make population control a vast dilemma throughout the countryside. When the government has attempted to notch up the pressures, abuses have grown. In some areas, officials have tracked the menstrual cycles of all the married women of entire villages or neighborhoods for years, then organized community meetings to put intense pressure on women who were slow to get abortions when they were found to be pregnant without authorization. Often women in such places have been pressured into abortions in the last three months of pregnancy. In a few places, there has been a reappearance of one of ancient China's darkest practices, the killing of baby girls. Now it has a latter-day purpose of leading to a second chance to try for a boy while staying within the quota.

In 1985, *The Washington Post* published a series of articles by my friend and colleague, Michael Weisskopf, detailing the terms of China's population-control issues, in the countryside and the cities alike. I read Mike's articles with a sense that he had done a distinguished job of laying out one of the most excruciating dilemmas facing whoever tries to govern the world's most populous country as it seeks to modernize. But because of its timing, the series quickly became involved in the controversy over abortion far away in the United States. Anti-abortion forces seized upon some of its most sensational elements to help their campaign in Congress against American contributions to United Nations population programs. The vote in Congress put a powerful spotlight on China, casting its population program in a harshly negative light. Chinese officials angrily denied that forced abortions were part of the national policy, an argument that was true as far as it went. But the pressures needed to slow the country's population growth rates, including incentives for officials who succeeded and penalties for those who failed, were often very intense. Evidence abounded that many officials had gone far beyond the means approved by the government, and that the government lacked an effective means of keeping these officials in line. Already faced with mounting pressures against strictness from within the country, the government had been allowing piecemeal relaxations for nearly a year by the time Mike's articles appeared. Now, despite repeated attempts to mount a propaganda counteroffensive against the publicity out of Washington, Beijing's policy underwent new relaxations, followed by rounds of directives against abuses like forced abortions.

The relaxation promptly threw China back onto the other horn of the dilemma. By 1985, the population strictures devised in the early 1980s had brought the growth rate down to 1.1 percent, one of the lowest in the Third World, after a decade in which it had sometimes exceeded 2 percent. That figure is far closer to the United States rate of 0.9 percent than it is to, say, India's rate of about 2 percent, itself by no means the highest in the third World. But by 1986, the rate was up to 1.41 percent, and in 1987 it was 1.44 percent. To many Chinese planners and foreign economists, numbers like those are the arithmetic of despair. Baby boom children of the late Maoist years are still in the family-forming ages, and at the 1987 growth rate, China's population, which was 1.08 billion that year, would reach 1.5 billion around 2010. China's limited arable land already is severely strained to provide food, cooking oils and other necessities. Many believe population growth on the 1987 scale could make the country an intolerable place to live. By late 1987 and early 1988, population control was getting new priority from officials in Beijing. As if on cue, foreign newsmen were traveling the country and again detailing the abuses spawned by the new pressures.

It is women, vastly more than men, who feel the weight of attempts to control the growth of the world's biggest population. In a country where informed estimates hold that about one pregnancy in three ends in abortion, it is the woman who carries the child and who therefore feels the full bore of the social, political, economic and sometimes physical pressures that are used by officials desperate to head off pay cuts and other punishments for failing to limit births. Scientific knowledge—for example, the fact that the father has more role than the mother in determining a baby's gender—has not penetrated far into the countryside. Official newspapers abound with reports of mothers beaten by their in-laws or husbands after producing a girl as the family's one child. In some areas, women who accept the IUD must accept with it periodic home visits by female officials who check to see that the device is still in place. For millions of women of child-bearing age, the arithmetic of population conspires with the goals of modernizers to create pressures women in many other societies would find unbearable. Relief from these pressures is not in sight in this century.

———

Many writers on women's and educational topics—and most of my Chinese acquaintances—take it as a given of life that women applicants to universities, especially engineering and scientific schools, have to score dozens of points higher on examinations than men. Chinese girls, like girls in many countries, tend to get higher grades than boys all through the junior high and high school years. But only in teachers' colleges—whose graduates are often required to start life in low-paid, low-prestige middle school jobs few educated people want—do women number comparably with men at the college level. In March 1986, the English-language editions of *Women of China,* the country's international propaganda magazine on women's affairs, reported that women currently accounted for more than 40 percent of the work force but only 26 percent of college students. Taken in combination with the fact that college women are enrolled disproportionately in teachers' colleges, the clear implication for the future is that males will overwhelmingly dominate the pool of educated people available to lead the modernization.

What is true of education is true several times over in hiring and promotions. Newspapers and magazines publish a steady stream of articles on the difficulties women have in getting promotions, or jobs commensurate with their credentials, or, in many cases, any jobs at all. So many women's federation officials told me, and so many publications reported, about prejudice among factory directors and government agency heads, that I stopped taking notes on the subject within a year after arriving in Beijing and simply adopted it as part of the lore. The usual explanation is that women have so much protection under women's rights laws that they frequently take time off for pregnancy, childbirth, or menstrual privileges and become unreliable workers.

A typical study, in Henan Province in 1982, found that 70 percent of factory directors openly acknowledged that they systematically looked for excuses to avoid hiring women for key jobs, especially as technicians, engineers, or scientists. Problems of women who do not go to college can be worse, once they finish or leave middle school or high school, than those of college graduates—perhaps a point of resemblance between the status of Chinese and Western women. In the early 1980s, a little-publicized face of the youth unemployment problem left over from the Cultural Revolution was the overwhelming predominance of young female junior high and high school graduates among the large urban category the government called "job-awaiting youths." In Chongqing, officials of the local women's federation told me that 21,000 of the 28,000 young people unemployed in the spring of 1983 were female. Women's federation branches and labor bureaus in other cities I visited that year reported roughly comparable proportions of females among their unemployed youths.

If getting a job can be hard for a woman, each step above the entry level typically becomes many times harder. On one 1983 trip to five industrial cities, I kept track of the numbers of male and female officials, factory managers, and other high-ranking personnel brought forward in response to my interview requests. Not counting officials of local branches of the women's federation, all of whom were female, a total of five out of sixty-three factory officials and technicians, and six out of seventy-one government officials or specialists, were women.

The trip included a stop in Nanjing, at a time when newspapers were making frequent references to a woman who had just been named governor of Jiangsu Province, of which Nanjing is the capital. She was the first female provincial governor in China's post-1949 history. Amid the stream of publicity about her appointment, I met three senior managers of Jiangsu Province's then-new Jinling Hotel, a symbol of the province's progressive government and the first international-standard hotel to attempt an all-Chinese management. The new hotel's managers had all been sent off for months or years of training, either at American or Swiss hotel management schools, or as deputy managers in European or American hotels of the departments they would head at the Jinling. A vastly more urbane lot than most Chinese hotel managers, they were at home speaking the international lingo of their trade, a language far beyond the abilities of their counterparts elsewhere in the country. But I was also impressed that all three were male, and that the staff members who brought us tea throughout our interview were, without exception, female.

The stop in Nanjing also brought out that when the new governor was promoted from deputy governor, her replacement as a deputy was male, so that the net number of women at the top of the Jiangsu provincial government remained what it had been—one. A year later, the country got its first female provincial Communist party first secretary. At the next level up, among the handful of women in the rarefied atmosphere of the Communist party Politburo and Secretariat, anyone who was not the widow of one of the top Communists of the revolutionary generation was a rarity and remained so when a new Politburo was named in October 1987, a few months after I had left China.

Both men and women consciously see a direct and often circular relationship between the difficulty women face in winning advancement and the way couples divide up their housework. Li Ganzhong, a member of the standing committee of the Beijing branch of the women's federation who attended the interview with Miss Jia and Dong Liya, summarized the situation this way: "Often a woman will take on more of the household burden in order to let her husband concentrate on his job." Under Deng Xiaoping's reforms, this tendency has been if anything intensified, now that it is again respectable to study as a way of preparing for advancement. My friends consistently reported that if household burdens forced a choice as to who would study in hope of promotion, it was the man who would go for the job advancement and the woman who would take on more of the chores. That, Mrs. Li and numerous other officials of the women's federation said, was the only realistic choice a couple could make, given the man's far better chance of getting a promotion. In an economy still heavy with official allocations amid shortages, the main benefit of a promotion still is less likely to be the modest pay raise and more likely to be the bigger apartment, bigger bonuses, access to rare recreational facilities, cards to shop in the special stores that carry goods available only, or more regularly, to the privileged, and similar perquisites that accumulate with rising rank. "Once advancement comes," Mrs. Li said, "then some of the benefits will be things both can enjoy. That is why many times the wife will feel her best chance is to help her husband, because he has much more likelihood of advancement."

This tendency of married women to put their husbands' careers first is of course not unique to China. Women in most Western societies often find themselves in comparable dilemmas. But I developed a strong sense that the entire system of sexual assumptions, of which this is only one major adult manifestation, is far more widespread and powerful than in the West. Many of these assumptions are carried over from Confucian tradition, which taught that society is naturally and properly hierarchical, with women subordinate to men, and that dire consequences result when these "natural" relationships are upset. Today, after nearly forty years of convoluted changes in the Communist party's doctrines, timeless sexual assumptions have proven more powerful than any antidote a Marxist-Leninist system has been able to devise. These assumptions begin early in childhood, and they have forcefully reasserted themselves as Deng Xiaoping's reform policies have spread through the society.

By 1985, newspapers were frequently reporting that, in many rural areas, it was getting harder and harder to enforce the requirement that families send their daughters to school. Farm parents have long questioned the point of any more than minimal literacy for their daughters, and as the communes were dismantled the easy means of enforcing this rule was lost. At the same time, as family farming reasserts itself, parents find more and more uses for their daughters at home. The tendency of parents not to educate daughters extends upward through the educational system, and by high school most of the relatively few drop-outs are girls, a pattern precisely the opposite of most Western countries. By college age, parents become increasingly conscious that their daughters are about to get married, which means in most areas that the bride will become part of the groom's family. Their sons, however, carry the family name and will remain part of the family after marriage. If parents have both sons and daughters, and if they need the added income a college-age child can provide by working instead of going to school, the sons will usually to go school and the daughters will usually stay home and help earn money, or do the housework, or both.

The conflicting and contradictory crosscurrents in the way the reforms play out into the lives of women often seem most striking and hardest to comprehend in the countryside. In 1985, my reporting for a series of articles on farmers leaving the land impressed upon me the fact that it is the men who are leaving, while one or two women in the prime of life stay behind to go on swinging the hoe and doing the back-breaking work that maintains the family's claim to a tiny patch of the earth. A few weeks later in Beijing, I mentioned this to a colleague, Rick Hornik, the *Time* magazine correspondent. "The feminization of agriculture," he replied with a knowing smile. He had written about much the same process, he said, when he worked for *Time* in Eastern Europe and reported on the much less radical reforms in Czechoslovakia and Hungary that the Chinese had studied before embarking on their decollectivization.

Rick's phrase aptly summarized the most striking face of what I saw changing in rural women's lives, but the effects of the reforms in most parts of the countryside I visited were as complex and hard to characterize as any facet of life in the Deng Xiaoping years. Farm women had rarely, even in the most doctrinaire years of Maoist egalitarianism, been treated as equals of men. When Chinese farmers were most rigidly collectivized into Mao's "People's Communes," women filled their full share of the long lines of peasants who swung hoes in unison and worked their way in ranks across the fields pictured in countless propaganda photographs of rosy-cheeked peasants. "In China," leaders of the women's federation told me time and again, "we have a saying that women hold up half the sky."

Those propaganda photos of long lines of men and women inching their way together across the loess or the rice paddy were one Maoist way of portraying womanhood holding up its half of the sky. Those were the years when things were, according to the dogma of the time, so equal that peasants were paid, not in money or in grain, but in "work points," recorded in the production brigade's books to become the basis of distribution of any surplus at the end of the year. What the captions on the propaganda pictures never mentioned was that, even in those days of egalitarian rhetoric, a woman was given fewer work points than a man for a day in the fields. Today, a woman who labors alone for long months on the family plot knows that compensation will depend, not on arbitrary rules that give women fewer "work points," but on how much she can make the family plot produce. On the other hand, how much control or influence she will have over the use of the money her work produces is likely to depend on local marriage customs in the part of China where she lives.

The Maoist collectivization did produce institutional arrangements to help women in ways that attracted worldwide attention. Probably the most publicized was the commune or brigade day-care center, which freed farm women in some villages, but by no means most, from child care while they took their required turns in the fields. Not long after the dismantling of the communes in 1983 and 1984, it became clear that many of the localities that had established communal nurseries were now abandoning them along with the communes. In Shandong, in southern provinces like Guangdong and Fujian, on communes outside Shanghai, in suburban townships outside Beijing, in Sichuan— virtually every place I went in the countryside—I began to see more and more mothers taking small children with them to the work place.

In Guangdong, in 1985, I watched a mother mix cement while her baby rode on her back, a practice I had not seen in China, though I remembered it from the early 1970s in Hong Kong, where women of the Hakka minority are a major construction force, as they are in much of Guangdong. Nearby, two toddlers perhaps two years old played in a lumber pile at the same construction site, while their mothers worked together on a frame for poured concrete. Everywhere I went, I felt, I saw not only fewer men in the fields but also more country women tending infants and toddlers as they worked. International agency officials, who traveled to all parts of the countryside from Beijing and saw places to which correspondents rarely got permission to go, told me that they were finding much the same. "There is of course no way to know a firm number," UNICEF agent Carl Taylor had told me in late 1985, "but it is clear that thousands of day-care centers have been closed across the countryside."

For significant numbers of women, the chance to tend their own or their families' children, even while working, is a welcome end to a degree of regimentation many peasants deeply disliked. And for some rural women, this requires less effort than for others. For some farm women, the new wave of cottage industries that is part of the reforms, as well as the new freedom to raise as many chickens and sell as many eggs as they can, have meant a chance to go back to caring for their own children even while substantially improving their economic situation compared with the recent past. For many rural women, these short-run benefits often obscure the fact that their husbands and sons are now advancing even faster than they are, and that the economic gap between the sexes may now be growing faster than ever in many parts of the countryside. Other rural women are making a go of small businesses, as restaurant owners, tailors, shopkeepers, or owners of nurseries that sell shrubs and saplings to green-starved cities. It is not unusual—though it is far from typical—for such women to experience periods when they earn substantially more than their husbands.

In the city and in the countryside, women often are being affected by the reforms of the Deng Xiaoping years in ways no one intended or predicted. As the Communist party stepped up the pressure for birth control under the one-child policy in 1981 and 1982, one grotesque side effect was a resurgence of female infanticide in some parts of the countryside. If there could be only one child, some families seemed to feel, it would have to be a male heir. Killing defective babies has been a common practice for centuries in many parts of the countryside, a practice the entire society often deals with by trying not to notice it. That being born female could be a sufficient defect to make the baby a candidate for death had long been part of this practice in the pre-Communist countryside. Foreign population experts have sought to quantify this practice by estimating how much the male-female ratio in actual population figures deviates from what might have been expected. This is a hotly controversial issue among the small community of demographers who attempt to work with China's population figures, and I am neither competent nor inclined to join the controversy. In general, though I am yet to be convinced that any of these calculations is reliable in its specifics, I am inclined to believe that female infanticide did increase significantly in some parts of the countryside in the early 1980s and may not have dropped back to earlier levels even by 1987. The Chinese Communist party had claimed to have made massive strides against this rural practice since 1949, but by the time I arrived, in late 1982, newspapers in some provinces were carrying public, open appeals from the provincial leaders to control an increase in the killing of baby girls. Premier Zhao Ziyang thought the problem widespread enough that he included an appeal for new efforts against it in his annual report to the National People's Congress the next year.[2]

In cities, a comparably undesired effect on women stems from the increasing pressure for efficiency and profits felt by factory directors. Chinese newspapers since early 1985 have published classic "teaching by negative example" articles about factory directors who have sought to improve efficiency at the expense of women workers. One such article told of Liu Jianzhong, who apparently thought he knew just what to do when he came under pressure for profits.[3] He ordered all the women in his factory who were age forty-five or older to take early retirement, at some 40 percent of their pay instead of the 70 percent they would receive at age fifty, the normal retirement age for women. But the story, whether real or apocryphal, as some of the negative examples are, is another case study in the conflicting forces the reforms have set loose in the lives of women. The women Mr. Liu had ordered into early retirement, the paper reported, took their case to court. In the end, it was Mr. Liu who lost his job.

Going to court is not a step Chinese take lightly. Chinese have for centuries avoided contact with courts for any purpose. The person who ends up in court, whether as plaintiff or as defendant, not only carries a fear of exposing himself to the authorities but also a sense of shame at having failed to live life in a properly harmonious way. The system of laws and courts was at best rudimentary by 1949 and was scarcely improved upon by the Communist party during its first decade and a half in power. When courts and lawyers' offices were closed during the Cultural Revolution, even that limited system was shattered. Construction of a legal system was just resuming in 1982, partly to reassure foreign businessmen that recourse to recognizable laws and institutions would be possible if they came to invest and work in China. For women, a stronger legal system struck me as a clear necessity if the women's rights written into the laws passed in the 1950s and after were to become part of daily life.

By the time I left China, the first stirrings of women's use of this fledgling legal system were suggesting the courtroom's potential as a forum for women. In particular, more and more women who had long suffered with abusive husbands were seeking divorce. "What would be the first result if the housing shortage were solved?" Lu Wufan, a factory translator in his early thirties, liked to ask me. "First thing, the divorce rate would go up. All the women whose husbands beat them or whose mothers-in-law are overbearing, if they could find other places to live, they'd get divorced right away." And, I thought to myself, if they could bring themselves to believe in resort to the law and the courts as a way of solving anything. By the time I left China, the housing shortage was showing the first signs of easing. The divorce rate, though still a fraction of American or European levels, was up for the sixth straight year. As always in China, the substantial majority of the applicants were women.

In the nearly five years I lived in Beijing, the lives of most of my women friends improved substantially. But the most palpable improvements did not stem from any changes in their status vis-à-vis men. Rather, the improvements I saw were part of the society's generally rising standard of living, and of the Communist party's tolerance of a degree of personal freedom, especially freedom of movement and travel. The middle 1980s also was a period of debate, perhaps the broadest seen by the Communist world since Lenin's time, on the role of women in socialist society. It became possible for women and men to use the columns of major mass-circulation newspapers and magazines to debate issues that had been closed for decades. Would it not be better, writers were permitted to ask in print, if mothers were permitted to stay home at partial salary for a few years, rather than a few months, to take care of their children? Shouldn't women normally work as late into life as men, rather than being retired five years younger? Didn't the country need to reexamine the levels of heavy physical labor to which a woman might be assigned by the state?

Might it not still be socialism, even if some women were permitted to decide that they preferred to tend a home rather than to go out to work at all?

These issues had been officially decided within a few years after the Communist party won power. For some three decades, the traditional Marxist answers were not open to challenge. But in the new atmosphere of reform, it had become possible to challenge them publicly and to debate them in detail over a period of years. The issues had not been resolved by the time I left China, but the freedom to challenge them, and the fact that both sexes were active in the debate, struck me as significant steps for women. Previously, a Communist party overwhelmingly dominated by men had simply decided such issues and had handed its decisions down for women to accept without debate. I felt less sure whether, on balance, women were making economic and personal progress as rapidly as men. But most of the women I knew seemed, for the moment, to be preoccupied with how much better life is now than it was a few years ago. They were not much inclined to ask themselves whether men had it even better.

6

"Politics
Is a Dirty Business"

From north and a bit west of Beijing, a string of shallow, elaborately gardened artificial lakes meanders into the city, punctuating one branch of the capital's water-supply canal system. The lakes were dug to create scenic centerpieces for some of the favorite pleasure grounds of the Ming and the Qing, the final two dynasties. Farthest from the city is a broad lake at the Yuan Ming Yuan, the ruins of the old summer palace that was looted and torched by British and French troops in the nineteenth century. Next is Kunming Lake, setting of the final dynastic summer palace, the Yi He Yuan, which still stands today, part of every foreign tourist's time in Beijing, perhaps best known as the site of the famous marble boat. The imperious Empress Dowager Tsu Hsi ordered a costly dredging and enlargement of Kunming Lake, and construction of the new palace on its shores, to replace the more elaborate structures upstream that had been left in ashes by the foreigners. The marble boat was an afterthought, the dowager's personal touch, a contemptuous answer to modernizers in her nephew's court. She financed its construction with money that had been appropriated to create her country's first modern navy.

From Kunming Lake, the canal flows south and a bit east toward the city for a few miles without further interruption by pleasure lakes.

123

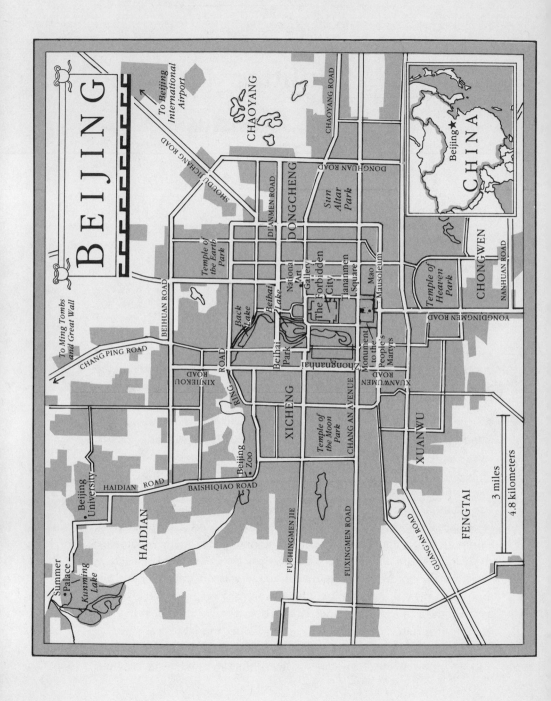

But just after it passes under the Beijing No. 2 Ring Road, a six-lane divided highway that scars the land where the historic Ming Dynasty city wall stood crumbling until the 1950s, it feeds into a large, unadorned pond. This one lake was left ungardened by the emperors, as if they were prudently reserving space for future use by members of their ever-growing courts and by their endlessly proliferating royal offspring. It is best known among Beijing people today as Back Lake, a name that may have grown out of its location, just inside the old wall's Desheng Gate, for a northern gate is a rear gate in the way Chinese houses, courtyards, and cities are laid out.

A narrow, worn, and yellowed marble bridge in the imperial style arches over the bottleneck where the waters of Back Lake begin their passage toward one of the capital's favorite public parks. North Lake, Beihai in Chinese, was once the privileged playground of low-rank concubines, mandarins, and eunuchs. From North Lake, the waters pass to Middle Lake (Zhonghai), and from Middle Lake to South Lake (Nanhai), used by the emperors as extensions of the palace grounds, laid out roughly from north to south alongside the western moat of the Forbidden City, the monumental main palace complex.

The dynasties early overflowed their main palaces, and they assigned high mandarins, generals, and even petty princes to live in lesser palaces on the shores of these pleasure grounds. Even these did not suffice, and scores of once-sumptuous traditional courtyard-style houses, all facing the south in obedience to Chinese tradition, now stand nearby in latter-day shabbiness. Many were built as homes of mandarins, merchants, scholars, generals, eunuchs, and sometimes the quasi-princely sons of minor concubines—people who had means to live graciously and who needed to live near the emperor's court. Dotted along streets and alleys throughout the neighborhoods east, north, and west of the Forbidden City, they once housed elegant rosewood chairs and tables, landscape and calligraphy scrolls, lacquered screens, elaborately carved family altars, and mahogany sideboards deeply incised with dragons and phoenixes. Today, many of them house restaurants, repair shops, and musty government offices.

On a crisp November day in 1983, Fang Xiuqing, a thirty-one-year-old daughter of a well-known old revolutionary in Shaanxi Province, guided me through the alleys of northern Beijing as I drove us to Back Lake, where she had promised to show me "something foreigners don't known about." From beside a public boathouse on the southeast shore, she pointed across the water to two large American-style houses that looked as if they had been transplanted from a 1950s neighborhood in Grosse Point Shores. Standing on spacious, tree-shaded shoreline lots, even two-story houses seemed to tower over the low, dark roofs and occasional red-brick public toilets of the aging one-story houses along the twisting Beijing lanes beyond. The buff brick exteriors and octagonal stairwell windows of the two houses formed a luxurious contrast with the unrelenting gray monotone of their surroundings.

The nearer of the two houses belonged to Ye Jianying, one of the bona fide legends of the Communist revolution, a general credited with saving Mao's life on the Long March and lionized in the 1950s as one of the ten marshals of the People's Liberation Army. Marshal Ye's name had continued to grow even through the Cultural Revolution, when he managed to rebound to the heights of the party with only brief falls from power, despite towering fights with radicals like Jiang Qing, Mao's wife. In one shouting match with Jiang Qing, Fang Xiuqing told me, Marshal Ye broke his little finger by smashing his fist on a table to make a point. In his eighties by 1983, and so enfeebled by age that he could rarely leave his house, the old guerrilla had such a formidable reputation that, despite his years, he was still a member of the innermost of all inner circles, the six-member Standing Committee of the Politburo of the Communist party Central Committee. That made him, by official designation, one of the six most powerful men in China. The other big buff brick house belonged to one of the old marshal's closest army cronies, Yang Chengwu, a general who had briefly served as chief of staff of the PLA but had ended his career in such deep trouble with Deng Xiaoping that even Marshal Ye could not get him anything significant to do.

The houses looked like something out of the 1950s because they were. When Mao's Communist armies took over Beijing in 1949, Marshal Ye became the party's first military mayor of Beijing. It soon turned out that history had been reserving the shores of Back Lake not for courtiers and courtesans of future princes but for a privileged handful among the inner circles and close followers of the guerrilla armies. Across the lake from Marshal Ye's and General Yang's stands today a still grander house, that of Soong Ching-ling, the widow of Sun Yat-sen, leader of the 1911 revolution that overthrew the final dynasty. Madame Soong's sister is Soong Mei-ling, the widow of Chiang Kai-shek, head of the Nationalist party the Communists had driven from the Mainland. Soong Ching-ling thus was important both because she could help the party borrow some of her husband's aura and because she was the only member of her own rich and influential family who openly favored the Communists and chose to live in China after they won power. Her house at Back Lake, on Soong family land, was one in a string of special privileges that added up to an extended proselytization by the Communist party's highest recruiters. This wooing of Madame Soong ended in one of those peculiar deathbed conversions that are familiar wherever there are true believers in an established religion. Soong Ching-ling had rejected all blandishments to join the Communist party all her life, so it was not until 1981, when doctors were sure she could never rise up out of her terminal coma and protest, that the country's top Communists gathered at her bedside for full last rites. As her life ebbed, they publicly pronounced her a Comrade. Now her house is open to tourists, courtesy of the Soong Ching-ling Foundation, itself a type of agency that became possible only with Mao safely gone from the scene.

After the last dynasty fell in 1911, Chiang Kai-shek's Nationalist party eventually established its capital more than 500 miles to the south, in Nanjing. With the seat of power moved so far away, the neighborhoods around the old imperial palaces and pleasure grounds in Beijing lost much of their vitality and virtually all of their political inhabitants over the decades. Then, on October 1, 1949, Mao strode into the very heart of these neighborhoods, stood atop Tiananmen, the Gate of Heavenly Peace, and declared a new People's Republic of China. Still deep in civil war even though the Nationalist armies were mostly on the run, the new Communist rulers were conscious of the aura and symbols of power that lingered yet in the old imperial precincts. The Forbidden City itself, built 600 years earlier, was no longer useful except as a museum, which it soon became. But the old palaces and walled pleasure grounds next door at Middle Lake and South Lake were perfect places for controversial and inexperienced new rulers to borrow some political legitimacy from history. The party soon took them over, combined the names of the two lakes into one word, *Zhongnanhai,* and converted the playgrounds of princes and mandarins into the working and living center of a new elite that would rule, from this walled and gardened lakeside sanctuary, in the name of equality.

In a city where recreation facilities are scarce and the masses even now resort daily to construction sites and highway divider strips to find space for their leisure, the custom of pleasure grounds for the ruling elite soon took on a touch of modernization with establishment of a complex called Three Gates. At this army-run recreation center, sandwiched into the imperial precincts between Coal Hill and the entrance to Beihai Park, high enough rank in the army or the party can carry with it the right to order up private showings of foreign movies to your taste in one of four theaters, to work out in one of several gyms, to swim in a pool reserved for the elite, or, as Deng Xiaoping and Hu Yaobang are said to do, to reserve a room for a card game.

Before long, power resumed its habit of spilling out of the palaces and into the neighborhoods near the moats and lakes. Fang Xiuqing guided me, in November 1983, on drives past the steel-gated courtyard houses of half a dozen Politburo members and of Zhang Aiping, the minister of defense. Most were old homes, long since out of the hands of the families of the mandarins and merchants who had built them to be near the court. "Most of these people have houses or apartments in Zhongnanhai," Fang Xiuqing said. "But their children hate to live inside Zhongnanhai. Every time they go in or out, and every time a friend comes to visit, they have to deal with so many guards, at the gate, and in their section of the compound, and at their home. That's why people want to have houses outside." In my remaining years in Beijing, other Chinese friends would guide me past the houses of other top Communists, including one built by a middle-rank Qing Dynasty mandarin and later owned by a rich merchant, a spacious triple-courtyard compound a few lanes north of the Forbidden City. Since shortly after the Communists arrived in Beijing, this classic mandarin-style, south-facing compound, grown comfortably shabby by the time I first saw it in 1986, had been home to Hu

Yaobang, who would later be deposed as head of the Communist party, and his wife, their four married children and their families, and his party-assigned personal secretary.

I soon began to realize that large areas near Back Lake were particularly larded with the homes of top military officers. Their houses, and those of many of the party's civilian elite as well, are entered through heavy gray steel gates. At eye level, each of these gates has a small horizontal slot. Whenever a foreigner or other suspicious-looking stranger approaches, this slot clanks open and a pair of eyes peers out. I once went back to old Marshal Ye's house to take a picture of his gate. As I walked back to the car, I heard a much louder clank from the gate and saw the faces of onlookers from the neighborhood turn ashen. "Who sent you here?" a youthful voice from behind demanded in Chinese. I turned to see the broad gate standing ajar, the first time I had ever seen it unlocked, and a teen-aged PLA soldier walking a few yards behind me. To the visible relief of the onlookers— as well as of the foreigner with the camera—he seemed eager to believe when I said I had merely been taking a picture of a schoolgirl who had fortuitously walked past as I knelt down to shoot.

Inside the gray gates of these generals' and politicians' houses is a life most Chinese would never imagine. "The first time my father took me and my sister to a party at Ye Jianying's house," Fang Xiuqing said on the way home from Back Lake, "I saw how big it was, and all the furniture, and I was so afraid I grabbed my sister's arm and said if the people ever find out there will surely be another revolution. So many rooms, and so many soldiers and other people to work there. And he has other places, too—two more in Beijing, where other relatives live, and one in Shanghai, and one in Guangzhou." Fang Xiuqing herself was a child of considerable privilege by any ordinary Chinese standard, having grown up in a well-connected provincial party second secretary's house with a car, driver, housekeeper, and easy access to the meats, clothing, bicycles, entertainment tickets, and other rationed goods the masses rarely get, or get only after long waits. Based on several visits to Ye Jianying's house with her parents, she estimated that the people regularly assigned to the old marshal's house must number about twenty. She said they include three private secretaries, two housekeepers, two cooks, two army orderlies, three army drivers for two cars and one jeep, and perhaps half a dozen guards who rotate on gate duty and often serve as personal errand boys and messengers. In the old guerilla's enfeebled later years, two army nurses also were on full-time assignment to his house.

In the following years, Fang Xiuqing and other friends would now and then point out additional centers of privileged living, most of them rather less grand than Marshal Ye's and more nearly on the scale Fang Xiuqing herself and some of my other friends had known in their youth. Many seemed unprepossessing at first glance. In central Beijing, for example, behind larger buildings in a cul-de-sac off Newspaper Alley and less than half a block east of Capital Theater, a turn north between open mounds of coal on the left and overflowing green garbage cans on the right leads to a charcoal-gray, four-story structure marked only by the number "69." Its style marks it as one of the first apartment blocks put up for the new elite in the 1950s, when Beijing's architecture added a series of period pieces that mixed Stalinist and Chinese elements into what was supposed to become the new socialist look. Buildings in this distinctive style, known among many foreign residents as "Sino-Stalin Gothic," are still dotted all over Beijing, reminders of the heady years when thousands of Soviet advisers were demonstrating Moscow's version of the Marxist-Leninist way to drag China into the twentieth century.

It took a second look to realize that 69 Newspaper Alley was no ordinary apartment house. Cars were the first giveaway. In ten minutes parked on Newspaper Alley one morning, I watched fourteen Mercedes and Toyota Crown sedans slip out from behind the garbage heaps and the coal piles. The building's windows are bigger and farther apart than in the rest of the neighborhood, a tip-off of the much larger size of the rooms inside. "You should see how high the ceilings are," Ming Yueliang, a friend who often visited relatives there, told me. "And they have parquet floors and polished wood around the windows and doors." In a city where it is a privilege to have a tiny three-room flat with a bare cement floor and whitewashed walls, these were special apartments.

69 Newspaper Alley is owned by the Ministry of Foreign Affairs. It is reserved for Chinese diplomats of ambassadorial rank and above.

Today, China's foreign service increasingly consists of men and women trained specifically for diplomacy in institutes and universities, and a new and bigger apartment house has been built to make room for a growing number of ambassadors. But 69 Newspaper Alley lives on, still in its original use from the days when Premier Zhou Enlai personally ran the country's diplomacy. In those early years, experience gained working with Zhou Enlai in the guerrilla decades, especially at Chongqing during World War II, when the Communists needed contact with the Americans, often was an ambassador's main qualification. Comparable housing has sheltered most of the old elite of the guerrilla generation for more than three decades in every provincial capital and every major city. In surroundings like these, Fang Xiuqing and thousands of other daughters and sons have grown up with the privileges their fathers acquired when victory suddenly ended their decades as active fighters. But these daughters and sons of the old revolutionaries, and now granddaughters and grandsons as well, have lived lives diametrically opposite to those of their elders.

In the political litmus test the Communist party applied in passing out privileges after 1949, the right color to have was Red. The best proof that you were Red was your record in the revolution. But once the parents were certified Red, the status of children and sometimes grandchildren was assured. They would enjoy the cars, the unrationed meat and clothing, the servants—indeed, would grow up taking them for granted—and few would ever have to risk calamity on the battlefield. In a country where Redness determined rank, and rank determined privilege, in a society where privilege was a far more negotiable currency than money, this new generation of the revolutionary elite grew up with a very special kind of privilege. As children of parents who had fought and bled to prove they were Red, the members of this new generation of revolutionary families were born Red.

Whenever I visited the neighborhoods around Back Lake, I was struck by the young women. Fashions were only in the very early stages of change when I arrived in China in October 1982, but even when they still wore the baggy blues that had been the standard of the Maoist decades, many of the young women here had a difference.

Their clothing was better cut and less faded, their shoes were more often leather than corduroy, and their hair looked professionally cut and recently washed. Their hands were exceptional, the skin smooth and unmarked by hard work, the fingernails intact and well tended. After I was told that this neighborhood was more heavily peppered than most with old guerrilla leaders, I began to develop the impression that the men who had fought to make everyone equal had found means to ensure that their daughters would grow up, in Orwell's phrase, more equal than others. These well-tended daughters and their brothers grew up knowing that having been born Red made them special.

For most Chinese, education beyond junior high school is a remote prospect, or at best an unlikely one. Only a relative few pass the tests to get into high school. College is scarcely worth dreaming about unless it is clear from a young age that you have exceptional ability and motivation. Shortly after I arrived in Beijing in October 1982, Chinese university professors I met estimated that fewer than 1 percent of college-aged people would find places in a university, institute or normal school the next fall. In the spring of 1987, with campuses at last mostly back to normal two decades after the depredations of the Great Helmsman's Red Guards, one of the same professors estimated that slightly over 2 percent would find places that fall. The continuing poverty of the educational system, thirty-eight years after the Communist party won power, will starve the economy of desperately needed human materials well into the next century and will silently mock Deng Xiaoping's modernization ambitions for decades. It also makes education the ultimate privilege, a point many in the revolutionary elite understood from the outset. By the time my assignment ended, I was fairly well acquainted with more than a dozen young men and women of the born-Red generation. Every one of them had graduated from a college-level institution. About half spoke English well enough that we rarely used Chinese when we talked.

Except for a few years when colleges were reopening late in the Cultural Revolution, college admission has always been by examination. For most people who hope to get into college, the year before the exam is a time of immense exertion and tension. I asked some of my born-Red friends how it could be that every one of them passed the examinations. Ming Yueliang smiled. "Almost every university and institute has a back door," he explained. "I did not rank high enough on the test to beat the other candidates, and neither did my older brother. But our test scores showed we could handle the work, and our father found schools that would make places for us." Other friends who were not privileged to be born Red told of arriving at their campuses for freshman year and finding that a small "new group" of freshmen, most of whom turned out to be from well-connected families, would arrive a few days after the main group.

The tiny percentage of the college-age population that finds its way into higher education is an instant elite by force of the sheer scarcity and importance of the education they get in a severely undereducated society. But the born Red form a super-elite within this educated elite. At school vacations and breaks, some of them can get tickets on airplanes to go home while their less privileged classmates spend whole days in line at railroad stations, hoping for a standing-room ticket on an overcrowded train. Some of my friends told of hometown professors who owed their politician fathers a favor and who had volunteered to tutor them during summer vacation if they ran into academic problems. Other students had managed to change their college majors, a feat rarely accomplished in a system that centrally assigns most students to a major upon admission to a university or institute.

Their elite status continues into life beyond college. Graduation itself is traumatic for most students, for it is the time to await nervously the state placement office's decision about where you will work. For thousands of new graduates each year, this means assignment to remote and rugged places like the deserts of Xinjiang Province, or the mountains and barren plateaus of Tibet. These are places where the poverty is even deeper than in most of the country, places where Han Chinese are regarded as foreign overlords by the local people, who speak unfamiliar tongues, eat unfamiliar foods and worship unfamiliar deities. Carla Kirkwood, an American graduate student who worked in my office, told me in a state of some agitation the story of some friends who were graduating in 1985 from the Beijing Aeronautical Institute. Teachers urged them to volunteer for service in the blazing and barren deserts of Xinjiang, assuring them that there was scant chance they would have to go but that volunteering would look good on their records. "Almost everyone who volunteered was actually assigned to Xinjiang," she said. A few weeks later, she reported that a handful who had influential parents managed to get reassigned, and a few others simply refused to go, defying a government threat that refusal would mean they would never get a state job assignment. "The rest are leaving for Xinjiang this week," she said.

"I want you to see the apartment where I'm staying in Beijing," Fang Xiuqing said one afternoon. What she was about to show me was in fact a vignette of how the born-Red generations exchange privilege, or *guanxi,* as a form of currency. *Guanxi* is a word often translated into English as "connections," but it has far more subtle and elaborate meanings in Chinese. The large apartment complex was, in this case, home to low-ranking bureaucrats of a large government ministry. She led me up four flights of the usual dark, dusty concrete stairwell, crammed with the usual black bicycles and rusting stoves and tools, into the usual three cramped, cement-floored rooms, each with a single electrical outlet and a single fluorescent tube for lighting. "This is where I sleep when I am here alone," she said, pointing out a tiny room with one window and a small day bed. "This is where we sleep when my boy friend is here for the night," she added, pointing into a somewhat larger room with a triple window and a double bed.

It was the first time she had mentioned a boy friend, but her tone was so matter-of-fact that it was clear the relationship was a long-standing one. As she guided me through the rooms, I wondered how Fang Xiuqing came to have this apartment. In, say, Washington or Hong Kong, I might not have thought much about what she was telling me. But China in 1983 was a country where young city couples usually deferred marriage for years waiting for an apartment, and Beijing was a capital where newlyweds often had to cram in for years with in-laws for lack of space elsewhere. Here was an unmarried young woman whose residence card was not from Beijing, whose work unit was far away in Shaanxi Province, who nevertheless had ready access to a spartan but hard-to-get apartment in the national capital.

I could not resist asking Fang Xiuqing how she got access to the apartment. She smiled and answered by simply pronouncing the name of an elderly Politburo member. I asked her to explain how it worked. In the division of labor among top Communists, it turned out, the Politburo member's responsibilities had long included Shaanxi Province. Her father had known the old man in a People's Liberation Army division in the civil war, and their mutual *guanxi* had ripened during the years of her father's high rank in Shaanxi. So whenever she was going to Beijing, she would call up the old Politburo member and he would arrange a place to live. Most often, as in this case, it would be in the Beijing apartment of his unmarried male secretary. The male secretaries, she explained, sometimes are fast-rising younger Communists, assigned, in an arrangement that reminded me of U.S. Supreme Court law clerks, to work with Politburo members and other top Communists, a chance to learn the ropes of the party's inner sanctum and to build their own *guanxi* networks on their way up. The Politburo member's responsibilities also included the ministry that owned this apartment, she explained, and that was why the secretary happened to be assigned quarters in this compound. Politburo members and their secretaries often are away from Beijing on business, and both often also have living quarters in the provinces that come under the Politburo member's purview. So for each secretary there may be at any moment one or more unused apartments, in the capital or in the provinces, which become part of the currency on the born-Red network. Over time I would learn that these and other privileged apartments are regularly borrowed and lent, providing the young born Red with a privacy and mobility ordinary people do not know exists. The secretaries, of course, often garden and mine their own *guanxi* with the born-Red progeny of the top Communists they serve, trading favors, inner-party gossip, and privileges, until they themselves often build up key roles in the network.

Officially, Lu Xiaowei is a translator for a flashlight factory in Shijiazhuang, the capital of Hebei, the province that surrounds Beijing. But by the time I met him in 1982, it had been more than a year since he made most of his income by his assigned work. Instead, as the flow of tourists began to rise, he began to wangle or simply steal time off from his job, which rarely had any work, and head for the Beijing airport. When he spotted a mild-looking, English-speaking tourist, he would strike up a conversation. If the talk went well, he would eventually offer to be the tourist's guide for a few days, promising to take him places an official government-assigned tour guide would never put on an itinerary. Lu Xiaowei would also take care of anything the tourist hadn't already arranged, booking rooms and planes, buying meals, hiring cars and taxis, all with individual rather than tour-group service and with much better English than a China Travel Service guide was likely to have. And he didn't charge a fee or take a cut—he gave the tourist the original receipts from the hotels and restaurants.

The secret was that the tourist would give Lu Xiaowei foreign exchange certificates, the premium scrip that foreigners receive when they change their hard currency. Lu would pay for as much as possible with local "People's Money," the domestic currency, which he would buy at bargain rates on the black market in exchange for some of the premium certificates the foreigners gave him. By this simple money-changing operation, he could make more in a day than most workers earned in a month. He soon became addicted to the income, drinking beer and eating in expensive restaurants, until during the high tourist season he would use up his annual leave, his sick time and all the days he could persuade his bosses not to report his absence, which often added up to more time than his sick time and his official leave put together.

Lu Xiaowei liked to talk about the line of work he had invented for himself. He was proud that, at age twenty-eight, he was already one of the few hundred thousand city dwellers who had found ways to make Deng Xiaoping's "opening to the outside world" work to their personal benefit. Every city has come to have its thousands of Lu Xiaoweis mining the burgeoning gray areas of a rapidly changing economy, raking in the easy money and basking in the reputation of one who has learned how to use the system. In a society that is only beginning to make way for genuine entrepreneurs, many of these young people don't even notice when they step across the line from entrepreneurship to hustling. But whether as entrepreneurs or as hustlers, they are petty operatives compared with some of their born-Red contemporaries. As the country opens the way to its Lu Xiaoweis to invent new ways to profit, it is often members of the born-Red generations, with their superior *guanxi* and their higher levels of education, who are making the big scores.

———————————

One of the first effects of the reforms was abrupt change in the nature of privilege itself. Suddenly, it became possible again not only to go to college but even to go overseas to college. Upon graduation from a Chinese university, the list of possible job assignments suddenly included firms that supply translators and office workers to foreign companies, where it would be possible to gain access to imported clothing and electronic goods, be sent abroad for training, possibly eventually find a way to live overseas in a richer and more comfortable country. The new "special economic zones," built in Shenzhen next to Hong Kong and in other southern coastal areas as windows to take in foreign technology and develop export trade, offered high pay and abundant room for wheeling and dealing. Every province and every autonomous city opened its own international business arm, patterned and usually named after the China International Trust and Investment Corporation, a half-private and half-state hybrid organized and financed in hope of promoting exports and attracting investment.

The young men and women of the born-Red generation had grown up comfortable with always having a piece of whatever action there was. Now, As Deng Xiaoping's reforms created myriad new opportunities to wheel and deal, money became a currency just as negotiable as privilege, and the scope of the action itself multiplied several thousandfold in a matter of a few years. As of 1988, eleven of my born-Red friends and acquaintances are now in the United States. In a few cases, their born-Red connections have continued to help them in America. One student I know, closely connected with a senior military officer, has for three years received monthly payments of $1,000 from a Japanese who does business with the People's Liberation Army. Another, the son of a guerrilla general from Hunan, Mao's home province, has found a job with the local investment and trust corporation and now makes extended trading trips to Hong Kong, Europe, and the United States several times a year. Another, the son of a senior Communist party newspaper editor with close ties to Deng Xiaoping, became the editor of one of the myriad new business magazines that have sprung up under the reforms, then found a job in Shenzhen, the special economic zone adjoining Hong Kong, then headed for the States to study for a master's degree in business administration. Aside from the progeny of top national leaders, whose operations were the common gossip of the circuit, each of my born-Red friends and acquaintances knew of many others who had found ways to combine the advantages of being born Red with the new action suddenly opening up in the newly loosening and expanding economy. As they do, many old revolutionary families are now going, in the span of a generation or two and often while the founding guerrilla leader is still alive, from the vanguard of Mao's peasant armies to the vanguard of entrepreneurship in Deng's new-look socialism.

When I arrived in 1982, the six most powerful men in China, the members of the Politburo's Standing Committee, were Deng Xiaoping, Hu Yaobang, Zhao Ziyang, Ye Jianying, Li Xiannian, and Chen Yun. Their offspring had diverse reputations. Ye Jianying's large family was widely regarded among my born-Red friends as a nest of privilege-seekers and expert *guanxi* manipulators who often skirted the edges of what society would tolerate even in the progeny of a revered leader. One of his sons, Ye Xuanping, now the governor of Guangdong Province, near Hong Kong, was counted as an example of probity, as if the family needed at least one major exception to prove the rule. Premier Zhao Ziyang's own reputation was never questioned, but his son, Zhao Jin, was a topic of endless fascination among gossips on the network. He had a reputation as a playboy among some young born-Red women, and he sometimes had business dealings that caused a buzz along the born-Red network. But he always managed to avoid outright unacceptability, though one company he dealt with in Hong Kong came under active investigation before I left. Chen Yun, though he was a frequent critic of Deng's policies, nevertheless was given the sensitive chairmanship of the party's internal watchdog agency, the Central Discipline and Inspection Commission, mainly because he was everyone's choice as the party's outstanding example of personal uprightness. Chen Yun has rubbed many people the wrong way over the years, but none of my born-Red friends had ever heard of any shady dealings in his family.

To many young people, the ultimate piece of the action now is a chance to live abroad, especially in the United States. At a 1987 press conference, He Dongchang, vice-chairman of the State Education Commission, estimated that some 30,000 young people had gone overseas to study since it had become possible to do so in the late 1970s. More than half had gone to the United States. This previously unimaginable privilege, like all the others, has had a compelling tendency to gravitate toward the top of the society, to the children and grandchildren of the top Beijing Communists and of the major provincial and city officials and party secretaries. One of the reasons I was able to have friends and acquaintances among young members of the born-Red generations was that so many wanted advice on how to apply for student visas to the United States, and help in preparing applications. They have no monopoly on study chances, but they patently do have advantages. Not the least of their advantages has been the tendency of various American officials to look more attentively at, and sometimes to invite or court, an application from someone they know to be well connected. Several times that I knew of, born-Red candidates who had been turned down when they first applied later obtained their visas after seeing to it that, on the second try, the identity of their influential parent was made known to the visa officer.

One friend was fond of telling about an early delegation that visited Ohio in the late 1970s, with a granddaughter of President Li Xiannian as head translator. A second translator with better English caught the eye of Governor Rhodes's staff and was offered a scholarship to Ohio State University. When she mentioned who the head translator was, the university also offered the president's granddaughter a scholarship. Neither of the two was permitted to accept those scholarships at that time, but President Li's granddaughter eventually found another chance and did study in America. I knew of several other cases in which American universities courted the children and grandchildren of top revolutionaries, with varying results.

Sometimes, the children of the very highest try to avoid publicity by taking assumed names while they are in the United States. Zhao Ziyang's son, Zhao Jin, for example, studied in Pennsylvania under the name Chen Xueliang, friends of his told me. The Communist party now and then clamps down on study in America by the progeny of the high ranking, sometimes on egalitarian grounds and sometimes citing fear of a developing "American clique" among younger members of leading families. But these rounds of new rules mostly affect the families of middle-ranking Communists, not the highest. By the time I left China, I had confirmed, mainly through talks with young friends in positions to know, that at least one son or daughter, or grandson or granddaughter, of each of the six top Communists on Deng Xiaoping's first Politburo Standing Committee—including family members of the highly reputable Chen Yun—had found a way to go to college in America.

On February 2, 1986, front pages and radio and television newscasts were dominated by accounts of an unprecedented event, the executions of three young men, all the sons of high-ranking Shanghai officials. The three had been convicted of gang-raping two women, raping or attempting to rape three others, and "committing adultery with or acting indecently toward" forty-two others between 1981 and 1984. The young men had used their fathers' rank to attract girls to parties with promises not only of excitement but of help in getting job transfers and foreign study opportunities. One of the young men was the son of a former second secretary of the Shanghai Communist party committee. His family was the highest-ranking Communist party family in three decades to be affected by such an exemplary execution.

The courts had been excuting thousands of criminals annually since 1983. Most of them were young men who had been involved in violent crimes or "crimes against the state," like embezzling. None had ever received so much official publicity. The way the Communist party–controlled papers and broadcasts drenched China with the news set the three Shanghai executions apart and identified them as a matter of high politics far more than a matter of criminal law. They were, in effect, a brutal form of official apology for how far the party had permitted its officials, and their sons and daughters, to use and abuse their positions. To make the apology explicit, the *People's Daily,* the country's leading newspaper and prime organ of the Communist party Central Committee, commented: "In our country, extraordinary citizens free from the binding of the law are not allowed to exist."

By the time of the execution announcement, the news media had been building up to it for months with reports on a campaign designed to clean up the party's image with the public. After years of intermittently decrying abuses by high-level party officials and their offspring in crisis terms, the party was telling the masses it was ready to act severely, to make public examples of the wrongdoers. The first news articles about this campaign brought forth among my born-Red friends and acquaintances a rash of reports speculating which households among the top leaders would be affected. These reports were remarkably detailed, and the details rarely varied from one telling to the next. Based on my previous experiences with reports on the born-Red network, I felt that the stories, though obviously second- or third-hand, were essentially authentic accounts of findings from internal Communist party investigations, some of them still in progress, and others completed and under review as to what action should be taken.

According to these reports, one Politburo member's son had been found out after taking more than half a million dollars worth of Chinese money from the government. Another Politburo member's son had accidentally been found, by workmen packing the family goods for a move from a big party-assigned house to a bigger one, to have two large sacks of currency. An investigation was said to have revealed that he had peddled his father's influence to a businessman in a western province. Several other stories touched on sons of other men high in the party, including other Central Committee members. Friends and acquaintances who told me these stories regarded them not as rumors but as facts. Some had known one or two of the Shanghai execution victims, and waited in horrified fascination to see who among their privileged friends or acquaintances would be next.

It was not to be. The Shanghai executions turned out to be, not the beginning of public and exemplary punishment for criminal sons and grandsons of the high-ranking, but the full extent of it. Instead of pressing on into the political quicksand of genuinely high-level wrongdoing, late in February the party offered up the Shanghai executions one last time as proof that even the powerful must answer to the law. It was the kind of final honk the party uses to announce that a job is finished. Then, as the weather broke, the campaign melted away like winter snow in spring sunshine. By summer, the newspaper space once given to that campaign was in use for a new form of proof of the party's sincerity in rooting out crime—an appeal to common criminals to turn themselves in and get amnesty or leniency.

"They think they can solve these things by hurting people," Ming Yueliang had said earlier, in 1983, as alleys in Beijing and other cities began to blossom with large white posters, each bearing an oversized red checkmark confirming the first waves of executions. "These are all young men who didn't have any jobs and only had very poor educations, and if they had had jobs I don't think they would have done such wrong things." After he had heard of the Shanghai executions in 1986, I asked if he had known any of the three. "Yes," he said, "I did know one of those boys, and everyone had heard about their sex parties. These were just the unlucky ones, the ones the party chose to make an example. The Communist party always finds it easier to be against sex. But don't ever believe that the same can happen to the really high people. Life inside the party is already full of vendettas that come from political struggles. If they made a public example of one Politburo member's son, well, maybe most are honest enough, but there are still too many who have this kind of problem, and he'd find a way to get even. There would be a whole new set of vendettas, and they could never end." If the campaign ever did reach the inner sanctums, the party had chosen not to publicize the example. The news media had never again mentioned exemplary punishments of comparably high-level party officials and their offspring by the time I left China.

Fang Xiuqing was fourteen years old in August 1966, when Mao Zedong's teen-aged Red Guards came to her family's home. They declared that her father, who had won a degree of fame in Mao's revolution and had risen to be a general in the People's Liberation Army and a party secretary in Shaanxi Province, was a class enemy and a traitor. She remembers little from that day, but she recalls that her father did not come home again for more than three years, that she rarely saw her mother for most of that time, that her two older brothers also soon disappeared, and that three other families soon moved in and occupied all but the two smallest rooms of their house. She and her eleven-year-old sister occupied one of the two tiny rooms, Xiuqing sleeping on the floor and the younger sister on the one bed the Red Guards had left them. The other room was crammed full of the family's belongings and was sealed. As winter set in, Xiuqing went to the locked room to get warm clothing for herself and her younger sister. "But some Red Guards found out, and they came and beat me and took our winter clothing away," she told me.

For three years, the two girls had only each other at home. Their father, they eventually learned, was in jail. Their mother and brothers had been ordered to the countryside to work on farms. "A friend of my mother's found out and secretly brought us warm clothing and simple things to eat," she said. "We lived mainly on sweet potatoes." Eventually, her brothers and then her mother came home. A man she had seen only a few times before came and took Xiuqing to a place she remembers only as a small, plain room with a few low, wooden stools. There, she saw her father for the first time in three years. "He was so thin and so pale, I cried when I saw him. But he held me and told me everything would soon be all right," she said. A few weeks later he came home. Within the year, his "case" was reinvestigated, and it turned out he was a loyal Communist after all.

In reality, the difference had been one of politics. He was jailed because he had a run-in with top followers of Lin Biao, the defense minister who was Mao's designated successor-to-be through most of the Cultural Revolution years. As Lin Biao's power began to slip, it became possible to let Xiuqing's father and thousands of other Cultural Revolution inmates out of jail. In the next few years, as Lin Biao's erstwhile radical allies among the Cultural Revolutionaries also began to slip, her father was given back his old job in the innermost councils of the provincial Communist party. With the job came the driver and the clanking, squeaking blue Shanghai-brand sedan that identified him on the street as a man of position. They got back their house, too, as soon as space could be found for the other families who had occupied it. One thing that was taken away while the Cultural Revolutionaries had the old guerrilla locked up could not be given back. He had lost his right arm, just below the shoulder, to the beatings of tormentors early in his confinement.

The details vary, but most of my born-Red friends and acquaintances have comparable stories of how the Cultural Revolution created large and chilling gaps in their privileged upbringing. Two never again saw their fathers, who had fought in Mao's real revolution but died in confinement at the hands of the young Maoist zealots who eagerly accepted the Great Helmsman's invitation to take a turn at playing revolutionist. Among most of my friends and acquaintances who were born into old revolutionary families, the vendettas of the Cultural Revolution have indelibly marked their attitudes toward the Communist party that their parents or grandparents helped bring to power in 1949. But it is not the only factor that has shaped their attitudes. For many, the experience of growing up amid the inner machinations of a ruling party in a one-party state has left its own mark, with or without the added trauma of an upheaval like the Cultural Revolution. The country abounds with examples of sons and grandsons of the old revolutionary families who have risen steadily within the Communist party, but very substantial numbers of the offspring of the old guerrilla families also shun the party with genuine dread, despite the privileged life it has brought them. "My father always wanted me to join the party," Fang Xiuqing said. "He said it was the only way to be sure of getting a good chance in life, because now the party is in power. But when he died, he knew that I would never join. It is the only time I ever deliberately chose to do something I knew would disappoint him. But I saw his life, the people he had to hurt even though they were loyal to him, and the people who had to do things that hurt him, and I can never imagine a life like that."

The senior editor's son, who had worked his way from business editor to Shenzhen businessman to business administration student, arrived at a similar conclusion from a different direction: "If I have to cut throats, I want to do it for profit, not for politics." Still others have preferred to retreat into art or music, rather than take up the chance they inherited to join the ruling party in a one-party state. Such conclusions, I was to learn, were not strictly limited to the younger members of the old revolutionary families. Dong Biwu was one of the larger-than-life figures from the guerrilla decades, a close associate of Mao's from the Long March and Yenan days. Fang Xiuqing was a friend of one of his sons. A few months after Dong Biwu died in 1975, the son told Xiuqing that the old man had called his boys to his bedroom to give them a final bit of advice. What the son quoted his father as saying, after a lifetime as a Communist party guerrilla and politician, sounded not greatly different from what other aging politicians, in other cultures, have sometimes said to their children. "Politics," the old revolutionary had warned, "is a dirty business."

7

Students
in the Streets

New Year's Day of 1987 was minutes from ending, but thousands of college students were still in formation, their footsteps muffled by a thin coating of snow that fell gently as they walked through the night, toward the city center from the university quarter northwest of Beijing. Their walk had taken shape spontaneously two hours earlier, when thousands had poured out of dormitories at Beijing University and erupted into the streets to protest police detention of student demonstrators at Tiananmen Square in the center of town on New Year's morning and afternoon. As they walked, the thin, fresh coating of powdery snow reflected the streetlights, brightening the scene as if nature had added stage lighting especially for this event. By the time midnight approached, the students had already swept through three police cordons, each time stopping first at a blockaded intersection to link arms ten abreast for maybe thirty or forty rows back, letting the rest of the column catch up to form tighter ranks. Their formation fixed, they advanced slowly and deliberately into the police lines, singing "The March of the Volunteers," the Chinese Communist party's national anthem, and "The Internationale," the song of most Marxist movements around the globe.

Just where they were going was still not clear, not to most of the

145

students and certainly not to any of the scores of foreign correspondents who had rushed into the snowy night to watch what had turned into one of the biggest spontaneous demonstrations in Beijing since the celebrations after Jiang Qing and her radical allies were jailed, ending the Cultural Revolution. I had linked up for the night with Patrice DeBeer, Beijing correspondent of the French newspaper *Le Monde*. "When we were in university, I marched to that song," Patrice reflected as another round of "The Internationale" began. "We were all proud young leftists. It never occurred to me in those days that it might become a song of counterrevolution." Patrice decided to make one more stab at asking where the students were headed. "Where are you going?" he asked the nearest student in standard northern Chinese. The student looked puzzled for an instant, then grinned as if delighted by his own cleverness. "I'm going to democracy," he said.

Student demonstrations, most of them stressing political themes like "democracy" and "freedom," had punctuated the late fall and early winter for two months, in about a dozen cities. They had reached their first crescendo twelve days earlier in Shanghai. Tens of thousands of student demonstrators had been joined by even bigger numbers of off-duty workers on a Sunday afternoon that capped three days of the most tumultuous street scenes Shanghai had witnessed since the Cultural Revolution. Demonstrations had come only slowly to Beijing, where the vast majority of students at Beijing University had held back and said they would not join in. Even on that New Year's Day, after more than a week of campus posters promising demonstrations at Tiananmen on New Year's morning, only a few hundred students tried to demonstrate. But tales of their being brusquely thrown into police jeeps, and the fact that they were still not back on campus by nightfall, seemed to provide what had previously been lacking in Beijing—a dramatic local grievance that could personalize issues that had previously seemed abstract. An urgency had come to the issue for the moment, but the student who said he was "going to democracy" reflected an air of spontaneity and holiday-making that still permeated much of the New Year's night demonstration in Beijing, as it had many of those in other cities.

More than a week would pass before we would learn that, by the time the student smiled and told Patrice he was on his way to democracy, the top national leadership of the Communist party had already met in a crisis session that did not reflect the holiday mood of the streets. The existence of that session was still a tightly guarded inner-party secret—and therefore, under the law, a state secret—as the students walked through the snow in Beijing. Many of the students had no more way than anyone else of knowing that their demonstrations had already provoked the crisis meeting, much less any way of knowing that the country's top Communists had agreed to do far more than merely crack down on the student demonstrations that had provided the occasion for the meeting. Two more weeks would pass before it would be made public that the aging Communist veterans, none present as young as the country's legal retirement age, had agreed to do no less than sack the head of their own party, Hu Yaobang. His offense had been to permit an atmosphere of free expression that had built up over several years to a level that made street demonstrations and deliberate defiance of the police thinkable, for an instant, in a country normally better known for the tightness of its social controls.

For years, these same old white heads who would sack Hu Yaobang had stood before official audiences, stiffly reading party-approved speeches that often included solemn reassurances that "the leadership of the Chinese Communist party" had created a unified land. As the official line had put it time and again: "In China, there is no problem of a gap between the old and the young." Now they were setting out on a crackdown that was to make palpable a truth almost everyone else in the society had noticed for at least three years: In China, generation gaps exist not merely between the wrinkled revolutionaries of the Long March and the unfurrowed faces of today's college campuses, but even between men of different ages and persuasions who all participated in the revolution. China's history in the twentieth century has been so tumultuous that great extremes of difference in experience can separate generations that are only a few years apart. And within any of these generations, there can exist further cleavages created by the turmoil of extraordinary events.

The Chinese Communist party was already nearly three decades old when it won power in 1949, a struggle long enough to give men of more than one generation claims to the political legitimacy conferred by participation in legendary Red Army feats. Hu Yaobang, for example, participated in the revolution but is about a decade younger than the octogenarian Leninists and Stalinists who were scattered throughout the party's upper councils until October 1987. He shares with those older men of the Long March an ability to lay down the party line in words that smart. As recently as March 1985, for example, he had appeared before Chinese journalists, who showed signs of itching for freer working conditions, and had reminded them at length that their job is to be "the mouthpiece of the party."[1] But he differs from the older men in that he is far less intimidated by the political fractiousness of the people, and certainly he is much less fearful of unorthodox ideas. In this respect, he sometimes seems to be a transitional figure, still dedicated to authority but prepared to contemplate some modest measure of the untidiness that free expression entails, willing to let the still-evolving Chinese version of Marxism stand a few risks, maybe even a few lumps, at the hands of other ideas.

———————

Under Hu Yaobang's stewardship of the party, expression had broadened steadily since late 1983, when the party had choked off in midstream its own drive against what Deng Xiaoping had labeled "Spiritual Pollution." That campaign was directed against pornography and instances of corruption specifically targeted by Deng and other old revolutionaries. But it had quickly run out of hand, as middle-level party functionaries used it as an excuse to wipe out a broad range of the economic reforms that Deng and his associates had struggled to introduce. After Hu Yaobang and other reform-minded top Communists had persuaded Deng to choke off the spiritual pollution crusade, voices began to be heard questioning party policy on a broad range of issues. By late 1984, publications of all kinds were witness to what may have been the broadest debate of women's issues in any Marxist country since Lenin's time. By January of 1986, scientists and social scientists were demanding, and seemed on the verge of getting, legal protection against Communist party interference in their research.

As this debate broadened into the fall of 1986, a few voices, including some rather respectably placed ones, began to be heard suggesting that Marxism, if its adherents really believed in it, ought to be sturdy enough to withstand challenges on its own turf by other systems of thought. A few voices even suggested that China might conceivably be governable by some system other than "the People's Democratic Dictatorship." Aging hard-line Leninists invoke this phrase from the official litany as if deaf to how mischievously their own Orwellian Newspeak mocks the sterility of their political ideas.

Some of the questioning voices, most prominently that of Fang Lizhi, an internationally known astrophysicist and vice-president of the national University of Science and Technology in Hefei, have come from within the middle levels of the Communist party. Fang would later be expelled from the party and reassigned to the Beijing Observatory, where he would have less contact with students. But he has come to represent a third generation, people who have come to maturity after the Communist party had won power. Most of them are not born Red, and none of them has any claim to Long March legitimacy. They have staked their futures on ability and education, and their adult lives have included scant or no experience of the Old China or of the revolutionary struggle. As men and women in the prime of life, some of them have been sufficiently bloodied in the Cultural Revolution that the last thing they are afraid of is an idea. Some people I met in this generation have seemed far more eager to get on with a quest for the modern world than to protect an orthodoxy they had not helped to import from the Soviet Union.

But these are only one face of their own generation. A broader face is the long ranks of the tens of thousands of the educated who grew comfortably into the Soviet system that was installed in the early 1950s. They graduated from Soviet-style universities and language and technical institutes before Mao began the systematic demolition of a still-fledgling higher education system as a central goal of the Cultural Revolution. Thousands of these people, now in the productive primes of their lives, went to the Soviet Union to study at Moscow's premier institutes, or studied in China under Russian professors, or learned their jobs under the thousands of Soviet advisers in the 1950s and early 1960s. Tens of thousands more graduated from the Soviet-style institutes built with Russian help in Stalin's and Khrushchev's time. Most of these, too, suffered in the Cultural Revolution. But for many educated people who are today in the prime of life, the lesson taught by the tumult of the Red Guard years is not the importance of the individual or the value of an idea. Rather, it is the imperative of order above all else. As the debate of the mid-1980s broadened, I came to feel that, at least among the educated, no generation is more deeply divided than these men and women in the prime of life, a handful of them stripped of their political fears by having survived the Cultural Revolution, but the majority comfortable within an essentially undemanding system, and little inclined to take political risks.

Probably no generation of Chinese has been more written about by foreigners than those who reached their middle and late thirties during my years in Beijing. Whether born Red into one of the founding families or simply born Chinese, they were born just as or just after the Communist party came to power. They are people who know pre-1949 society mainly as a topic of endless harangues at the interminable political meetings that still punctuate the lives of many city folk. In most of their lives, political consciousness began in the teen years, when Chairman Mao stood atop the Gate of Heavenly Peace and called on them to join the Cultural Revolution. Many to this day get stars in their eyes when they recall the heady sense that the summons was direct and personal. They were to take to the streets, defend the chairman from his enemies, "demolish the headquarters of the Capitalist Roaders" and "make revolution." Today, many of these people, former Red Guards and the victims of Red Guards alike, feel a profound sense of betrayal. Many, those who wore Red Guard armbands and those to whom the same armbands became an emblem of terror, routinely speak of themselves as "victims of the Cultural Revolution." In important ways, this self-description fits them even more aptly than it does the older teachers, writers, and Communists whom the Red Guards persecuted. As I left China, some twenty years after the white heat of the Cultural Revolution, the Communist party press still struggled with scant effect to persuade these people in their thirties that they are not members of a lost generation.

"We were excited. We had been taught that the people who had made our revolution were heroes, and now we were to have our

chance at 'making revolution.' Our hero and our country needed us,"
Lin Sanjin, a friend whom I frequently saw both in China and in
America, told me before he left to start college at age thirty-three at an
American university. "We had no idea what Mao was really doing.
But he told us to destroy the party, and we destroyed the party. He
told us to close our schools, and we closed all the universities and high
schools in Fuzhou and beat the principals and kicked the teachers. He
told us to struggle against rightists, and we dragged rightists out of
their houses and spit on them and made them wear signboards and
dunce caps and chased them through the streets. How did we know
who were rightists? Someone from the 'revolutionary headquarters'
told us. Some of these rightists were our neighbors; some were friends
of our parents. Maybe their crime was that they were intellectuals,
people who had graduated from high school or university, or people
who didn't join The Left soon enough. Maybe their fathers or uncles
or grandfathers had been businessmen or landlords before 1949.
Sometimes they were parents of Red Guards, and then their sons or
daughters had to make 'clear class stands,' which meant getting up in
front of the audience and kicking and cursing their own father or
mother harder than anyone else was doing. Can you understand what
that meant in a society where respect for your elders, especially your
own parents, is the first virtue?

"Then we were told our job was completed, that the army would
handle the rest of the revolution. And then I began to wonder when
my school would open again, whether I'd ever go to college, whether
I had a future." Lin Sanjin was twenty-one by the time his high school
reopened, so he never got past his sophomore year, but he was given
a diploma anyway. After several unsuccessful attempts to get into an
American university, he decided to fake a high school record and have
a friend take the Test on English as a Foreign Language. He planned
to work illegally in the States, because he had no scholarship and his
family could only put together enough cash to support him for a few
weeks. "That's a lesson I had to learn in the Cultural Revolution,
getting by the best way I could," he said.

The closing of universities and institutes in 1966, including medical
schools, foreclosed higher education for all but a scant handful from
this generation. When they were permitted to reopen in 1972, insti-

tutions of higher education were in an atrophied state from which some had not recovered fully by the the time I left China, twenty-one years after the Cultural Revolutionaries had closed them. In October 1972, on my first trip to China, I had visited the Sun Yat-sen Medical College in Guangzhou, the provincial capital just north of Hong Kong, where I was chief of *The Baltimore Sun*'s bureau from 1970 to 1973. On that 1972 visit, I had seen a campus eerily lacking the one commodity that defines most colleges—students. Although my visit was during daylight hours of a weekday, and although my official handlers were assigned to see that I got the best possible impression, in several hours on campus I never saw a class in session and saw only two groups of students, both doing calisthenics in unison near a sidewalk. My official greeting was by the nine pairs of baggy blue pants, nine blue Mao jackets, and nine red plastic Mao badges of the school's administration, then called its "revolutionary committee." None of these rote figures seemed ready to welcome the foreigner one bit less dourly than the next, and I began to wonder whether any of them spoke English, a language usually found in abundance among medical faculties. Only by deliberately cracking a feeble pun, and watching to see who snickered or groaned out of turn before the translation, did I finally discover that indeed there were at least two English speakers. I was told the school would start with a few hundred high school or junior high graduates. Their two or three years of schooling would include a substantial portion of "politics" and a big chunk of factory and field work, to keep them in touch with the masses they would serve. Then they would be doctors, qualified to treat patients or to teach the next generation of medical students.

I went back to Sun Yat-sen Medical College in Guangzhou in 1985 to see what had changed. Classes seemed to be in normal session, and students were visible strolling and chatting everywhere on the campus. I was greeted by the school's president and two faculty members, each attired in necktie, three-piece suit, and black wool topcoat. The president greeted me in English, and my translator had to help only once or twice in an interview that lasted nearly an hour. But when it came time to discuss the school's rehabilitation, what impressed me was how much work remained even then, just to get back to where the school had been before the Cultural Revolution had closed it nineteen years earlier. The president told me that in the spring of 1986—fully twenty academic years after the Red Guards had arrived to close it and drive most of the faculty off into the countryside—the college would for the first time graduate a class that had completed the full six-year, Soviet-style course that had prevailed before the Cultural Revolution. Then three more years would pass before the school could graduate a six-year class with as many students as it had graduated annually before the Cultural Revolution.

———

What was true at Sun Yat-sen Medical College was true in varying degrees at many of the dozens of Chinese campuses I visited. It often seemed that the job of putting campuses back together after the trauma of the Cultural Revolution was proceeding more slowly than had the original job of building them between 1949 and 1966. Furthermore, for more than a decade new professors had not been trained or had been trained in stunted, abbreviated programs often distorted by the bizarre political content of the Cultural Revolution. For these reasons, long after the event, today's college-aged people continued to be victims of the Cultural Revolution. But members of today's college-aged generation rarely speak of themselves as victims of those tumultuous years. That manmade cataclysm was somebody else's experience, something that came and went while today's newly adult Chinese were not yet old enough to have political ideas.

Wu Qi, a professor of automation at Qinghua University, had a daughter in college during most of my years in China. He once described to me how his daughter's generation appears from his perspective. Most Chinese who speak of a generation gap, he said, are talking either about differences between the pre-1949 generation and people who grew up after the Communists won power, or else about differences between older folk and the Cultural Revolution generation. But for Professor Wu and many other parents I met, an altogether new generation gap is developing out of the unprecedented experiences of teen-agers who are now reaching college age. These young people were perhaps ten years old in 1978, when Deng Xiaoping began to consolidate his position as first among unequals in the post-Mao Politburo. Deng's policy, formally made the Party Line at the Communist Party Congress in 1982, was that the country's primary task for the foreseeable future was not revolution, as Mao had preached, but economic development.

Deng Xiaoping's ability to sustain such a drastic change of direction at the political center has, for about a decade now, dramatically changed the experience of coming of age. "It is not that my daughter never experienced Old China, with its warlords and landlords and Japanese overlords and constant fighting and catastrophes," Professor Wu explained. "It is not even that she was too young to understand much during the Cultural Revolution. It is that, from the time she was old enough to begin to understand such things, she has never known anything but political stability, peace and steadily increasing prosperity." No other generation of Chinese alive today has passed its entire adolescence amid nothing but political stability, peace and steadily increasing prosperity.

People about the age of Professor Wu's daughter are a critically important generation. They are part of a major population bulge created by a baby boom just before the birth-control policy became much more strict, about a decade ago. Substantially more than half of the population is under thirty and that is expected to remain true well into the 1990s. People like Professor Wu's daughter thus represent a large and growing proportion of the population. The immense gap between their experience of life and that of even, for example, the generation of new leaders in their late fifties and early sixties now working under Zhao Ziyang will be one of the givens of society and politics for decades to come.

"For people my daughter's age," Professor Wu commented, "The Communist party is, not the people who drove away the old order, but the people who seem always to have been in charge." Professor Wu stopped tactfully short of spelling out the obvious implication— that the Communist party has now been in power long enough that members of the biggest generation in the country's history think of it, not in terms of contrast with the old order it destroyed, but in terms of what it seemed to be as they grew up. Like most governments, it tends to get more blame for what has not been done than credit for any progress. Given the immensity of what the Communist party now calls Mao's "mistakes," even the most objective observer might reasonably argue that what has not been done since 1949 exceeds what has been. Add to this the impatience of a generation that is rapidly discovering what the rest of the world was doing with those same decades, and it is not hard to understand why the glories of making proletarian revolution are no longer salable among adolescents and young adults.

By early 1986, when Professor Wu and I discussed the generations during the last of three times we met on the campus at Qinghua, the Deng Xiaoping years could be counted as no more than nine years old by the most inclusive reckoning. But Deng's time at the top had already become the longest period China had seen in more than a century that could fit the description Wu Qi gave of his daughter's growing-up years. More than any since perhaps the early 1920s, today's college-aged generation, especially in the cities but increasingly in large areas of the countryside, is a generation of rising expectations. People coming of age today have already begun to take boom boxes, color televisions and refrigerators for granted. Few that I met, either among my private friends or among people I interviewed in more structured settings, are willing to marry before they are sure these basics, and usually a set of modern furniture, are secured. Many have begun to experiment with cameras, motorbikes and ten-speed bicycles. Many older or middle-aged people, and some in the Cultural Revolution generation, often volunteered some degree of concern that the pace of change under Deng Xiaoping may be faster than the society can tolerate or digest. But among my acquaintances in the generation now of college age, I had to suggest that idea myself. The answer was uniformly a gasp or a shake of the head and a quick and emphatic, "No—not fast enough, not fast enough."

Most people I met in this emerging generation are essentially mystified, and many are impatient and annoyed, when the older heads in the Communist party stand up at political meetings to start in on the litany of evils of the Old China. "We are supposed to be grateful to the Communist party for doing away with those things," Wang Yuping, a newly graduated accountant for a government ministry in Beijing, told me early in 1987. "But everybody knows that was almost forty years ago, and all the good they can claim to have done was thirty years or more ago, and now they say everything the party did under Chairman Mao was a mistake. When they call a political meeting at our ministry, the women knit and the men put economics or engineering books inside their political book covers and study something they can use." I saw Wang Yuping once or twice a month for several years. Two years earlier, when he was still a student in Beijing, he had told me he was considering joining the Communist party. "It's still the surest way to get ahead," he had said then. I asked in the spring of 1987 if he still thought about joining. "Nobody I know really thinks the party matters much any more," he said. "I'd rather perfect my English and try to get a job with a foreign company. I was lucky to get assigned to this ministry, because it has lots of business with foreign companies. Once I know the ministry well and have better English, I think I can find a good job with a foreign company, or maybe with a Chinese company in Hong Kong or overseas."

If any single phrase could describe my impression of this generation of Chinese, it would be "a piece of the action." A decade of concentration on the economy, instead of on revolution, had dramatically multiplied the available action by the time I left Beijing. Most of the newest and best opportunities are in the growing and rapidly opening economy, which means they are outside the Communist party. For the first time since 1949, the party has tolerated major nonparty avenues to success and even modest degrees of economic power. Government jobs, and work in state factories, are still appealing for the security they offer. But the party itself has serious and rapidly increasing trouble recruiting the people it wants. Not only potential new recruits to the party, but Communists of all ages, often after decades of working their way into political jobs of some modest consequence, are now looking about and discovering that there is often more to hope for outside the party than in it. The party's press has been awash for more than four years in articles decrying the tendency of middle-level party officials to use their positions to set themselves up in business, or to favor a relative or friend who has gone into business. The party has attempted to set forth rules and regulations to restrict the private business interests of its members, and especially of its officials, but in some cases this has simply tempted some people to do something previously unimagined. I never saw any published figures on the subject, but at least a few people—numbers large enough that the party has felt a need to warn against the problem publicly—have given up half a lifetime in the party and have resigned in order to pursue better chances in the economy.

The tendency of Communist party members to husband private interests is not unknown in Leninist societies and is a well documented fact of Soviet, East European, Cuban, and Vietnamese life. What is different today in China is an atmosphere in which opportunity is often much greater outside the ruling party than inside. This reversal of the usual Leninist order of things is in turn part of a new milieu in which many of the older moorings of life, ideological as well as practical, seem to have come loose. The ancient Confucian certainties, a system of thought that prescribed how to behave in most of life's major passages, were officially abandoned when the Communist party came to power in 1949. In their place was installed a Stalinist-Leninist thought system, to which Mao steadily applied increasing doses of his own idiosyncratic variant of Marxism. The orthodoxy of the Maoist decades sought to replace the hierarchic thought system of Confucianism, in which everyone had a place and knew whom to honor and whom to despise, with an iconoclastic ethic based in one of the most extreme egalitarian ideals ever imposed upon a large society. But for most people I talked with in five years in China, by the time the Cultural Revolution ended, what it had proved was just how painfully and ludicrously futile their lives could be made by Mao's pursuit of his social ideas. Then Mao died. The communes he had built were officially dismantled, and Chinese were told that most of their sacrifices in his three decades in power had merely helped him carry out "serious mistakes."

Mao's successors have been for the most part preoccupied with trying to make the government, the party and the economy function. That leaves scant time for serious application to replacing the certainties of thought and ethics that have been shattered by the revolution and Mao's Cultural Revolution. Their few forays into philosophy have been less than equal to the rapidly increasing complexity their economic and political programs are introducing into what had been an essentially simple, if impoverished, society. In some ways, the most convincing philosophical statement they have produced is one Deng

Xiaoping has made several times: "Our goal is to have relative prosperity for the Chinese people. Just to extricate one-fifth of the human race from poverty would be a major achievement."[2] That is an eloquently simple statement of purpose, but it is not a system of ethics, much less an all-embracing, religionlike thought system, capable of explaining everything from heaven to earth, like the ones Chinese have been used to having under Confucianism and Maoism.

I once spent much of an hour in my apartment in Beijing arguing with Michel Oksenberg, a China scholar at The University of Michigan and the friend who later persuaded me to attempt these pages, over whether China needs such a system of thought. Mike said, in essence, yes, that the country does not yet have a national economy or a network of institutions capable of knitting together its many subcultures, so it needs the unifying force of a single, all-embracing ideology. I argued that ideologies were not part of the solution but part of the problem, and that if China truly wants the modern world (and only the Chinese themselves can answer that question) then it would have to ease away from its tradition of relying on thought systems that take on the force of a state religion. But there is no doubt that Mike's point applies today and that, at least for now, many people of all ages feel morally very much at sea in these years of change.

That feeling was palpable everywhere I went, and it was most pervasive among those college-aged students and workers who have experienced none of the earlier tumults and traumas that seemed for so long to be part of the very definition of growing up Chinese. Older generations are at least bound together by vivid common memories of Japanese overlords, or of Red Guard street battles. But among the newly adult, the casting about for something to cling to, something to give a sense of being special or being part of something bigger, is visible everywhere. People now approaching or newly arrived at adulthood are increasingly money-oriented, determined to have life's material "goodies," eager to learn foreign ways like dancing and skirts and long hair. Even their brothers and sisters, only a few years older, express surprise at how young they begin to experiment with sex. Several of my friends estimated that perhaps as many as half of the urban young people in this age group now have had at least one sex partner by the time they are past twenty. Others seek meaning in religion. In the dozen or so church services I attended, I was impressed by steadily growing numbers of young adults, especially in Protestant congregations.

My own sense was that, among these younger people, the urge to acquire music tapes and electrical appliances, the desire to learn English in order to get a better job, the passion to chase money, the vogue to experiment with sex, and the impulse to explore Christianity and Buddhism all seemed to spring from a single source. The best description I can give of that source is a search for identity or a sense of place or belonging. These are young people coming of age in a society that has rejected both its old certainties and its new, and has replaced them mainly with a drive for national prosperity. The new party line under which they grow up holds that the individual's best contribution to the national goal is to ensure his own prosperity.

This atmosphere of rising expectations amid loose moorings extends beyond the economy and well into the political attitudes of many young adults. The party itself has done much to contribute to rising political expectations. Most top-level Communists have shown awareness, albeit in varying degrees, of the extent to which the existing jerry-built, half-Stalinist, half-Maoist political structure, and especially the existing form of the Communist party, has come to hold back development now that the strategy is changing in the direction of a more open economy. Deng Xiaoping, Zhao Ziyang, and Hu Yaobang talked for more than three years of the need to reshape the party, and they made a few steps toward actually doing so at a national Communist Party Conference in 1985. Two years later, in October 1987, Deng forced the retirement of the last few orthodox Leninists from the top councils of the party, and he himself joined them in giving up all but one of his top posts—head of the military.

Deng Xiaoping and his reformist allies spoke of the need for political and governmental reform to bring the political structure into line with the party's plans for the economy and to reduce the party's weight as a drag on the economy. Such talk seemed to open the way to debate of fundamental political issues, precisely at the time Hu Yaobang was allowing a rapid broadening of expression in many fields. Some members of the young adult generation, vaguely aware of the past role of students in prodding their elders to change, sensing that the land was passing through what could prove to be formative times, and themselves feeling that change was not nearly fast enough, seemed by 1985 to be casting about for ways to press their elders for speed. On the day the Communist Party Conference opened in the fall of 1985, students in several major cities, including Beijing and Shanghai, the symbolic centers of past student movements, attempted demonstrations. They adopted a politically safe theme, opposition to Japan, a topic on which Chinese of many generations can agree, albeit for differing reasons.

Many foreign diplomats and journalists have suspected ever since that that day's demonstrations were too well orchestrated in too many places to have been purely student operations. China does, in fact, have a long history of attempts by leaders to use students in their factional disputes. The Red Guards and the Cultural Revolution were, in a sense, the ultimate case in point, the Great Helmsman's attempt to use the country's youth to overwhelm rivals within the party who had banded together to block his most radical dreams of collectivization. But a suspicion is a long way from a fact, and the subject seemed unlikely to produce a story worth the concentration that would have been required to get to the bottom of it. I left without ever feeling that I had heard a satisfying answer either way as to whether the 1985 student demonstrations sprang from the minds of the students, or from the needs of a faction within the party.

But even if the 1985 student demonstrations were inspired from higher up, they still were in some sense part of a series of events across the country that suggested increasing willingness by the young to take to the streets. Through 1984 and 1985, soccer games produced a series of outbursts, most notably in Beijing when the Chinese national team lost to tiny Hong Kong and was thereby bumped out of the Asian Cup tournament. The wrath of the fans first turned toward their own team and coach, for losing. But when police finally escorted the players to safety under the stands of Beijing's big Workers' Stadium, the fans spilled out onto the streets and began to rock buses and to surround foreigners' cars. Lewis Theiler, a UPI photographer who tried to take pictures, was drenched in spit, two cars were overturned, and the handful of policemen who had been on hand to direct traffic disappeared.

A few months later, I was in Nanjing and heard a commotion outside my hotel. I went down to the street to find thousands of young men surging through the bicycle lanes to protest an official's call at a soccer game. Local and foreign friends who lived in other cities reported similar outbursts among soccer fans, most of them young workers, in half a dozen places. In the late summer of 1985, Beijing bus drivers got into the act. They had long been promised pay raises to help cope with prices that were rising as more and more staples went off the price control system, but the pay increases were repeatedly delayed. One afternoon, the rush-hour crowds at most major bus stops on Chang An Boulevard, the main street of downtown Beijing, swelled out into the streets, severely disrupting rush-hour traffic. The drivers on several prime routes had gone on strike for the day. Chinese friends later told me that some of the younger drivers had taken the extraordinary step of driving their buses to deliver their protest at a gate of Zhongnanhai, the walled Communist party headquarters compound next door to the Forbidden City.

For the most part, the Communist party leadership under Hu Yaobang adopted a strategy of conciliation toward these and other demonstrators during 1984, 1985, and most of 1986. It was a strategy that seemed to be paying off in peace, especially on the campuses, throughout the spring semester of the 1985–86 school year. But by late November of 1986, students were demonstrating again in some cities. The first demonstrations we heard about in Beijing were in Hefei, the capital of Anhui Province and seat of the prestigious national University of Science and Technology. By mid-December, demonstrating seemed to be on the verge of contagion, with perhaps half a dozen cities known to have had street protests of varying sizes and durations. Most of my colleagues and I in Beijing either had written or were preparing pieces noting that student demonstrations were again in the wind, and that this time the recurring themes were "democracy" and "freedom," rather than the safer anti-Japanese themes of a year earlier. But none of us was prepared for what was about to happen.

The big story began unremarkably on Thursday afternoon of the week before Christmas 1986, with a few hundred students from

Shanghai's Tongji University in the streets. They could not have been unaware of the demonstrations of the preceding weeks in other cities, but their immediate concern was for schoolmates who they said had been manhandled by police during a pop music concert a few days before. Students said an American singing act, Jan and Dean, had, as part of its routine, invited audience participation. But the police apparently felt some of the students went too far.

Shanghai's reformist mayor, Jiang Zemin, went to Tongji that Thursday night, apparently to pursue the party's policy of dealing with demonstrations by conciliation and persuasion. Students said later that his tone had been conciliatory, but that many students nevertheless ended the evening with a feeling that their right to demonstrate had been challenged. On Friday afternoon, the number of students swelled into the thousands and the demonstrators reached the Shanghai Bund, the waterfront row of New York–style buildings left over from the freebooting decades of foreign domination of Shanghai before the Communist rise to power in 1949. Additional universities were represented, and the tone switched from one mainly emphasizing the concert grievance to one in which placards and slogans for "democracy" and "freedom" began to dominate the scene. Sensing that their numbers were still swelling and that the authorities were not sure just what to do, many students determined to carry their demonstrations into the weekend. A Chinese friend I talked with on the telephone from Beijing that Friday night described a scene in which hundreds of policemen had cordoned off several blocks of the Bund. Thousands of students milled about behind the police lines and seemed to be bedding down for the night.

The change of venue from little-known provincial cities to Shanghai, which is, with Beijing, one of the two Chinese city names Americans are most likely to recognize, was sure to change the impact of this story on American readers. And what my friend described on the Bund was already a scene unlike anything since the Democracy Wall months in Beijing, as Deng Xiaoping consolidated his power. I talked soon afterward with Dan Southerland, a friend from my Vietnam and Hong Kong days of eighteen years earlier who now lived across the hall as *The Washington Post* Beijing correspondent. We agreed to join forces on the Shanghai story. Dan would go to Shanghai as soon as he could on Saturday, and I would stay in Beijing to handle official reactions and keep track of the newspapers and the Xinhua News Agency wire, all of which was available earlier and more easily in Beijing than in Shanghai.

The events Dan and other correspondents saw in Shanghai in the next two days put China onto front pages and evening TV newscasts as it had not been since late 1980, during the trial of Mao's widow, Jiang Qing. On Saturday, students from more of Shanghai's universities joined in the demonstration, swelling the numbers well over 10,000 by Dan's estimate. On Sunday, the demonstrators included not only students but also off-duty workers and Sunday shoppers, as many young people from the normal throngs of day-off shoppers joined in the marching, chanting, singing, and placard-carrying. The crowd basically controlled not only the Bund area but the main city square several miles away. Dan estimated that some 50,000 people filled the square, and police repeatedly failed in attempts to limit entry to the square by linking arms and forming cordons with iron railings. Dan estimated that at least 20,000 more demonstrated in the Bund area.

That weekend saw an abrupt reversal in the Communist party's approach to student demonstrators. On Saturday, Xinhua, the official news agency, carried an interview in which an unidentified but obviously high-ranking education official continued with the benign style of the preceding two or three years. Less than twenty four hours later, even as the demonstrations were swelling to their peak in Shanghai's streets, the agency published an article that quoted a Shanghai city government spokesman as denouncing the student demonstrators for a long list of illegal acts. The allegations including beating thirty-one policemen, breaking into the city council offices, and "releasing leaflets," which is prohibited in a country where publishing is permitted only under licenses supervised by the Communist party. That bill of particulars would have been more than enough to justify, in the terms usually applied by the Chinese Communist party, the use of force to put down the demonstrations. But as it happened, force was not needed. Feeling that I had already seen the most dramatic likely turn in the official propaganda line, I wanted to look at the streets in Shanghai and went there Monday. But the students had run out of gas with their huge success on Sunday and needed rest after four days of virtually nonstop organizing and demonstrating. There were knots of excited people at the two main scenes of the big demonstrations, but by Monday the young workers were back at their offices and factories, the authorities were getting their bearings, and the police were taking advantage of the students' exhaustion to reclaim control of the square and the Bund.

A day in Shanghai talking with students left me with one impression that did not fade during the coming weeks, namely, that while the students use words like "democracy" and "freedom," it is extremely hard to know what content those words have in their minds. These are people who show all the results of having grown up in a Leninist society in which the schools, like the media, are part of a political indoctrination system. While it was clear that the indoctrination had failed to win real loyalty to the system, it was equally clear that it had kept these students from gaining a useful knowledge of any other system. The system no longer kept these students from trying on printed T-shirts, faded jeans, and down jackets, but they were still a long way from knowing much of life outside China beyond these superficialities. Talks during that day and others to come suggested that to many of them, banners they raised demanding "freedom of the press," for example, basically meant that newspapers should give less biased treatment to the students' own demonstrations. As to what "democracy" might consist of, there was no discernible shape to their ideas. Fundamentals like contested elections, alternative political parties, or secret ballots were not part of their conceptual vocabulary. They seemed to know that they wanted more scope to express themselves and more access to the system in some form, and it was clear that they were not buying much of what the Communist party was selling. But specifically what they wanted was another question. When the scene of demonstrations shifted to Beijing, I continued to ask questions along these lines, and I continued to have a sense that the fundamentals were absent.

The Shanghai demonstrations were essentially over, and I went back to Beijing Tuesday. I got back just in time to see the beginnings of yet another change of venue. For the next two weeks, the skirmishing between the generations would be mainly in the national capital, where the country's most prized demonstration targets are located.

Students at Beijing's most famous universities had been generally quiescent as their fellows elsewhere spilled into the streets in late November and most of December. Most of the students my colleagues and I had seen at Beijing University, the city's premier arts and sciences campus, and at Qinghua University, the capital's best-known engineering and scientific school, had said they did not expect to join in any street demonstrations, though posters and the occasional rally had begun to become part of campus life during those weeks. For decades, the prestige and activism of those two schools have made them almost the definers of student demonstrations in Beijing. Beijing University, in particular, was the one students from other colleges in the capital were likely to look to. If Beijing University joined in, there had been a real demonstration; if not, there had not.

As the Shanghai demonstrations lost steam, posters at Qinghua called for a mass meeting for the night I got back to Beijing, December 23, to discuss the Shanghai rallies. They invited university officials to meet with them at the main auditorium that evening. Instead, the students later said, the administration unexpectedly announced that a movie would be shown in the same auditorium at the same time. That was a blunder that brought student demonstrators into the streets of Beijing for the first of what would be several times. With the movie scheduled for the auditorium, some 4,000 or 5,000 students—angry about press coverage of the Shanghai demonstrations but wanting to talk with the campus administrators, not to demonstrate—instead found themselves milling about in the cold with no place to meet. Voices began to be raised for street demonstrations. Student association leaders who opposed the idea found that more than 1,000 of the students ignored their official leaders and followed the demonstrators out through the gates. The first destination was Beijing University, one of a series of attempts students from other campuses would make to goad students at Beijing University into joining the action. After walking the mile and a half from Qinghua to Beijing University, the students talked their way inside the gates and gained a few hundred more followers. The students walked into the night in the general direction of downtown Beijing, but they lacked organization and leadership. Eyewitnesses later reported that their numbers dwindled as they walked. About two hours beyond Beijing University, they were down to a few hundred as they reached a police roadblock at the northwestern edge of Beijing proper. The police, apparently recognizing the fading nature of the protest, avoided confrontation and let the students cross White Stone Bridge, where the roadblock had been set up. But once past the police, the remaining student demonstrators seemed to run out of gas and headed back to their campuses.

By Christmas, with demonstrators all but out of sight in Shanghai and demonstrations in other cities failing to gain much attention, a few students at Beijing University were beginning to urge their schoolmates to take the lead in keeping the action alive. Posters and leaflets began to appear on the campus calling for some unspecified kind of demonstration at Tiananmen Square, the vast Chinese version of Moscow's Red Square, early on New Year's Day. In visits to Beijing University, my colleagues and I found posters, occasional rallies and a certain level of excitement, but none of the electricity that would have suggested an ability to pull off a major demonstration. Most students still seemed to show little or no interest in joining any challege to the authorities.

But the change of venue to Beijing, and the call for demonstrations at a place as symbolic as Tiananmen Square, where Mao's preserved and refrigerated corpse lies on permanent display in a mausoleum hastily thrown up as a Chinese counterpart to Lenin's in Red Square, seemed to throw the Communist party Old Guard into high gear. To foreign visitors and to most Chinese tourists as well, Tiananmen is a place to experience the grandeur of the imperial past. It is the entrance to the splendors of the Forbidden City, where the Ming and Qing emperors ruled the country for four centuries. The Gate of Heavenly Peace, at the head of the square, is where Mao stood on October 1, 1949, to declare the birth of the People's Republic: "Today, the Chinese people have stood up."

But to the men who headed the Communist party in the winter of 1986–87, history in Tiananmen Square was fresher. At the center of the square stands the Monument to the People's Martyrs, where demonstrators massed in rallies that made clear the depth of public disgust with the Cultural Revolution as Mao was dying. It soon became clear that any attempt to carry calls for "democracy" and "freedom" all the way to this symbolic beige obelisk would meet massive official resistance. Older and more orthodox Marxists who had retired from the propaganda apparatus suddenly began to appear in public and to make what seemed to be definitive pronouncements, including vivid denunciations of student demonstrators. The *People's Daily* challenged the students in terms rarely used since Deng Xiaoping had replaced Cultural Revolution rhetoric with political compromise and modernization. The paper admonished the students not to fall into "opposition to the people,"[3] the direst warning known to the liturgy of Leninism. Although education officials in charge of dealing with the students sought to sustain the conciliatory approach they had maintained for more than a year, the Communist party propaganda organs, clearly back in the hands of the orthodox older heads in the Politburo, promoted an atmosphere of high crisis. On December 29, the Beijing *Daily News* spoke of meddling in student affairs by Taiwan agents, and of "secret and conspiratorial schemes" by "hostile elements against the socialist system." Taking implicit aim at the Voice of America, which had reported extensively on the demonstrations as had other Western news media, the paper accused "a foreign radio station broadcasting in Chinese" of helping to spread word of the plans for a New Year's Day demonstration.

By New Year's Day, most of the English-speaking correspondents in Beijing were developing the practice of working together much as correspondents do in newsier places. Particularly on this day, which was to prove long, active and at some points unpredictable or confusing, we frequently pooled information. The following account of this Friday and of the extraordinary night that followed is, accordingly, in significant measure the product of that pooling. For some parts of it, especially for my picture of some of the midday events around Tiananmen Square, I am more indebted to my colleagues' observations than to my own.

The prospects of major demonstrations in Beijing seemed slight, but by early New Year's Day there was no room to doubt that the Communist party was taking the few posters and leaflets at Beijing University very seriously. Having seen their Shanghai comrades caught off guard as the numbers of demonstrators grew exponentially for four straight days, Beijing's Communist party leadership had served notice early in the week by having the municipal government announce an ordinance banning public demonstrations at places like Tiananmen and requiring permits to demonstrate anywhere else—effectively also a ban, given the political atmosphere in the capital after Shanghai demonstrations got out of hand.

The Beijing municipal government's tangible preparations began in earnest well before dawn of New Year's Day. A small fleet of Beijing's ubiquitous blue-and-white street-watering trucks appeared in the center of town well after midnight and systematically sprinkled every inch of Tiananmen Square, an area big enough to contain thirty American football fields, including end zones. In the chill of Beijing's below-freezing January weather, the water trucks succeeded in making a vast and treacherous ice rink of a public space that is normally swept meticulously clean every time a few snowflakes fall. In the morning, I walked through the streets east of the square and southwest of the municipal government complex, a usual staging area for Beijing police whenever action is likely in the center of town. I saw several police squadrons come out from behind steel gates of official compounds and form ranks in the streets. Dozens of police buses, ranks of red-white-and-blue police jeeps, fire trucks, and water cannons, all were parked in numbers exceeding anything I had seen in that area in four years in Beijing.

I arrived at Tiananmen about 8 A.M., just in time to see some of the thousands of policemen at the scene begin to make rectangular formations and to clear spectators out of all but a few hundred square yards of the north end of the square. Busloads of children were arriving, to join in government-organized New Year's Day programs that would occupy the center of the square for part of the hours when the demonstrators were likely to make their moves. Ranks of policemen in some of the inner locations in the square were reinforced by school-children where police lines were thin.

Some of the campus posters had called for demonstrations at 9 A.M., but promptness was unlikely because students did not dare come to the scene in a body. Instead, they traveled individually, by bus, by bicycle, and on foot. By 9:30 A.M. students still seemed outnumbered by tourists, and maybe even by the scores of foreign correspondents who had come to watch. But young Chinese were beginning to form small knots here and there in one area not yet cleared by the police, in the north end of the square, on Chang An Avenue across from the heroic-sized Mao portrait that still gazes down expressionless from the Gate of Heavenly Peace.

Shortly after 10 A.M., as the knots of students began to grow, police began to move in formation from west to east to clear the last few hundred square yards at the north end of the square. But the new police pressure on the students created a bulge in the line of policemen assigned to keep demonstrators out of the area already cleared. A few hundred of the students seemed to take that momentary distortion in the police formation as their chance. They passed quickly through the police line and went slipping and sliding across the fresh ice, taking the inner police lines and their school-child fillers by surprise with their sheer audacity.

Before there had really been a contest, a few hundred students had their first and, as it would turn out, best victory of the day, reaching the sacrosanct and forbidden precincts of the Monument to the People's Martyrs. In front of the monument, they sang "The Internationale" and "The March of the Volunteers." It was the first of scores of times those two songs would be heard that day and night. Then the students dispersed, and many of them eased into the surrounding crowds of holidaymakers, tourists and onlookers before the police could pull together and start chasing them. A handful were seen being hauled off by police and thrown into red-white-and-blue jeeps and police vans, the first few of dozens who would be detained that morning and afternoon.

Skirmishing in the Tiananmen area continued intermittently into the afternoon. Students would filter through the usual pedestrian crowds and would form into loose marching units, sometimes numbering as many as perhaps 1,000. When satisfied that their numbers were adequate, they would unroll one or two "democracy" or "freedom" or "oppose conservatism" banners. But the banners were evanescent. Most were written on long sheets of computer paper, and each one that went up was in shreds as soon as the students began to scatter when the police moved in. Each time the students made a new move, the police would close in from several directions, grabbing however many students they could and wrestling them into the backs of vehicles. By midafternoon the outnumbered and arrest-depleted demonstrators were no longer able to form up into a big enough body to make an impression. The daylight phase of the New Year's activities petered out well before the afternoon rush hour.

By nightfall both sides had scored points, but the most dramatic action lay ahead. The students had managed a surprisingly successful daylight foray against authorities who had spent more than a week marshalling public opinion, organizing the police and devising tactics like icing Tiananmen Square. Demonstrators started the day by getting all the way to the forbidden monument at the center of Tiananmen Square itself, several times briefly forming small parade units and raising banners at the fringes of the square. On the police side, the demonstrations had been kept from going on for any length of time that might encourage bystanders and holidaymakers to join in, as had happened in Shanghai on the Sunday before Christmas.

But the forcible and highly visible seizure of students, which had been central to the police strategy during the day, was to prove costly in the second round that night. At Beijing University, thousands of students, excited by the events at Tiananmen and angry that their detained schoolmates still were not back on campus, gathered in front of the main auditorium by 8 P.M. This time it soon became clear that the question was not whether Beijing University would join in, but what it would take to bring calm back to the campus.

Democracy and freedom were no longer abstractions being urged by students from other campuses. The police in downtown Beijing had been by no means brutal in breaking up the students' formations, but they had used some force. Reports of plainclothesmen training cameras and video recorders on students, of uniformed men chasing students across the ice, of students running, writhing and shouting in futile attempts to escape detention, of schoolmates being manhandled and thrown into the backs of vans at Tiananmen, passed from mouth to ear through the crowd outside the auditorium. All these accounts, and the continuing absence after nightfall of two or three dozen students detained during the day, personalized the issues and provided the local spark that previously had been missing at Beijing University. Neighborhood residents jogged to the university's traditional-style red west gate, near the auditorium, to check out the roars from the crowd, which they had heard inside their brick-and-cement walkup apartments several streets away. A large delegation of students was dispatched to the home of Ding Shisun, the university president. He came to meet the crowd, which had grown to include half or more of the student body, and about 9:30 P.M. he agreed to try to get the students out of detention. He promised to report back to the crowd by 11:30.

It was too little and too late. After the crowd in front of the auditorium had dispersed, hundreds of charged-up students trotted across the campus to the dormitory area and began to move from room to room in small groups. By 10:30 P.M., students were pouring out of the dormitories around the campus's main gate, many of them still pulling on gloves and puffy down jackets as they ran. For a few minutes, the sound of running feet seemed to drown out the shouts. By this time, Patrice DeBeer and I had been inside the campus for perhaps an hour, mainly talking with Chinese and foreign students and foreign teachers we met as the rally ended. As we walked across the campus toward the main gate, there was one loud roar from a crowd, and by the time we got there only stragglers remained inside the gate. We hurried back across the campus to get Patrice's car. By the time we caught up with the students, they had already walked through their first police cordon, just around a corner from the gate. Several thousand students were walking toward downtown Beijing, some eleven kilometers away, and we began to follow their procession, sometimes riding alongside, sometimes parking a bit ahead and going back to walk a kilometer or two with the group, sometimes stopping to make telephone calls to our colleagues.

After two or three encounters with police cordons, it became clear that the police were under orders not to use force. They would have been badly outnumbered at any of the places where they had set up cordons. No more than 200 or 300 police were in the street at any of the points they tried to block. The students had gained recruits from Qinghua University and from People's University and had picked up substantial numbers of young sympathizers as they walked. At the peak their column seemed to number well over 5,000 for a time. Some of my colleagues estimated as high as 10,000. Each time the students came to a police cordon, they stopped to solidify their column and then walked forward into the police lines, singing "The Internationale." And each time, a second or two before there would have been physical contact, the police line gave way and let the students pass.

The students chanted slogans for "democracy" and "freedom" and against "conservatism" and sang "The Internationale" uncountable times, but there is no way to guess what might have happened if one of the police cordons had tried to hold its ground. Still, the police lines served a very useful tactical purpose for the authorities. At each cordon, the students had to slow down to regroup and form the head of their column into a knot strong enough to feel confident in challenging the police. Each time the column stopped, a police car carrying a university vice-president arrived from the rear. Through a loudspeaker mounted on the top of the car, the vice-president urged the students at the rear of the column to go back to the campus. "Your friends are being released by the police," he said in one speech I wrote down as he spoke. "Buses will come to this corner soon to take you back to the campus to meet your friends as they come home. You should go back and greet them. Wait here for the bus." Each time, a few hundred or sometimes as many as a thousand would stay behind. By the time the students turned east onto Chang An Avenue, they knew that this time the police were not likely to stop them from going all the way to Tiananmen Square, but there were no more than 1,500 left in their column.

After watching the students maneuver past the seventh and most formidable police cordon, just north of the Diaoyutai State Guest House, where the government puts up foreign heads of government and state, Patrice and I decided to go back to the campus to see if students were, in fact, coming back from detention. At the main Beijing University gate, students and our colleagues described scenes in which handfuls of returning students had been let out of cars and hoisted onto the shoulders of small crowds of students still on the campus. Some of the returnees made speeches and told of their experiences in detention, which seemed to consist mainly of long waiting periods between hours of questioning about the demonstrations. Their classmates welcomed them with chants and shouts and carried some of them into the campus on their shoulders. Students said that they had seen some twenty or so return from detention, but that at least half a dozen or a dozen had not yet come back.

When we got back to the column of demonstrators, it was down to somewhere between 1,000 and 1,500. Most of the students had dropped off along the way, but a few hundred young people had finally joined up from small crowds that had been tagging along on the sidewalks without moving into the street. Soon after the students turned eastward onto Chang An Avenue, they met up with something new—an intersection where a few dozen policemen sat in their buses without forming a cordon. By this time it was nearly 3 A.M., but the students now knew that the police had completely dropped any attempt to stop them. Now nothing but snow and fatigue lay between them and two great and forbidden demonstration targets—Zhongnanhai, the headquarters and official residence of China's top Communists, and then Tiananmen Square a block farther east. As they passed Xidan Street, the center of the Democracy Wall movement eight years earlier, it was clear that even at this symbolic spot the police were not longer going to get out of their buses and form a barrier. One student stepped out of the column to shout chants directly into one of the police videotape cameras that had followed the column of demonstrators since soon after it left the campus.

By the time they reached the old princes' and concubines' palaces that now serve as the Communist party headquarters at Zhongnanhai, a few hundred yards beyond Democracy Wall, the demonstrators had returned to the political spirit they had started with. "Democratic freedom is not the end of socialism," was one of their chants at that point. Opposite the monumental flagpole that marks the ornate red entrance to Zhongnanhai, they ignored a police loudspeaker that forbade them to stop. "Oppose conservatism," they chanted several times. Then they sang "The Internationale" one more time, worked through several more chants, and moved on.

A few hundred more yards brought them, about 3:30 A.M., to the same north end of Tiananmen that students and police had physically contested by daylight. This time, the police presence had been reduced to no more than a few hundred green uniforms in the vast square, far more than are normally present at night but nowhere near enough to contest the scene with the students. A small knot of waiting foreign television cameramen and news photographers provided an eery greeting as their lights cast long shadows of the demonstrators into empty pedestrian crosswalks that by day had been crammed with tourists. The students first claimed their victory, and taunted the police, by walking the full length of the square's northern end, the area most contested with police by daylight. Then they turned south and walked down the east side of the square, opposite the monumental history museum, where additional tussles had taken place between students and policemen by daylight.

By this time, the students were openly mocking instructions that came over a loudspeaker atop a police jeep that drove alongside their column. "Please walk in the street outside the railing," the loudspeaker said. The students veered to the right, in order to walk in the square itself, inside the railing. "Please walk faster," the loudspeaker said, "Walk slower; walk slower," student voices said, and the column slowed down. "Don't go inside the square," the loudspeaker said. The students turned right and headed for the center of the square, walking between the Monument to the People's Martyrs and the Mao mausoleum. "Don't go up to the monument," the loudspeaker said. The students walked up to the front of the monument and formed themselves into an oval at its base, so they could hear their leaders. "Don't stay inside this area," the loudspeaker said. "Please move on." Half of the students sat down on the frigid pavement. "Students who are sitting, please stand up," the speaker said. Most of those who had remained standing sat down.

Then the loudspeaker fell silent, and after it stayed that way for a few minutes, some of the students began to stand up and do dances and calisthenics to keep warm. Their presence in front of the monument confronted the authorities with the reality that dawn, and the Saturday morning office-and-tourist rush at Tiananmen, were hours away. That raised the prospect of having to choose between a highly visible demonstration at a place the authorities had expressly forbidden, or an equally visible and potentially inflammatory confrontation. The authorities chose to meet the students' only demands—the release of the last remaining detainees from the day before. Not long after

6 A.M., with the last of their schoolmates free, the student demonstrators boarded buses provided by the city and headed back to their campuses.

─────────────

With their schoolmates free, the relatively few true activists among the Beijing University students again began to find it hard to get demonstrations going in the next few days, even on campus. The students were into their examination period, and most were concerned with their own studies. As they took their last exams, many headed home to help their parents prepare for the coming holiday, Chinese New Year, which is as important in Chinese family life as Christmas and New Year's all in a single three-day celebration. There was much anger at the antagonistic and blatantly one-sided coverage their demonstrations had received in the Communist party–controlled press, and some students organized a campus ceremony to burn copies of the Beijing *Daily News* a few days after New Year's. Students I talked with on the campus said that, while they had always vaguely heard and suspected that their news media distorted information to fit the party's needs, this was their first experience of actually seeing an event take place and then reading what the party permitted the newspapers to say about it. "Really disgusting," a commonplace expression of anger in Chinese, was a staple remark by students during these days.

With characteristic Leninist thoroughness, the party set about making use of the holiday period to head off any chance of student demonstrations in the spring semester. Provincial newspapers and radio broadcasts carried a steady flow of appeals to parents to talk with their sons and daughters when they came home for Chinese New Year and persuade them that they should stick to the books when they got back to school. Directives went down ordering provincial and local officials to organize direct contact with parents to see that they complied. The second semester saw no more significant demonstrations, and from a newsman's point of view the story changed in character.

By mid-January 1987, the action was in the inner councils of the Chinese Communist party. There, the eruption of the country's multiple generation gaps into weeks of student demonstrations had given the aging orthodox Leninists an occasion to make a major push, after years of frustration at the hands of the reformers. The spread of reform, and especially the broadening debate that Hu Yaobang had tolerated and sometimes seemed to encourage, had long offended their preference for tidiness and stimulated their fears of a loss of control. Long before the students began to demonstrate, through much of 1986, the control-minded elements in the party had been complaining, often rather publicly, that reform had gone too far. Now, the student demonstrations seemed to broaden the concern for control, persuading other officials that there might indeed be reason to fear a challenge to the Communist party's role in the society. By all accounts, it was during the student demonstrations that Deng Xiaoping himself first told the assembled leadership of the depth of his doubts about his lifetime protege's stewardship of the party. The student demonstrations, while not the cause of Hu Yaobang's fall, seemed an opportunity that had long been awaited by his opponents to take advantage of inner-party discomfort with the pace and extent of the reforms.

For the next few months, the Chinese Communist party would speak with two voices. One of those voices would belong to men like Zhao Ziyang, the premier and new acting party secretary, who would stress the need to place strict limits on the conservative reaction and keep it from cutting into the economic heart of the reforms. The other voice would broadcast the attitudes of the older and more orthodox Leninists, who used the moment to regain control of the propaganda apparatus and then used the media to press the advantage they had found in the student demonstrations. It would be a period when most of the news from China would be of reformists purged from the party or from key government jobs, and of conservative victories, especially in the party's important propaganda department. It would be a time when Zhao Ziyang and his followers would seem preoccupied with a struggle to keep their economic policies, which had seemed firmly in place a year before, from being vitiated by the backlash. The work of rebuilding the top leadership would begin to take shape only months later, in October, with the convening of a long-scheduled Communist Party Congress.

8
Will China Make It?

No student demonstrations were reported in Bin Xian, a county in frigid Heilongjiang Province in northeastern China, in the winter of 1986–87. But for officials of the Bin Xian Communist party committee, students in the streets hundreds of miles away in Shanghai, Beijing, and other cities would turn out to have a very personal meaning. Officials in Bin Xian happened to be facing career-threatening challenges just as the Shanghai and Beijing students took to the streets in December and early January. Liu Binyan, a *People's Daily* reporter who had used the new freedom of the reform atmosphere to become the country's most famous investigative journalist, had accused the Bin Xian party committee of having formed "the social foundation" for Wang Shouxin, an embezzler whose case had become one of the more publicized in a plethora of corruption proceedings. But more orthodox-minded elements in the Politburo were gaining strength after the fall of Hu Yaobang in the wake of the student demonstrations. Now, Liu Binyan was among a handful of prominent intellectuals, once protected by Hu, who were very publicly expelled from the Communist party in February 1987, as bad examples of the "bourgeois liberal thinking" Hu had countenanced.

Scarcely a month after the Communist party announced its expulsion of Liu Binyan, the Heilongjiang propaganda media reversed course and began to portray the Bin Xian leaders as victims of a false accuser.[1] News articles restored good names to the Bin Xian Communists, not because some new evidence was uncovered or some new witness had stepped forward to exonerate them, but because the reporter who had accused them was now himself in deep political disfavor. Such was the course of justice, some eight years after Deng Xiaoping began to consolidate his power and accelerate the country's reforms, that the fate of the accused still might hang less on the facts of the case than on the political fortunes of the accuser. Not only in Bin Xian but also in the Shanghai Marine Institute, in the Xi'an City Communist party committee, in the Gansu Province Communist party propaganda department, in the Sichuan Provincial Writers Association, reputations were rising or falling in inverse relationship to the criticism or praise people had received from Liu Binyan in his years of fame.

As I read news reports of this nationwide reversal of Liu Binyan's investigations, I was impressed by the power of old ways, both ancient and Maoist, to live on into the years of rapid reform Deng Xiaoping and his allies have sponsored. It is neither possible nor necessary for a foreign commentator to reach a judgment on each of the cases brought to light by Liu's investigations. But it is impossible to miss certain patterns in ways of handling these cases. In those patterns lie clues that help us to understand how very far away the modern world still is, despite the dramatic developments since Deng Xiaoping came to power as the 1970s were ending. What became clear as province after province reversed Liu's findings was the extent to which truth and justice are still political concepts, issues to be decided more by power relationships, and sometimes by struggles, than by reliance on impartial laws and procedures. That reality must form an important part of the background of any attempt to assess the accomplishments and prospects of China's newest effort to find its way into the modern world.

Ancient Confucian culture demanded reliance on good men far more than on laws and institutions, and it had a strong tendency to judge the person rather than the act. Maoist revolutionaries established "people's justice" and "people's courts," explicitly as instruments of the class struggle that Mao saw as the heart of Marxist doctrine, and explicitly not as an impartial fact-finding system. Neither of these systems laid much groundwork for modern concepts of independent inquiry or the use of facts within a system of laws to sort out right and wrong. For all of my years in Beijing, Deng's reformers had been conducting "legal education" drives in most major cities, to urge both officials and the public to rely more on the law as a much-needed step toward modernization. Now, the Liu Binyan cases forcefully demonstrated the persisting power of both the hundreds of years of Confucian tradition and the decades of Maoist preaching. From the Confucian centuries came the tendency to judge the man—in these cases, the accuser—rather than apply a set of laws to a set of facts. From the Maoist decades came the tendency to extend political struggle into the application of justice. These swift reversals of years of Liu Binyan's investigative work suggest that, even as Chinese cast about at a conscious level for new intellectual and spiritual moorings, for many years they will inevitably reach out reflexively, often unconsciously, to solve today's problems by grasping at ways handed down from grandparents of the Confucian generations and parents of the Maoist generation.

The 1986–87 student demonstrations were still reverberating through the polity when I left China in the summer of 1987. I left with a sense that, on the one hand, the reforms of the Deng Xiaoping years would survive that particular challenge, but that, on the other hand, it was still much too soon to conclude that the reforms had set a fixed course into full participation in the twenty-first century. My four years and ten months had persuaded me that the reforms are widely popular and are bringing improvements in daily life that many, probably most, individuals can readily feel. Only a relative handful are genuinely well off even by Third World standards, the society is still far more closed than open, and availabilities of goods, especially manufactured items, are still measured more by degrees of scarcity than by degrees of plenty. But travel and thought are far less restricted than ten years ago, most basic food staples and a growing list of manufactured items have gone off ration coupons, and even most of what is scarce is far less so today than it was as the reforms were beginning in the late 1970s.

"We very deeply respect Mr. Deng Xiaoping for what has happened in China since he came to power," the parents of a student I had helped with an application to an American college told me during a dinner they offered me in thanks. The time was just before the demonstrations started late in 1986. Like many in those months, they seemed eager to talk about times in which their own lives were measurably changing. These were two soft-spoken, middle-aged, well-educated, middle-level government bureaucrats. The father spoke English well enough that we alternated between his English and my Chinese, which by 1986 was good enough for most ordinary conversations. They acknowledged a persisting distaste for the way some young people now dance and the ways some young women now dress, disgust at pornographic Hong Kong videotapes their sons had seen and later told them about, and deep uncertainty at the scary unpredictability of prices compared with the total predictability of their government paychecks. But they could point to both tangible and intangible changes in their own daily lives. The mother gestured about the usual minuscule, cement-floored apartment, pointing to a Shanghai-made color television and a Japanese-made stereo in the living room, a Japanese-made refrigerator next to the dining room table, a Chinese-made washing machine in the bathroom. She listed the year when each had been purchased, all since 1979. "Only that came before the reforms," she said, pointing to a powerful, three-speed, Chinese-made electric fan in the one bedroom.

As dusk passed into darkness outside the windows of their third-floor walkup, the father told of having being able to get train tickets to go to his father's funeral four days away in Fujian Province, of now being able to read a favorite newspaper that had been out of publication for twelve years because of the Cultural Revolution, of getting the refrigerator home by finding a private delivery man with a flatbed tricycle, a line of work that had been illegal in Beijing until a few months before they bought the new fridge. He said he now sometimes takes his sons fishing along a Beijing canal during evening hours that had formerly been taken up by mandatory "political study" meetings, and that on the way to work he often eats a breakfast of scallion-flavored pancakes bought near bus stops from vendors who had been banned from the streets for more than a decade. The wife proudly brought out a new pair of jeans and a new blouse she had bought from one of Beijing's new night street bazaars. The one in their neighborhood had opened a year earlier. No one thought it necessary to mention that it would never have occurred to their son to try for an American university had he reached college age ten years earlier.

———

"No one dared to imagine in 1976 that we might live like this in 1986," the father said. Their experience of the reforms, multiplied by millions of households in cities, towns and villages, adds up to a potential constituency that would make wholesale reversal of Deng Xiaoping's work a risky undertaking. In that sense, I ended my assignment feeling that there is a certain extent to which what has been done since Mao died cannot be undone. Surely there is no early prospect of going back to the days of Red Guard rallies, burning temples, and the Mao Cult. The polity was actively rejecting that way of life even while Mao was not yet dead.

But a wide range of possible policy choices lies between that rejected model and the reforms now being led by Zhao Ziyang under Deng's sponsorship. Within the polity are many constituencies that have reason to dislike today's course, and many of these will retain at least a potential political potency for years or decades to come. At the top today, by far the most publicized of these constituencies consists mainly of some of the old revolutionaries, members and former members of the Communist party Central Committee and its Politburo. Some of these people are uneasy about a few of the changes they see going on around them; some are revolted by what they regard as a rampant return of capitalism; many fall somewhere along a scale between these degrees of discontent. Right below them stands another potential constituency, its dimensions and political dynamic untested but its time soon to come. One face of this potential constituency for a more conservative course is the People's Republic's first generation of overseas students, the thousands who studied in the Soviet Union and Eastern Europe in the years of Sino-Soviet closeness in the 1950s. It is reasonable to assume that many of these people, now in their fifties and about to come into their years of greatest power and influence, came back from Stalinist Russia with damaged or even shattered illusions. One of them, Li Peng, the new premier, has hinted as much, telling American interviewers that there is no chance of ever going back to any relationship like the one the Soviets and the Chinese had in those heady years just after 1949.

Li Peng describes himself as a prime leader of the reforms, but his generation is deeply steeped in the ways of a tightly centralized economy. Without ever consciously doubting that they were leading the way to reform, some members of this generation could yet prove to be intellectual captives of their own Stalinist educations. Li Peng is himself a power-dam engineer who came up through a series of Stalinist-style big-project assignments. Many foreign diplomats and scholars see in his public utterances the outlines of a reform plan that would differ in fundamental ways from the work Zhao Ziyang has done for the past decade. They suggest that Li's China might have a more centralized economy with more state planning, less private enterprise, less personal freedom and less freedom of political and social expression than Zhao's has had. Whether or not that assessment of Li is accurate, it is reasonable to assume that among the thousands of returned Soviet students of his generation, there must be many who find the current experiments strange and disturbing. To whatever extent such people exist, it is fair to guess that they have some potential to form into a future constituency for an approach to economics and governance that would differ markedly from the one that has succeeded thus far under Zhao Ziyang.

So even now that people have had, and for the most part very much liked, a taste of Deng's and Zhao's ways, it is not hard to see where important constituencies might form up to try to push the country back, not to Maoism, but toward a less open and partially recentralized society. One additional source of such constituents might well be the generations educated in Soviet-style ways within China in the years after the revolution. After 1949, the few existing colleges and universities, many of them built by foreign missionaries, were restructured along Soviet lines into narrowly vocational training, rather than the broader liberal arts and sciences tradition some originally had. Ranks of new universities and institutes were opened, also along Soviet lines. They trained students in the then-new ways of the centralized system, with initiative to rest essentially in the hands of state planners rather than enterprise managers. These institutes and universities were the core of higher education until the Cultural Revolution closed them in 1966. It remains to be seen how comfortable their pre-Cultural Revolution graduates, now in their forties and fifties, can feel as the new system decentralizes decision making and seeks to give autonomy to local managers. It is logical to assume that many may find things disturbingly unfamiliar as more and more is done outside the state plan, as markets set more prices and planners set fewer, as prices regulate more and more economic activity and planners regulate less and less, as the privately owned sector, even among manufacturing plants, grows much faster than the state and demands bigger and bigger shares of the energy and raw materials that state plants always find in chronically short supply.

Another potential constituency for a more traditionally Leninist, more economically and politically centralized system exists within the middle and upper-middle ranks of the Communist party itself. This constituency extensively overlaps with the Soviet-trained, but includes large additional numbers of the less educated. Among the more than 40 million who hold party cards, the overwhelming majority have joined since 1949, and additional large numbers only after it became clear that Mao's Red Armies were headed for victory in the civil war. Though the Communist party still retains much of its conspiratorial secrecy, it has been decades since its principal attraction to new members was the thrill of throwing out a failed government and seizing power in the name of the people. The few young people who acknowledged to me that they might like to join the party uniformly said their purpose would be to "get ahead." They said this without embarrassment, as a simple matter of fact that everyone understood about party membership. At the middle and upper-middle levels of the party today are a few million who have invested decades of their lives doing precisely that—getting ahead. By these decades of personal sacrifice, they have established their *guanxi* networks of friends and acquaintances and have worked their way into the positions of power or influence that bring with them a broad range of licit and illicit privileges.

Now, the reformers at the top of the party are reinventing the system. Every month comes a demand that these people in the middle and upper-middle levels give up some further increment of the power, influence and privilege that they have worked and suffered long to accumulate. More and more economic decisions are supposed to be put into the hands of professional managers. More and more planning is supposed to devolve to lower and lower levels. At the middle and upper-middle levels, each such change means less power, less influence, less ability to repay favors or to claim them. Many of these middle and upper-middle Communists have sensed from the outset that the new ways would require that they begin to contemplate their own creeping irrelevance. Some have responded by using their party positions as launching pads to join up with the new system. They are sources of many of the complaints, both public and private, about corruption spreading through the party via the reforms, for they often use their party connections to set themselves or their relatives and friends up in lucrative businesses. But in many cases, the personality that has been attracted to the party way of getting ahead has been less entrepreneurial, more inclined to trade privileges than to pile up money, more inclined to work within an established and understood system than to freewheel in the new atmosphere. From these ranks have come many of the middle and upper-middle Communists who have found ways to subvert the new system, to cling to their old power, influence and connections in substance, even when forced to give them up in form. These Communists, many of them types who would find soulmates among political hacks in a Chicago or Boston election district, will find fewer and fewer roles to play in the new system. Yet they will have important voices within the party for years to come, perhaps decades. Any force at the top of the Communist party that might push for more centralization and a more traditionally Leninist system could be expected to have substantial appeal among some of these people.

In many cases, local party and government cadres have not needed support from the center to begin working in ways that undermine the reforms. The party and government have made several attempts at administrative decentralization, pushing powers long reserved to the province or even the center down to the city or county level. But in thousands of cases, local officials have used this new authority to gather more power into their own hands, demanding *guanxi* transactions for routine decisions and, in turn, becoming more obstructive to factory and enterprise directors, and to private and cooperative businesses, than the central and provincial authorities had been. The experience with administrative decentralization has produced innumerable case studies in the complexity of moving a country as big and diverse as China onto a single course, and the inherent difficulty of relaxing the grip of decades of centralized and bureaucratic decision making. At the level where these local cadres function, administrative decentralization has pumped political and economic power into the offices of many of the same petty officials and bureaucrats whose hands the reformers are trying to pry off the levers of economic power in order to let market forces play a fuller role in the economy.

It is among the elites of the old system, then, that the potential leadership and shock troops of any move back toward a more closed society might be found. That is how it has been for the past hundred years—whenever China has undergone reform, the mandarins or the warlords or the Maoist true believers of the existing system have found ways to marshal a resistance. Today, those forces might consist of the older Leninists in the Politburo, of some of the returned students and the China-trained graduates of the Soviet years, of some of the middle ranks of the party—and of some elements in that most mysterious of all the country's political institutions, the People's Liberation Army. The PLA has been for decades the great Black Box of Chinese politics, and only a few Western scholars are even now beginning to get some clues to its political workings and role. But Deng Xiaoping tells us by his actions that the PLA is not yet wholly and dependably on board with the reform program. Formally, the PLA is a two-headed organization, supervised by a Communist Party Military Commission and a State Military Commission, though the memberships of the two have been identical ever since the state commission was created in the mid-1980s. Deng sought throughout the middle 1980s to retire from his major posts, but even after divesting himself of many jobs at the 1987 Communist Party Congress, he remained head of both the party and the state military commissions. Hu Yaobang told the world why Deng could not give up either military role when interviewers asked him about the army in 1985. At the time, Hu was still secretary general of the party, a post that might have been

expected to entail chairmanship of the party's military commission.
Deng, he said, could settle any issue in the military with one sentence;
Hu or Zhao might need three or four sentences.

Deng's long years of delay in giving up either of the two military
commission posts say all that needs to be said about how far the
reformers dare to trust the army politically. Clearly, somewhere
within the PLA there are still powerful elements that are having trouble adjusting—to the newly decentralizing society, to the reduction by
some one million soldiers of the army itself, to the low budget priority
being given to defense in order to promote the civilian economy, and
to the removal of army units from college campuses, factories and
other reaches of the society soldiers had come to think of as their own.
Deng's personal authority has kept these elements from expressing
themselves. What elements these are, and how effectively they might
be able to join in any political coalition, are questions that no one I
know dares to answer in any detail. Only one thing seems clear;
somewhere within the great Black Box that is the People's Liberation
Army, there lurks something that Deng and his reformist allies do not
fully trust.

Most people seem to be enjoying the new relative freedoms and the
relative improvements in daily life that are coming with the reforms.
The expansion of personal freedom is measurable in the growing
ability of ordinary folk to travel about the country, or to open a small
business. It has also improved significantly the working prospects of a
foreign correspondent. In my first two years in Beijing, Chinese
acquaintances tended to act furtive about meeting with me. If we
chose to meet at a major institution like the Beijing Hotel, police
would often call my friend aside and write down the information on
his identity card. Several reported that their work units or their
neighborhood committees called them in afterward to warn how
dangerous a foreign correspondent could be. By the end of 1985,
police at most places had given up trying to track contacts between
Beijing people and foreigners in such detail, perhaps partly because
there were so many more foreigners. The furtive feeling was mostly

gone, though events still could send a chill through relations with local friends now and then.

While people clearly are enjoying new freedoms and higher incomes, there is no lack of potential sources of popular support or acceptance if a new leadership, backed by conservative elements in the old elites, were determined to move toward more social controls and a more centralized economy and polity. Wherever I went, I saw signs that, while many workers were enjoying the chance to prosper by working harder, some others seemed to be resenting the new demands. Life has been poor and simple under the old system, but except during the recurring waves of Maoist political turmoil, the work place has been essentially secure and undemanding for most city people. Professors put in few hours actually teaching compared with university teachers in the West. Factory workers have often worked in such overstaffed conditions that many could get away with skipping whole days or even weeks of work. Many people spend much of the workday gossiping, or in many cases I encountered, pursuing hobbies at the workplace.

Now, with the new emphasis on incentives, autonomy and profits, even some state factories have begun to expect more work for a day's pay. At the same time, some services are being removed from the welfare category and required to be more nearly financially self-supporting. In some places, hospitals and doctors now charge fees commensurate with the cost of services, rather than the token sums they had always asked when they could count on bigger state subsidies. In addition, the government's experiments with price reform and market forces have released inflation never before experienced under Communist party rule. For most, increased income has more than offset price increases. But significant numbers who live on fixed incomes—most painfully, perhaps, the country's already poorly paid schoolteachers—are feeling a severe pinch.

In the countryside, while a few farmers are now genuinely well off, especially in the suburbs of big cities, many more are experiencing far more modest improvements, or none, in their lives and incomes. After more than two years of widespread ballyhoo about the "10,000-yuan households"—families dotted across some counties who are earning annual incomes deemed obscene in the Maoist years—the news media came under top-level criticism in 1985 for overemphasizing these newly well-off peasants. There followed a period of stories emphasizing how many peasants in remote areas are still struggling to overcome poverty and describing how much remained to be done in the countryside. Articles about 10,000-yuan households have been less frequent ever since. In their place has grown up a genre of pieces about "red-eye disease," the Chinese-language equivalent of green-eyed envy. These articles relate the negative examples of peasants who do not advance as fast as their neighbors, and so resort to theft or vandalism to get even. In industry, a comparable genre of negative-example reports now tell of workers who met bad ends because they sought revenge, beating up the factory directors and coal-mine managers rather than digging in to work harder when their bosses disciplined them.

These articles, teaching poor peasants not to vandalize richer neighbors, and workers not to resist their bosses, stand in 180-degree opposition to the propaganda of the civil war and Cultural Revolution years, when the party's official news media made heroes of peasants who tore up the village landlord's turf and of workers who rebelled against their bosses. My own impression is that these articles reflect pockets of real resistance the reforms are meeting among some ordinary people. None of this adds up to a rebellion against the reforms, which are generally well received. But it suggests that there are pockets of persisting and, in some places, growing resentment. In addition, even among many who basically support the reforms, there are doubts about much of the untidiness that comes with them. Especially among middle-aged and older Chinese I met, but even also among some younger people, there is considerable discomfort about the return of highly visible inequalities in wealth and income, about the rapid changes in clothing styles, the spread of corruption, the growing numbers of foreigners, the changing sexual mores and the importation of pornography. Whenever the more social control—oriented and centralization-minded Leninists in the Politburo have sought to push back against the reforms, they have relied upon these sources of discomfort, especially sex and pornography, as some of their leading issues.

In the face of Deng Xiaoping's personal authority, and in no small measure because of his political savvy and sense of timing, success has never been more than partial and temporary for the various forces that might seek to reverse the reforms, or to divert them onto a recentralizing, control-oriented course. But the struggle to succeed Deng was already visibly beginning when I arrived in China in October 1982. It had already passed through some acute phases when I left in August 1987, with Deng still healthy and active. This struggle predictably will continue well beyond his death, until someone clearly wins out.

Deng Xiaoping labored mightily through the mid-1980s to arrange things so that his reformist allies could smoothly succeed him. At a Communist Party Conference, called in the fall of 1985 specifically to arrange for his own succession, he lined up the generations within the party in rank after rank, in an almost pyramidal fashion, setting the stage for himself to ease into inactivity and for his chosen successors to ease into power during his remaining lifetime. But he came to power in his seventies, too late in life to undertake the long process of changing the basic ways power is transferred. Stable political institutions of the kinds that promote smooth transitions cannot be planted quickly or easily. So Deng Xiaoping has had no choice but to rely on the old ways, putting men of his choice in place. He has done more than had ever before been attempted within those ways. He has tried to give his chosen successors years of high-visibility apprenticeship, and he has put large numbers of men in place, deep down into the system, hoping that they could form a political base for the few at the top.

But China's rulers have fought many losing battles through the centuries in their efforts to arrange their own successions. Even in the far simpler context of a hereditary ruling family, the frustration of emperors' attempts to say which son should succeed to the throne has been legendary. Some emperors resorted to secrecy, naming a son in a written document to be opened only after death. Even so, the secret might often leak out, leading to the destruction of the chosen successor. A typical case was the mighty Kang Xi emperor, the greatest in the Qing line. Each time he named a son as successor, the son became a target of the concubines, eunuchs, mandarins, and generals who inhabited the Forbidden City and its precincts. In time, each prince was so surrounded and seduced by factions among the courtesans and courtiers that at least two of his sons became bisexual playboys and lost all ability to concentrate on affairs of state. Twice, the great Kang Xi became disgusted and switched to a different son.

Neither the end of dynastic rule in 1911 nor the arrival of Mao Zedong's armies in Beijing in 1949 ended the frustrations of leaders in their attempts to provide for their own successions. Mao's first officially designated successor was the ill-fated Liu Shaoqi, whom Mao personally ordered out of power. Branded a "renegade, traitor and scab" by Mao's Cultural Revolutionaries, Liu died a prisoner and was posthumously given back his reputation only after his lifetime protégé, Deng Xiaoping, had won power. The next successor-designate was Marshal Lin Biao, the defense minister officially described by the Cultural Revolutionaries as Mao's "close comrade in arms." But the Great Helmsman's close comrade in arms tried to assassinate his mentor in order to inherit power. According to the Communist party version, Lin died in a plane crash in Outer Mongolia while trying to escape to the Soviet Union after his assassination plot had failed. Mao then, according to party versions, anointed a third would-be successor, Hua Guofeng, a fast-riser of the Cultural Revolution years. "With you in charge, I feel secure," the bedridden and dying Mao supposedly told the new heir-apparent. Initially, the remark was about Hua's handling of an investigation of Deng Xiaoping in Mao's fading years, but Hua's associates inflated it for broader use and he did, in fact, succeed to Mao's title, Chairman. But Deng and his allies eased Hua out of power almost effortlessly. After a failed suicide attempt and a long hospital stay in the early 1980s, Hua Guofeng today clings to his last high post, a seat on the Central Committee of the Communist party, by grace of Deng Xiaoping's preference for keeping all the stallions inside the corral, where they can be watched.

———

This recurring frustration of succession arrangements, under the dynasties and under the Communist party, has a common thread. That thread is the persisting Confucian preference for reliance on the individual ruler rather than on institutions, laws, procedures, and processes. China has no equivalent to the fixed term of office, which in modern societies makes transfers of power a routine and predictable part of political life. There is no equivalent to the vice-president, the fixed and predictable successor in case of unexpected death or disability. There is no place for a public debate or a vote of no-confidence or impeachment in case a ruler violates the law or loses his political base. Such constitutions as have existed since 1949 have been freely rewritten to accommodate each major shift in power and personnel, including most recently another rewriting to meet Deng Xiaoping's needs. It is, in modern terms, a political system without system, a world in which it is the institutional frameworks that are the interchangeable parts and the man who is indispensable. In this world, like many emperors before him, Mao could pass from the political scene only by death—not only because he himself loved power and trusted fewer and fewer of his colleagues but also because the system itself needed him as its emblem and legitimizer so long as he breathed. Deng Xiaoping, in his turn, inexorably found through the mid-1980s that the very fact of heading the system made him indispensable to it, even though he resisted any hint of a cult, steadily reduced the number and the grandeur of his political titles, and retreated with age into shorter and shorter working days.

The timeless character of Chinese governance, then, is the first place to look to understand why, much as the naming of a son by an emperor made the designated successor a focus of intrigue at court, Deng Xiaoping's very act of setting up a succession plan in 1985 touched off struggles that caused his plan to self-destruct barely sixteen months later. In that sense, the student demonstrations that gave the conservatives at court their opening in January 1987 was only the occasion, not the cause, of Hu Yaobang's fall. The effect has been not only to remove Hu himself from the chain of succession but also to move Zhao Ziyang abruptly out of the governmental jobs, where he has a demonstrated track record, and into a Communist party political role, for which he himself has said repeatedly he is not best suited.

At the 1987 Communist Party Congress, Deng Xiaoping was forced to concentrate on building a new succession plan to replace the one that had burst the preceding January. The new plan ratified at that congress put Zhao Ziyang in place as permanent party secretary and Li Peng in place as premier. But the same elements of compromise that make that alignment feasible under Deng's tutelage make it inherently unstable in his absence. Even with Deng still active, and with Li still only the acting premier, that instability began to show up in policy and power struggles between Zhao and Li that were reported by my colleagues in Beijing in the spring of 1988.[2] There is no way to foresee the outcome of those struggles, and even for some time after they are resolved it may not be altogether clear what has been the outcome. Given the popularity of the reforms, for example, any moves toward centralism and more social control would, in their first stages, be couched in reformist language and presented as further steps along the existing path, or at minimum as a way of trimming the sails to keep the reforms on course.

So the central question—Will China make it?—is largely a matter of whether China will go on trying to make it. For a decision in favor of recentralization and a return to deep social controls would be, in effect, a decision against reaching for full participation in the twenty-first century, or at least against reaching for full participation in what most commentators and analysts believe the twenty-first century will be. The world is already well into an age in which information itself is arguably the fastest-growing commodity being exchanged in international marketplaces. The country that marries up to, or stays married to, a traditional Leninist system takes a real risk of waking up one day to find that it has opted out of the twenty-first century world economy.

The most fundamental principle of social and political control in a traditional Leninist system is severe restriction of access to all forms of information. This is not merely a matter of controlling the propaganda media but of seeing that state decision making, and access to the most routine financial, economic, and political data, is tightly retained within the Communist party elite. In November 1986, the New York Stock Exchange conducted a symposium in the Great Hall of the People on world capital markets. After a few days of exposure to the Chinese system, several American experts remarked that many of their hosts seemed shocked by the amount of information they would have to disclose in order to borrow big sums in traditional international markets. China's willingness to disclose financial data is at best "marginal," David C. Batten, managing director of First Boston Corporation, said after one session. "They're going to have to provide more information if they want to participate."

A world in which personal and mainframe computers silently and instantaneously exchange book-length volumes of information, by satellite or telephone transmissions from opposite sides of the globe, is in no way compatible with the fundamentals of traditional Leninist political control. If a government limits the use of computers, or their ability to communicate with one another, it will limit the country's participation in the future world economy. If it does not, it will by that act permit freer exchange of information than any Leninist system has ever been able to tolerate. The current leadership under Zhao Ziyang shows signs of understanding this dilemma and of beginning to resolve it in favor of steadily growing openness. But the openness the modern world economy requires as the price of participation will entail political costs that many middle- and upper-middle-level Communists will be unwilling to pay. To many of them, every lost increment of control over information will represent a lost increment of political power as it has been practiced for the past four decades. Any attempt at full participation in the twenty-first century will require a vastly greater opening of the polity, economy, and society than has ever been contemplated by any government of China—dynastic, Nationalist or Communist.

Assuming that the society continues to want extensive modernization, and that the Communist party continues to pursue it, there remains a further central question: Can the Chinese make it happen? Any discussion of this question must begin with a definition of "making it" in the Chinese context. According to at least two important definitions, the answer would have to be a fairly firm *yes*. One essential aspect would consist of giving the substantial majority of individual Chinese a sense, over the coming years and decades, that things are better this year than last and hold good prospect of being better next year than this. That might be described as a "political minimum" definition of making it—enough sense of progress to make revolt unlikely. Today's leadership inherited from the Maoist decades such a low standard of living and such a closed society that there is plenty of room to go on providing that sense of incremental, overall improvement for the foreseeable future. There was no question in my own mind as I left China that, on the whole, people were feeling substantially better off than they had for a very long time, and that they were expecting each succeeding year to be better than the last.

In its other aspect, making it would consist of playing a much larger role in the world, and specifically in the world economy. Because of the self-imposed isolation of Mao's Cultural Revolution years, by that definition, too, there is still plenty of room left today for years and maybe decades of improvement along the lines already seen. China not only is well on the way to full membership in the world diplomatic community but also increasingly makes itself felt in the world economy. "I hope that some day the main issue between our two countries will be disputes over textile trade," one American diplomat liked to tell Chinese counterparts during my early years in Beijing. "Why," his listeners would usually ask, "would you want to see arguments over textiles?" "Textiles," the American diplomat would reply, "is the issue we argue over with our friends." By the time I left Beijing, China had leapt in a few years from insignificance as a U.S. textile supplier into a high-ranking position that had indeed made textiles one of the major recurring issues of China–U.S. diplomacy. American buyers were setting out to expand the range of simple manufactured goods China could supply, including plastics, tableware and bottom-of-the-line jogging shoes. Electronics components, though still a minor factor, were on the agendas of several trade meetings.

Both of these definitions are important to the Chinese people and to the world. Each will have much to do with the country's internal political stability, and with the stability of its foreign policy, for the rest of this century and well into the next. Either could conceivably be met, even after a return to a more closed society, polity and economy. But neither is equal to the ambitions of today's reformers. Deng Xiaoping has sometimes stated these as the right general goals: a quadrupling of the 1980 gross product by the end of this century; a West European standard of family income and living by the middle of the next century; and full participation as an equal member of the world economy by the end of the next century. The last of these strikes most foreign analysts as a very remote goal for the entire country, but it is possible to visualize a China with half a dozen or a dozen urban centers that might participate fully in the modern world by the end of the next century. If even that much is to happen, the economic and political changes that have seemed so dramatic in the Deng Xiaoping years will mark only the barest beginning compared with what must come in the next few decades.

What China's reformers are trying to do, no one else has ever successfully done. Essentially, they inherited a rigidly socialized economy patterned after the Soviet one of the Stalin years. That is the kind of milieu many Western economists like to call a "command economy," a world in which factories, farms and stores provide, not what the consumer wants to buy, but what the state tells them to provide. From this inherited starting point, the reformers are trying to make a transition to an economy with the flexibility, the incentives and the room for individual and local-level initiative that would be required to win a chance at a full share of the world economy, in the twenty-first century.

Exactly where today's reformers are trying to take their country, other than out of poverty, they themselves do not know, a reality to which some of the top Communists now and then confess. They say they are determined to keep the economy "socialist," but what "socialism with a Chinese face" will look like fifty or one hundred years from now, or even ten, they do not pretend to know. The Marxist world has no success story to offer as the precedent for this transition. A few East European countries have attempted to loosen their economic, social and political controls in varying degrees and with varying effects, but none has yet managed to move from the Leninist-Stalinist centralized system all the way to full participation in the world economy. Several have had to stop short because of pressure from Moscow. That pressure, at least, is one China will not have to deal with, for no one foresees any return to Soviet domination. Indeed, for however long Mikhail Gorbachev leads the Soviet Union into a more open system, Chinese reformers will have a readymade answer to any voices that speak out for control and recentralization. Why, after all, should China go back to the old Soviet ways when Moscow itself is now following along, ten years behind China's moves toward more openness? But some of East Europe's socialist countries also have found that their own Communist parties, with or without pressure from Moscow, are unable to tolerate the economic and political breathing space a genuinely modern economy would require. The Chinese Communist party is only in the earliest stages of reforming itself, and it is still far too soon to guess whether it may yet revert to the course set by its East European brothers.

If China does manage to make permanent its current departure from the Leninist-Stalinist mold, or at least to loosen its grip enough to permit a truly modern economy, the transition will be filled with monumental difficulties and perils, economic at least as much as political. The economy is studded with evidence of how hard it is to move all the way from the inflexibility of the Maoist years to a system that can respond in timely fashion to market forces. Reformers have tried countless times to decentralize decision making about basic questions, like what a factory should produce and where it should get its supplies. But it often seems that each wave of decentralization must be followed by a new wave of recentralization, often in response to forces unexpectedly set off by the reforms themselves.

Soon after offices closed one Tuesday afternoon in May 1985, large numbers of well-clothed and self-confident shoppers began to appear in marketplaces all over Beijing. Betraying a sense of urgency that is not common in the state-run markets, many of them bought far more than the usual one-day or two-day requirements that have been the typical shopping pattern of the Chinese people for centuries. "These are low-level Communist party members and government workers," a friend explained after taking me to a major state marketplace to watch. "They know something. My father says the party people in his work unit got word this afternoon that food prices will go up soon." Two days later, Beijing newspapers published the news that food-price reform, which had been introduced across the country a few cities at a time for the preceding year, would reach the national capital that weekend.

That rush of insiders into the marketplace to buy food was one of scores of big and little price-reform vignettes I learned about or witnessed, beginning in 1985. These incidents impressed on me how intricate and difficult it can be to move from the rigid command economy inherited from the Maoist years to the market-tempered economy today's reformers hope to establish. One major risk for the foreseeable future will be the public's deep political sensitivity to price increases. It is an acquired sensitivity, deeply etched into the Chinese psyche both by years of national price trauma and by decades of Communist party propaganda. As the Nationalist party government lost its grip on the country in the civil war years after World War II, the people lived through one of the world's great inflations, finally ending in one of those textbook periods in which wheelbarrows full of paper money literally wouldn't sustain a family for a day. Inflation became one of the Communist party's chief propaganda weapons against the Nationalists. When the Communists came to power, they set out to make good on their promise of stable prices and incomes. By the time Deng Xiaoping began his rise to power in the late 1970s, the Communist party proudly and frequently pointed out that inflation had been held within the one-percent-a-year range since soon after the Communists had won power in 1949.

The claim was not inaccurate, but the stability had been purchased at a Draconian cost. A crazyquilt of government subsidies and inflexible price controls had been pieced together, and the Communist party often regarded these controls and subsidies as a major way of buying political peace, especially in the often-volatile cities. Today the reformers have acknowledged what foreign economists have said for years—that the same patchwork system of wholly arbitrary prices that buys urban peace also distorts economic values of almost everything, severely drains national and local government revenues and, by the estimates of Chinese and foreign economists alike, acts as a massive drag on economic development. Chinese and foreign analysts are little short of unanimous in the view that one of the hardest tasks facing the reformers is to wean the economy from these bureaucrat-administered prices that make it impossible for market forces to regulate production and consumption.

Wang Jixian, director of the Chongqing municipal price-reform office, used coal as an example of how the old price system retarded the economy. When I visited him in 1985, he explained that home-heating coal is so politically sensitive that both price controls and heavy subsidies are used. Each worker who lives in a building that has no central heat, which means most houses and apartments, gets a cash coal subsidy. A family that has three or more working members and heats with coal is likely to make a profit on its coal subsidies through the winter months. And for factories, said Wang, "coal is what grain is to a man. If coal prices go up, then the factory's costs go up, and some factories might fail. So for many years, China's policy has been that it is better to keep 1,000 factories on heavily subsidized and controlled coal prices than to let a few factories fail. The losers have been the coal mines—they cannot invest, which means they cannot explore for new coal and they cannot install new equipment." Miners have long paid a more personal price. The cash-starved mines, unable to solve their most elementary production problems, have had little means to provide the luxury of safety equipment. China does not publish industrial accident statistics, but foreign analysts I spoke with all agreed that the country's mines appear to have one of the worst fatal-accident records in the world.

Reformers began to work on coal prices, and to expand state investment in the mines, as early as the late 1970s. The country's chronic coal shortages were easing impressively, though they were by no means cured, as I prepared to leave in 1987. But reforming prices on other fronts, especially in housing, consumer products and foodstuffs, has proved a much more delicate operation. "For a long time, our propaganda held that steady prices were a basic principle of our party and a guarantee of a stable life for the people," Xue Muqiao, a senior economist, wrote in an article reprinted in *Economic Daily* in 1985. "Now this propaganda is deeply rooted among the people and every time prices go up, people feel restless."[3] When Chongqing set out to reform food prices in 1985, Wang Jixian told me, the price-reform office set up a special telephone line to handle the public's complaints. With the first prolonged dry spell in the summer of 1985 came a wave of inflation in vegetable prices and the predictable wave of calls from the public. The city's government-run vegetable companies responded by sending trucks out to scour the countryside, buying up vegetables wherever they could, often at prices higher than they intended to charge when they resold the goods in the city's markets. Then the city sold the vegetables in state markets at big losses, to force the peasants to lower their prices in the free markets. The city vegetable companies were allowed to make up their losses by taking cash from $3.3 million the Chongqing government was still budgeting every year for food subsidies. "The nature of commerce should change once the reforms are in full effect," Wang said, "so after this period of adjustment there should come a time when we no longer need these subsidies."

But by the time I left in 1987, local governments all across the country were still heavily involved in similar subsidizing and dumping tactics to keep food prices within bounds. In many cities, the attempts to introduce market forces into the pricing system touched off bouts of inflation and rounds of public complaints the Communist party was unprepared to sustain. As 1986 ended, student demonstrators were making the rising cost of food one of the recurring issues on their banners. As the student demonstrations spread, the government announced that price reform at the consumer level would be drastically curtailed in 1987, an attempt to keep consumer prices stable and to keep popular discontent from spreading beyond the campuses. There was no suggestion yet of any real plan to reform housing rents, one of the most distorted pricing areas in the economy. Price reform continued in many areas, especially at the producer level. But in broad areas badly needing price reform, the reformers seemed prisoners of the Communist party's decades of subsidies, controls and no-inflation propaganda.

In the discussion of state factories earlier in this book, the implied central question is whether these large and small plants, the principal means of manufacture created by more than three decades of costly state-directed investment, can adjust to the new ways and can now make contributions to modernization that are in proportion to the painfully husbanded capital they represent. Most of these plants have long histories of extremely slack use of their capital. Starting at this low level of effectiveness, returns from the initial years of serious attempts at factory reform have been significant, despite widespread resistance and much continuing inefficiency. But Liu Guoguang, a vice-president of the Chinese Academy of Social Sciences, raised telling questions about the prospects of these factories when he delivered the

1987 Alexander Eckstein Lecture at the Center for Chinese Studies of The University of Michigan. Liu said, in effect, that it would be a long time before the state factories would become fully part of the new system.

Liu described an economy in which attempts at speedy reform contributed to severe overheating, especially in the fledgling private and cooperative industries, in late 1984 and early 1985. Overheating, in turn, created both economic and political pressures that required reimposition of central controls to bring inflation and disjointed growth under control. The experience was an object lesson in the difficulties and dangers any leadership will face in the transition from the rigid Maoist command economy to a system tempered by market forces. The period was marked by attempts to move rapidly, almost abruptly, from detailed state planning to a reliance on "economic levers," resembling the means many Western governments use to regulate capitalist economies. But the capitalist-style levers—fiscal policy, banking, interest rates, and a broad range of other economic controls—were not yet nearly equal to the job. Today, said Liu, they still are not developed to a point capable of doing as much as they do in capitalist countries, and China will live with a dual system "for a rather long time." In the lexicon of Chinese socialism, a rather long time is a period unlikely to end in this century.

In industry, Liu continued, managers will have to learn to work with two economic systems that are based on two diametrically opposite sets of rules. Further, these systems will not merely coexist separately but will also deeply interpenetrate and intermingle, as different state factories take different paths through the end of this century, and as state factories begin to establish working relationships with some of the private and cooperative factories that are rising up to challenge the older state plants. Some foreign analysts working in Beijing have argued that this dual system will suffice to bring China a substantial level of modernity. Their view is that the much more vigorous private and cooperative factories will, as one diplomat likes to put it, simply "surround" the less aggressive state factories, eventually becoming the dominant force in the manufacturing economy. That view has its appeal to the capitalist-oriented foreigner, but it has two major drawbacks in the Chinese context. It accepts as normal the continued severe under-performance by hundreds of thousands of plants that represent decades of squeezing investment capital out of an impoverished economy. Furthermore, China's reformers still feel constrained to insist that their economy will remain Marxist, and that state ownership will play the dominant role in industry—in short, that the private and cooperative sector must never be permitted to "surround" the state sector. Zhao Ziyang, then still the premier, implicitly rejected this scenario in April 1987, demanding that state factory officials stop undermining the reforms. "The reason why major enterprises are not vigorous and their enormous potential has not been fully tapped," Zhao said, "is that policies and measures to encourage the initiative of enterprises and employees have not been carried out."[4]

Zhao Ziyang's words add up to a fair one-sentence summary of what was described in more detail earlier in this book. But a long, dimly lit struggle will lie between the reformers' recognition that reforms are not being carried out at the factory level and success in bringing real systemic change to big enterprises that ought to be principal contributors to modernization. That struggle will be further complicated by the Marxist principle that all reform must proceed under a rubric of state ownership. Planners in Beijing have insisted that private and cooperative enterprises must never be more than a "supplement and a stimulus" to the state-owned sector. Du Runsheng estimated at a press conference that private and cooperative manufacturing would have to be limited to somewhere between 10 and 20 percent of the total. If the Communist party in fact carries out a long-term policy of tolerating only limited private and cooperative manufacturing, industrial growth seems likely to be distorted and self-limiting, for the state-owned sector, though it has seen improvements in the initial attempts at reform, shows few signs of being able to compete on its own with the dynamic new private and cooperative enterprises. The only way to keep some of the new capitalist and quasi-capitalist businesses from surrounding and eventually stifling some major state plants will be to put artificial restrictions on these aggressive new elements, while continuing to provide a broad range of subsidies and other costly crutches to the state enterprises.

Prices and manufacturing are two examples, drawn from a broad range of fields, in which reforms have made impressive initial progress, but have not yet reached sufficient mass and momentum to impart confidence that the remaining task will be completed. Given how very much has been accomplished in the short space of a decade, there is a danger of underestimating the enormity of the work that still faces China's reformers, and of failing to see formidable obstacles that still stand in the way of getting it done. The job of reopening schools and universities after the Cultural Revolution, for example, has been so daunting that it is tempting to accept that work, now virtually completed, as sufficient. In fact, it is scarcely a beginning. Schools remain hopelessly underfunded; university teaching methods work to elicit intellectual obedience rather than independent reasoning; and laboratories are backward and undersupplied. The legal system is scarcely far enough advanced to be characterized as in its infancy. It might more accurately be said to be in a late prenatal phase. Passenger trains have run on time since the early 1980s, but freight trains have barely begun to emerge from chaos after a full decade of effort. And the country shows only the initial signs of working toward political institutions that might one day help to ensure smooth, or at least nonviolent, leadership changes.

Leaders of China will not be without opportunities and advantages as they seek to build a new economy. The country's enormous rural population provides a huge built-in marketplace for city and town factories. This means that industrial growth can rely for many decades on a domestic market much like the large rural market that helped to fuel the early decades of U.S. industrial growth. But any leadership, regardless of its ideological coloration, will find that severe limitations and excruciating economic and political choices grow out of such immutables as the sheer size and age of China's society. Foreign economists in Beijing sometimes describe energy and transportation as the two critical constraints on China's economic growth. Both are, in fact, powerful constraints, but China has vast coal reserves that can fuel its growth, and both of these constraints are subject to eventual solution with concentrated effort. If the needed political and fiscal will can be found, the same is true, with much greater effort, of a less-discussed but equally powerful economic constraint, the education system, which starves the country of the human element that has been a major engine of modernization elsewhere in Asia.

But many of the factors that will most affect the economic and political future are far less tractable. A population of more than a billion people is already a heavy burden on resources of all kinds. Many societies find that urban life eventually helps to slow population growth, and many Chinese city dwellers are, in fact, voluntarily limiting their families. But some 700 or 800 million Chinese are rural, and rising prosperity will powerfully tempt many of them to find ways around the national birth control policies for at least a generation. How much human pressure the country's already scarce arable land can withstand, or even how much rural crowding a huge society can tolerate without social turmoil and political instability, may well be tested in decades to come. As population grows and the leadership seeks to bring peasants off the farms and into rural and small-town industries and commerce, land already deeply eroded and weary from thousands of years of agricultural pressure will now be put under immense new environmental strains, with unpredictable results.

Fundamental political issues in this enormous and variegated society will not necessarily resolve themselves as they have in countries that have already modernized along Western capitalist lines. More than one commentator has accurately pointed out, for example, that if Chinese freely elected a president or a parliament any time soon, the overwhelming majority who are rural might well vote for candidates who promised a course leading somewhere other than into the modern world. If future leaders do find the political will to tolerate dissent and allow freer flows of information, the country could face a long and potentially divisive political transition as its people adjust to these unaccustomed freedoms. It is hard to predict how well a country with weak institutional structures and a long history of recurring political fractiousness would hold together through such an adjustment.

I left China with a sense that I had been privileged to see nearly five years of potentially historic change. But I was aware that others before me have left China with similar feelings. Foreign commentators have been writing for nearly one hundred years that China has been standing poised to join the modern world, and that the next few years would see China burst upon the world scene as a major economic and political force. These enthusiasms of foreigners have accompanied events as long ago as the abortive reforms of the late nineteenth century, the fall of the Qing Dynasty in 1911, the victories of the Nationalist armies in the 1920s, and the rise to power of Mao's Red Army in 1949. Some of the voices that have participated in these enthusiasms have belonged to figures of far grander reputation than my own, but I am little inclined to join this distinguished company.

My sense is that the rapid and dramatic changes I saw are indeed potentially historic, but that the key word in the sentence may yet prove to be "potentially." It still seems too soon to feel certain that the Deng Xiaoping years will prove, in retrospect, to have been more than the greatest in a long line of ambitious starts. The possibility seems strong that China may now continue to open its economy, polity and society, internally and to the outside world, with many twists and turns but with a long-range trend toward openness and development. If it can safely navigate that politically and economically treacherous passage, which no other Leninist society has yet completed, that would in turn open up for the first time a very real possibility that some coastal cities might find themselves fully participating in the world economy late in the next century. But I do not believe there is yet any certainty to this outcome. For millions of people, the extraordinary adventure of the Deng Xiaoping years has already materially changed the very experience of being Chinese. But I left Beijing feeling that the country had not yet passed either the political or the economic point of no return.

Epilogue

Events seem to be bearing out caveats expressed in chapter eight almost faster than a book can be put into print. As these pages head for the press in the winter of 1988–89, China is half a year into an economic retrenchment of major proportions. In the space of a few months, the central political authorities in Beijing have reclaimed power over signing of major contracts, use of foreign currency, and basic investment decisions. They have announced plans to limit growth in the number of private enterprises and to clamp down on capital spending by localities. They have ordered a return to state control over the prices of long lists of consumer goods. The center is thus gathering back into the hands of its own planners and bureaucrats many of the powers Zhao Ziyang and his reformist allies struggled for a decade to release to lower levels and to the marketplace.

When this two-year retrenchment was announced in the summer of 1988, foreign businessmen were publicly assured that their investments in China would be unaffected. But big-scale changes of direction in China tend to have effects that central decision makers do not always announce at the outset, and may not at first anticipate or intend. By the fall of 1988, foreign businesses were reporting all the predictable problems of canceled contracts, delayed payments, sched-

205

ule setbacks, and difficulty in getting foreign exchange allotments to pay for work already done and goods already delivered. In November 1988 Beijing announced that, after all, a few big "nonproductive" foreign investment projects like hotels and office buildings would have to be postponed indefinitely, even though contracts had already been signed. Foreign investors in Beijing, Shanghai and Guangzhou waited to see who might be next.

Increasingly, economic retrenchment is accompanied by political, cultural and social retrenchment, until the entire process has gained dimensions and momentum that suggest it will become much deeper before there can be any new relaxation. Playwrights and movie directors are reporting new constraints, and intellectuals who challenge the Communist party's vested right of "leadership" are reporting a new intensity in the party's suggestions that they keep their opinions to themselves. Hu Qili, the Politburo's propaganda boss, called his colleagues together for four days in October 1988 and suggested that some newspaper editors be sent for "ideological refresher courses." To make sure it was clear who was in charge, the meeting was told that every publication in the country, except the eight key Communist Party Central Committee newspapers of which *People's Daily* is the flagship, would be getting half as much paper. "Control of the press," Hu asserted, "is a bigger problem than control of the economy."

So saying, he twice pronounced the watchword of this retrenchment: "control." As the preceding eight chapters of this book were completed in May 1988, Zhao Ziyang, the general secretary of the Communist party, and Li Peng, the premier, were struggling for primacy in economic policy. Zhao, who had been the premier and a major architect of the dramatic reforms through most of the 1980s, was fighting to protect the core of his program; namely, an opening, decentralizing and market-regulated economy patterned after China's fastest-growing Asian neighbors. By contrast, what Li most wants, it is now clear, is to reassert control. He has set out to reclaim for Beijing at least a very ample portion of the economic and other authority the central bureaucrats and politicians were losing when Zhao headed the government and Hu Yaobang headed the Communist party. He is working, in short, to undo very big parts of the reforms of the 1980s.

In May 1987, the public debate had still been cast in terms of the fight against "bourgeois liberalization" which had given conservatives in the Politburo their chance after the student demonstrations of the preceding winter. At that time, Zhao seemed successful in holding back conservative attempts to extend the campaign from politics into the economy. But between May 1987 and May 1988 the central dilemmas of China's modernization caught up with Zhao and gave Li his opportunity. One of those dilemmas is this: On the one hand, there will be no real modernization without an end to the jerrybuilt structure of arbitrary prices which distorts every corner of the economy. On the other hand, there can be no early abandonment of the old administered prices without passing through a difficult and possibly prolonged period of inflation and other economic dislocations. By the spring of 1988, inflation had grown from a major nuisance to an urgent political problem. Letters to the editor, wall posters, telephoned complaints to urban price-control offices, and the occasional street demonstration all warned of rising unrest. Still, Zhao argued that China should try to stay the course. He was urging more decentralization, not less, and urging that still more areas along the coast be freed up to seek opportunity in the form of exports and foreign investments.

By midsummer, consumer prices for June 1988 had been officially reported at 19 percent higher than a year earlier, inflation unprecedented in China under Communist rule. Zhao's course lost, at least for the time being, its political base within the inner councils of the Communist party. The party's central leadership switched to a crisis approach to inflation, and it became clear that there was to be no more debate. A subdued Zhao loyally adopted the new line, abandoning his calls for further reform and joining in the announcements of a two-year economic retrenchment. Since then, Li has consistently had the better of the match. By October 1988, it became clear that he had won the ears not only of a majority in the Politburo but also of Deng Xiaoping himself. "We have been bold enough," Deng was quoted as saying in newspaper dispatches out of Beijing. "Now we need to take our steps in a more cautious way." After ten years in which "boldness" had often been proclaimed as the chief virtue of the reformers, Deng's remark reads like a direct answer to what Zhao must have been arguing in the inner councils.

Premier Li's rise to primacy over Zhao in economic policy is not exclusively, nor even mainly, a matter of fighting inflation. There are many ways to do that, and not all require undoing so much of what Zhao's reformers spent the past decade doing. Zhao's current predicament has elements that suggest a Chinese Marxist application of the Peter Principle. By far Zhao's greatest years were spent as premier, a job in which his abundant policy and administrative skills were the basic tools of the trade. If his political skills and connections were less abundant, that was amply made up for by the political authority and astuteness of Deng Xiaoping and the far-reaching connections of Hu Yaobang. But when the party sacked Hu Yaobang as too politically permissive, Deng seemed to feel that Zhao's spectacularly successful years as premier marked him as the logical new head of the party. Zhao publicly raised some gingerly objections at the time, saying he felt more comfortable handling policy and administration than politics. Despite his new job, his public pronouncements have gone on dealing more with policy and economics, and less with politics, than might be expected of the head of a large Communist party. He has sometimes seemed a fish out of water.

Li Peng is proving to be a more well-rounded leader than Zhao, and a far more effective politician. After decades of service in the bureaucracy, his policy and administrative skills are substantial. And, possibly because he grew up under the wing of one of the Chinese Communist party's greatest politicians, Premier Zhou Enlai, whose adopted son he is, Li also has shown that his political connections and skills are developed beyond any level Zhao ever managed. Steadily and relentlessly, he has gathered to himself the primacy in economic policy that had been Zhao's through most of the eighties. But even as he has repeatedly demonstrated his ability, he has simultaneously demonstrated his discomfort with Zhao's still-incomplete experiments in freemarket economics, decontrolled prices, and decentralized authority. As he must, he has offered the expected reassurances that the current retrenchment is intended not to abort the reforms, but to keep them from going off course. Indeed, there is no reason to doubt that Li is completely sincere when he says over and over that he counts himself as an enthusiastic reformer. But Li's education in the Soviet Union, and his long decades as an engineer and administrator in the big-project world of Chinese electric power supply, seem to have inclined him toward that instinct for administrative order and social tidiness which is often the distinctive mark of the Marxist bureaucrat.

In a vast, diverse, poor, and sometimes politically fractious country, administrative order and social tidiness are concerns that cannot be ignored, especially in times that are alive with the rapid social changes accompanying economic development. The challenge any leader of China faces is to find a balance that satisfies those basic societal needs while creating an openness—a social, political, and economic breathing room—that will give the economy space to work its way up to a takeoff. The country is still only in the early stages of attempting a dangerous transition no other Leninist society has yet successfully managed. The danger Li Peng seems to have persuaded the Politburo to fear most at the moment is loss of control during the transition. It is beyond question that such a danger exists. But an excessive concentration on that risk carries with it a huge danger of its own, one made greater because it is more subtle and less immediately threatening. That is the danger of a half-done reform, the risk of a China that makes detectable progress every year but remains permanently consigned to wonder why its Asian neighbors still race ahead so much faster.

Mao's man-made disasters cleared the decks in ways that made the great reforms of the 1980s possible. Those years of the 1970s, when a nation demanded that its leaders guide it out of Maoism, were a moment that was unique in the history of Marxist societies. Deng Xiaoping seized that moment and put men like Zhao in charge to take advantage of it. It is hard to foresee another equally good chance to set a course toward real participation in the modern world. For more than 100 years, Chinese leaders had insisted that, while they wanted the modern world's goods for their people, they wanted them only on China's terms. For most of the 1980s, China has had, for the first time, a leadership willing to flirt with the spooky notion of entering the modern world more nearly on the modern world's own terms. The current retrenchment is not necessarily the beginning of a new retreat into the old way of thought. But its scope suggests that 1989 and 1990 may prove to be years that will profoundly influence the course of the world's most populous country far into the future.

The genie of modernization is not yet all the way out of the bottle in China, and it is too soon to say that a control-minded leadership would be unable to stopper the bottle for decades to come. The genie will not fully emerge until, as now appears to be true in South Korea and Taiwan, a middle class has developed economically and educationally to the point of being a force the government cannot repress. Marx understood the genie. He called the middle class the bourgeoisie and identified it as the force that had propelled Western nations out of medieval economies and polities and into the commercial-industrial world of the late nineteenth and early twentieth centuries. But Marxism came to China, as to most of the countries that adopted it, before there was a powerful middle class. Until Deng Xiaoping, China's Communist party devoted itself to suppressing the very middle class that Marx had identified as the propelling force of modernization. So the China Deng inherited in the late 1970s was still in very large part a medieval society. Its Communist party remains today an instrument far more at ease with a medieval centralization of powers than with the untidiness of trusting businessmen and consumers and voters to make their own decisions.

In such a party a real danger may remain, well into the early years of the next century, that the great reforms of the 1980s will end half done. If half-done reform is the product of Deng's unique historic moment, full participation in the world economy could be put off, except possibly in Guangzhou and Shanghai, to some time well beyond the twenty-first century. China would become, not the home of half a dozen or a dozen Hong Kongs and Taiwans, but a vast Hungary—another example of where Leninist societies go when their leaders draw back after discovering how inhospitable a modern economy is to the degree of social and political control Leninism has trained them to think they need.

Tokyo
December 1988

Notes

1. Cars and Cadres

1. This account relies on articles published in the Hong Kong newspaper *Wen Wei Po*, January and February 1986, translated by the staff of the Beijing bureau of *The Baltimore Sun*.

2. Starting in the Countryside

1. From "Address of Comrade Chen Yun to the Conference of the Communist Party of China." English translation distributed to foreign correspondents, 19 October 1985, by the Information Department of the Ministry of Foreign Affairs, Beijing.

2. "Comrade Tian Jiyun Reports on Rural Work," *Peasants Daily*, 24 January 1985, p. 1 (translated, *Baltimore Sun*).

4. Pop Stars, Preachers, Party Lines

1. This account relies on articles published in provincial newspapers, March 1985, translated by the staff of the Beijing bureau of *The Baltimore Sun*.

2. "What is Wrong with the Play 'Bus Stop'?" *Wen Yi Bao*, February 1984, p. 23 (translated, *Baltimore Sun*).

3. "Hu Yaobang Reports on the Work of Journalism," Hong Kong *Wen Wei Po*, 3 March 1985, p. 3 (translated, *Baltimore Sun*).

4. "New Freedom for Chinese Writers," Wang Meng, *Outlook Magazine,* October 1985, p. 42 (translated, *Baltimore Sun*).

5. Women: Big Strides, Forward, Backward, and Sideways

1. Surveys of urban housework, and of related domestic topics that touch on housework, first appeared in *Social Sciences in China,* vol. 1, no. 1, January 1981, and were published from time to time during the journal's first two years.
2. "Premier Zhao Ziyang Reports to the National People's Congress," Xinhua News Agency, English language daily report, 11 May 1983.
3. "Liu Jianzhong Solved Problems at the Expense of Women Workers," *Workers Daily,* 8 July 1986, p. 3 (translated *Baltimore Sun*).

7. Students in the Streets

1. "Hu Yaobang Reports on the Work of Journalism," Hong Kong *Wen Wei Po,* 3 March 1985, p. 3 (translated, *Baltimore Sun*).
2. Deng Xiaoping interview with Japanese visitors. Notes provided by Japanese resident correspondents in Beijing, March 1985.
3. Citations from newspapers throughout this account rely on translations prepared daily by the staff of the Beijing bureau of *The Baltimore Sun.*

8. Will China Make It?

1. This account relies on translations of provincial newspapers prepared by the staff of the Beijing bureau of *The Baltimore Sun.*
2. For example, "Two Chinese Leaders Are at Odds over Economy," *New York Times,* 4 March 1988, p. 6.
3. "Why Price Reform Is Different from Inflation," *Economic Daily,* 10 December 1985, p. 4 (translated, *Baltimore Sun*).
4. "Zhao Calls for More Initiative in Factories," *China Daily* (North American Edition), 27 April 1987, p. 1.

Index

John Woodruff has been a newspaper reporter and editor since graduating from Williams College in 1960. He joined *The Baltimore Sun* in December 1965. His initial assignment in Asia was as *The Sun*'s Vietnam War correspondent, based in Saigon, in 1969 and 1970. After Saigon he was assigned to Hong Kong, where he wrote about China from 1970 to 1973. He first visited China in October 1972, after Richard Nixon's meetings with Mao Zedong and Zhou Enlai, as the first Hong Kong–based American correspondent admitted to attend the Canton Trade Fair.

Woodruff was a member of the inaugural class of The University of Michigan Journalism Fellows in the academic year 1973–74, studying Japanese language and East Asian history, politics, and economics. He has studied Chinese politics, history, and language in Washington, D.C., at the School of Advanced International Studies of The Johns Hopkins University. He has been awarded the American Political Science Association Award for Distinguished Reporting of Public Affairs. During the period covered by this book, his dispatches from China and India were part of a *Baltimore Sun* team project that won the $10,000 International Hunger Journalism award in 1985. He has served as a member of the selection committee of The University of Michigan Journalism Fellows and as a juror for the Ernie Pyle Award of the Newspaper Guild.

This book is based on Woodruff's third tour in Asia, as chief of the Beijing bureau of *The Baltimore Sun*, from October 1982 to July 1987. It was written during the academic year 1987–88, while he was teaching as the Howard R. Marsh Visiting Professor of Communication at The University of Michigan. John Woodruff is now chief of the Tokyo bureau of *The Baltimore Sun*.